Routledge Revision: Ques

Jurisprudence
2011–2012

Routledge Q&A series

Each Routledge Q&A contains approximately 50 questions on topics commonly found on exam papers, with answer plans and comprehensive suggested answers. Each book also offers valuable advice as to how to approach and tackle exam questions and how to focus your revision effectively. New **Aim Higher** and **Common Pitfalls** boxes will also help you to identify how to go that little bit further in order to get the very best marks and highlight areas of confusion. And now there are further opportunities to hone and perfect your exam technique online.

New editions publishing in 2011:

Civil Liberties & Human Rights	Equity & Trusts
Commercial Law	European Union Law
Company Law	Evidence
Constitutional & Administrative Law	Family Law
Contract Law	Jurisprudence
Criminal Law	Land Law
Employment Law	Medical Law
English Legal System	Torts

For a full listing, visit **http://www.routledge.com/textbooks/revision**

Routledge Revision: Questions & Answers

Jurisprudence

2011–2012

David Brooke

Senior Lecturer in Law and Module Leader in Jurisprudence at Leeds Metropolitan University

Routledge
Taylor & Francis Group

LONDON AND NEW YORK

Fifth edition published 2011
by Routledge
2 Park Square, Milton Park, Abingdon, Oxon, OX14 4RN

Simultaneously published in the USA and Canada
by Routledge
270 Madison Avenue, New York, NY 10016

Routledge is an imprint of the Taylor & Francis Group, an informa business

© 2009, 2011 David Brooke

Previous editions published by Cavendish Publishing Limited
First edition   1993
Second edition   1995
Third edition   2001

Previous editions published by Routledge-Cavendish
Fourth edition   2009

Typeset in The Sans by RefineCatch Limited, Bungay, Suffolk
Printed and bound in Great Britain by TJ International Ltd, Padstow, Cornwall

British Library Cataloguing in Publication Data
A catalogue record for this book is available from the British Library

Library of Congress Cataloging in Publication Data
Brooke, David, 1966-
    Jurisprudence / David Brooke. – 5th ed.
        p. cm. – (Q&A, Routledge question & answers series)
    Rev. ed. of: Jurisprudence, 2009-2010. 4th ed. 2009
    Includes bibliographical references and index.
        ISBN 970-0-415-59915-3 (pbk : alk. paper) – ISBN 978-0-203-83280-6 (ebk)
        1. Jurisprudence–Examinations, questions, etc.   I. Brooke, David, 1966-
Jurisprudence, 2009-2010.   II. Title.
    K231.B76 2011
    340.0076–dc22   2010040385

ISBN13: 978–0–415–59915–3 (pbk)
ISBN13: 978–0–203–83280–6 (ebk)

Contents

Preface		vii
Table of Cases		ix
Table of Legislation		xi
Guide to the Companion Website		xiii
	Introduction	1
1	General Aspects of Jurisprudence	9
2	Precursors of Modern Jurisprudence	21
3	Natural Law	39
4	Common Law and Statute	65
5	Utilitarianism	83
6	Punishment	101
7	Legal Positivism	111
8	Authority	155
9	American Realism	173
10	The Nature of Law	185
11	Contemporary American Jurisprudence and Political Philosophy	199
12	Rights	211
13	Law and Morality	225
	Index	239

Preface

This collection of Questions and Answers has as its objective the provision of structured material designed to assist students preparing for first examinations in jurisprudence. The mode of presentation adopted involves the setting of a question of the type often asked in examinations of this nature, and the providing of an appropriate answer. The answers are not to be considered as 'model answers'; they are intended specifically to be illustrations of the type of answer required, with particular reference to content and structure.

The format is as follows:

Introduction to chapter. This indicates the subject matter to be covered by the questions.

Checklist. The relevant jurisprudential concepts to be tested are noted. They should be learned or revised carefully before the answer presented is considered.

Question. The rubric and its specific demands should be studied carefully. 'Comment', 'critically examine', 'outline' are not interchangeable terms; each requires its own pattern of answering.

Answer plan. This indicates the approach that is taken to the question and suggests a skeleton plan that is followed. Students should consider the advisability of planning an answer in this form; the production of a skeleton plan is a useful method of arranging content.

Answer. Content and structure are of major significance and ought to be noted carefully.

Notes. Details of suggested reading are given under this heading. Students who require guidance in the choice of general jurisprudence reading material might consider the following recommended texts: James Penner, *Jurisprudence* (2008) is an up to date and accessible guide to the subject (McCoubrey and White's textbook on Jurisprudence, edited by James Penner (2008, Oxford University Press); Brian Bix, *Jurisprudence: Theory and Context* (2009, Sweet and Maxwell) is recommended as a student text, and also see N E Simmonds, *Central Issues in Jurisprudence* (2008, Sweet and Maxwell). Raymond Wacks, *Understanding Jurisprudence* (2009, Oxford University Press) is useful. A valuable addition to any jurisprudential library is *A Dictionary of Legal Theory* (2004, Oxford University Press) by Brian Bix, which gives helpful definitions of many jurisprudential words and phrases. Further reading includes the following: Harris, *Legal Philosophies* (1997, 2nd revised edition, Lexis Nexis UK); Freeman, *Lloyd's Introduction to Jurisprudence* (2008, Sweet and Maxwell); Hart, *The Concept of Law* (1994, 2nd edition, Oxford University Press); Dworkin, *Law's Empire* (1986); Davies and Holdcroft, *Jurisprudence – Texts and Commentary* (1991, Butterworths). A very detailed and comprehensive commentary on jurisprudence is provided by Penner, Schiff and Nobles, *Jurisprudence and Legal Theory: Commentary and Materials* (2005, Oxford University Press). Please try to use the most up to date versions of textbooks where available.

In this fifth edition new questions appear throughout the book and new chapters appear on Common Law and Statute, Punishment and The Nature of Law.

David Brooke

July 2010

Table of Cases

A, Re (Children) (2000) 4 All ER 961 **222**

Airedale NHS Trust v Bland [1993] 1 All
ER 821 **218, 219**

Brown v Board of Education 347 US 483
(1954) **13**

Burnie Port Authority v General Jones Pty
Ltd (1994) 179 CLR 520 **80**

Chapman v Chapman (1954) AC 429 **68**

Donogue v Stevenson [1932] AC 562
60, 77

Entick v Carrington (1765) 19 St Tr 1029 **34**

Ibrahim v R (1914) AC 599 **75**

McLoughlin v O'Brien [1982] 1 AC 410
13, 60

Omychund v Barker (1744) 1 Atk 21; 26 ER
15 **61, 67**

R v Howe (1987) AC 417 **75–76**

R v Sargeant (1974) 60 Cr App R 74 **103**

Riggs v Palmer (1889) 115 NY 506 (Elmer's
case) **13, 182**

Savings and Loan Association v Topeka
22 L Ed (1875) **34**

Tennessee Valley Authority v Hll (1978)
437 US 153 **13**

Table of Legislation

UK LEGISLATION

Care Standards Act 2000 **85**
Civil Procedure Rules 1998
    r 32.14(1) **213**
Criminal Attempts Act 1981 **176**
Health Act 2006 **185**
Human Rights Act 1998 **88**
Land Charges Act 1972 **176**
Police and Criminal Evidence Act
    1984 **78**
Pollution Prevention and Control Act
    1999 **213**
Prison Rules 1964
    r 1 **105**

Public Order Act 1986 **202**
    s 23 **86**
Regulation of Investigatory Powers Act
    2000 **85**
Road Traffic Act 1988 **202**
Sale of Goods Act 1893 **66**
Sexual Offences Act 1967 **228, 229**
Terrorism Act 2000
    s 16 **213**
    s 22 **213**

LEGISLATION

European Convention on Human Rights
    1950
    Art 3 **92**

US LEGISLATION

Kansas Statutes 1971 **221**

Guide to the Companion Website

http://www.routledge.com/textbooks/revision

Visit the Routledge Q&A website to discover even more study tips and advice on getting those top marks.

On the Routledge revision website you'll find the following resources designed to enhance your revision on all areas of undergraduate law.

The Good, The Fair, & The Ugly

Good essays are the gateway to top marks. New to this edition, this interactive tutorial provides sample essays together with voice-over commentary and tips for successful exam essays, written by our Q&A authors themselves.

Multiple Choice Questions

Knowledge is the foundation of every good essay. Focusing on key examination themes, these MCQs have been written to test your knowledge and understanding of each subject in the book.

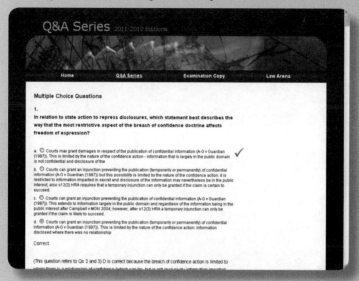

Bonus Q&As

Having studied our exam advice, put your revision into practice and test your essay writing skills with our additional online questions and answers.

Don't forget to check out even more revision guides and exam tools from Routledge!

Lawcards

Lawcards are your complete, pocket-sized guides to key examinable areas of undergraduate law.

Routledge Student Statutes

Comprehensive selections; clear, easy-to-use layout; alphabetical, chronological, and thematic indexes; and a competitive price make *Routledge Student Statutes* the statute book of choice for the serious law student.

Introduction

Jurisprudence is a difficult but rewarding subject, consisting as it does of philosophical enquiry applied to the study of the social institution and cultural phenomena called 'law'.

Jurisprudence allows us to step back from the grinding detail and rote learning of case law and statute inherent in other law subjects and allows us to ask fundamental questions of our and other legal systems. Jurisprudence then is a self-reflective exercise for law students asking such questions as: how is the law to be distinguished from the demands of a gangster? what are the minimum conditions necessary for the existence of a legal system? is there an ideal form of law to measure our own legal system against?

You might find it a relief not to have to wade through, and master, a large number of cases and statutory provisions – as demanded of you by say criminal law or land law. Studying jurisprudence can seem like 'coming up for air' after the tedium of usual law studies **but you will still have to read deeply, although in a different way: studying ideas, not case-law and concepts, not statutes**.

The study of jurisprudence can at first seem like a bewildering array of names such as Raz, Kelsen, Hart, Dworkin, Finnis, Austin, Bentham etc, and an equally bewildering list of jurisprudential theories: legal positivism of both hard and soft varieties, 'law as integrity', natural law, classical common law, the 'pure theory of law' etc. Do not panic, stay calm and carry on reading. Looking at the first question in this book might help you as it aims to place various legal thinkers in a 'mind map' with regard to the different perspectives legal theorists have on law.

Even before you look at question 1 of this book consider the following questions which will help you to **orientate** the particular legal theorist you are studying in the legal theorist's wider context:

(a) what did the legal theorist consider important questions to ask about 'law' and how did those concerns shape the legal theorist's theory of law?

(b) what political or religious views did the legal theorist hold which might have influenced the theorist's legal theory?

(c) was the legal theorist trying to build up his own theory and reputation by criticising (perhaps unfairly) the work of an earlier legal theorist?

(d) what have subsequent legal theorists said, criticised, or supported about the legal theorist's theory of law?

(e) what was the focus of the particular legal theorist? Was it to give an account of legal systems generally? (see Professor Hart) or was the theory limited to the justification of appellate adjudication in the Anglo-American legal systems? (see Professor Dworkin) or was the focus of the theorist upon some ideal legal system which is used to criticise actual legal systems? (see Professor Finnis);

(f) what is the contemporary significance of the legal theorist's work?

For a similar kind of checklist for studying jurisprudential theories, but more developed than the one above, try this quotation on methodology in studying jurisprudence successfully from modern legal theorist William Twining, who in interview with Raymundo Gama comments:

> for disciplined, charitable reading of juristic texts ... an approach involving three stages: the historical, the analytical, and the applied. The first stage (the historical) involves setting a particular text in the context of the author's time, situation and concerns (what was biting him/her). The analytical stage involves putting the text to the question: the reader converts the author's concerns into questions: What questions does this text address? What answers does it suggest? What are the reasons for the answers? Then: Do I agree with the questions? Do I agree with the answers? Do I agree with the reasons? At the third stage (the applied) reader explores the implications and detailed applications of answers and ideas supplied by the text. This helps to clarify the contemporary significance of the text, but also serves as a test of the validity, cogency and relevance of the text to the reader's concerns.

It is important to be clear what jurisprudence is not about. It is not about providing a definition for the use of the word 'law'. If it were jurisprudence would be of no more significance than a relatively short dictionary entry in the *Oxford English Dictionary*. 'Law' is a familiar word which we use without resort to any philosophical definition. As Professor Raz comments in his biographical note, following the death of Professor Hart, in *Utilitas* (1993):

> **The purpose of jurisprudence is not to instruct us in the use of "law" but to explore the law's essential relations to morality, force and society. The task of**

jurisprudence is misrepresented when it is conceived as a search for definition. It is in fact an exploration of the nature of an important social institution.

Therefore, jurisprudence is about the analysis of law as a social institution, studying law as a cultural phenomena. At its best, exemplified by the work of Professor Hart and Professor Raz for example, jurisprudence tells us something of value about the institution of law wherever it is found in whatever human society. This kind of 'general and descriptive' jurisprudence, of which Hart was the great master, can reveal universal truths about the social institution we call 'law'. Such general and descriptive insights include:

- ❖ all law claims legitimate moral authority. Whether law has that authority that it claims is a separate question (Raz);
- ❖ the emergence of a legal order brings the benefits to a society of certainty, efficiency and adaptability in the administration of the rules of that society. However these benefits should not be confused with the rule of law which is a separate issue (Hart);
- ❖ the essential conditions for a legal system to exist are that the legal officials accept the legal order as valid (for whatever reason) and that the bulk of the population generally obey the legal order (Hart);
- ❖ that all law is 'source based'. This is the concept that to identify the content and existence of law and laws you do not have to rely on a moral argument. Although law is often heavily influenced by morality, the actual identification of law is done using lawyerly techniques in the identification of sources such as legislation, custom or precedent (Raz);
- ❖ there are inevitably 'gaps in the law'. Law is 'gappy' because those persons laying down law in statute or judicial precedent cannot foresee the future infallibly. Circumstances may arise where there is a gap in the law because no one foresaw that actual set of circumstances. Also, law is 'gappy' because language is inherently indeterminate and vague and requires fresh determinations as to the exact meaning and application of words used in legal sources. One consequence of 'gaps in the law' is that in certain legal systems judges may have an inescapable law-making power to 'fill the gaps' in the law (Raz, Hart).

Such general and descriptive jurisprudence is to be contrasted with legal theory that is preoccupied with a particular legal culture, such as Dworkin's preoccupation with appellate adjudication in the Anglo-American legal system (see *Law's Empire* (1986)) or Galligan's focus on modern Western legal orders in *Law in Modern Society* (2007). The general and descriptive jurisprudence of Hart and Raz is to be contrasted also with Kelsen's *Pure Theory of Law*, which is excessively preoccupied with important questions concerning the 'normativity' and 'unity' of legal systems – but with those questions alone and therefore lacks **general explanatory power** of the social institution called law.

Professor Hart deserves a special place in the history of jurisprudence in the English speaking world. Before Hart's appointment as Oxford University Professor of Jurisprudence in 1953 jurisprudence in England was in the doldrums with no significant developments since Austin's publication of *The Province of Jurisprudence Determined* in 1832. There were of course jurisprudential developments abroad, most notably the Austrian Hans Kelsen and the work of the American legal realists in the United States. However in England jurisprudence had fallen into a deep trough, with most of the writing of legal philosophers concerned with the definition of a small number of notions such as 'law', 'rights', 'duties', 'possession', 'ownership' and 'legal persons.'

Professor Hart's *The Concept of Law*, a text aimed at students and based on Hart's Oxford lecture notes, was published in 1961, in many ways **'year zero'** for jurisprudence in England – the year in which Hart breathed new life into the dead subject of jurisprudence. As Professor Raz comments in his *Utilitas* biographical note for Hart:

> **he turned jurisprudence back into legal philosophy, as it had been of old, and helped to make it a bridge between students of law, politics, and philosophy.**

Professor Hart in *The Concept of Law* (1961) turned his back on providing a **definition of law** and instead focused attention on three recurrent issues about law which asked questions about law as a social institution:

❖ 'How does law differ from and how is it related to orders backed by threats?'
❖ 'How does legal obligation differ from, and how is it related to moral obligation?'
❖ 'What are rules and to what extent is law an affair of rules?'

For Hart 'definitions of law' had done little to answer these questions about the institution of law. There had been definitions of law offered by theorists before Hart, most famously by Austin (following Bentham and Hobbes), that **'law is the command of the sovereign'**. There have been definitions of law offered after Hart's era, most notably by Neil MacCormick in *Institutions of Law* who (influenced by Kelsen) defines **law as 'an institutional normative order'**. Such definitions of law may have some use as a way of quickly distinguishing law from other normative orders such as morality, but ultimately jurisprudence is not fundamentally about providing definitions of law but rather concerns the analysis of a fundamental, central and socially pervasive institution that is called 'law'.

One final note of caution concerning the use of terms such as 'natural lawyer' or 'legal positivist' to label particular legal theorists – labels are fine if used with caution. It is perfectly fine to comment that: **'Professor Finnis in *Natural Law and Natural Rights* (1980) breathed new life into the moribund natural law tradition.'** However labels are used wrongly if you are not sure what is meant by labelling Professor Raz for instance as 'a legal positivist'. Legal positivism is really only about the very simple idea that all law is identified from human or social sources, in other words that morality is not a criteria of legal validity. Many legal theorists agree with this concept called 'the sources thesis', including the 'natural lawyer' Professor Finnis. In some old jurisprudence books a fundamental dichotomy or division is mentioned between 'legal positivism' and 'natural law', as though a legal philosopher could not assent to the truth in legal positivism (that all law is 'source based') and be a natural lawyer as well. In fact the trend in legal theory today is to try not to rely on labels in identifying the work of particular legal theorists and instead just discuss the work of the theorist instead. Professor Raz, in the preface to the second edition of *The Authority of Law* (2009), comments: 'that we should move away from ways of classifying theories of law which serve to obscure rather than clarify' and later on in the same book Raz comments: **'the classification of theories into legal positivism and others is misleading and unhelpful.'**

Raz is joined in his dislike of labels by Neil MacCormick; who comments in *Institutions of Law* (2007) of the old distinction between legal positivism and natural law theory:

> it is better to reject the aforesaid dichotomy as based on a misleading account of the history of legal ideas than to trouble responding to the question: "Are you a positivist or a natural lawyer?"

The old distinction between legal positivism and natural law was based on the so-called separability thesis. Legal positivism allegedly held that there was no necessary connection between law and morality, whereas natural lawyers insisted that there was a necessary connection between law and morality. Today most legal positivists, such as Professor Raz and Professor Gardner, agree with the natural lawyers that there are necessary connections between law and morality – one such connection being that the law by its nature always claims legitimate moral authority. The essence of legal positivism is not that there is no necessary connection between law and morality but that to identify the law, **to work out the content of the law, you do not need to use a moral argument – the law can be worked out using lawyerly skills, such as the study of precedent or statute**.

With this 'sources thesis' of legal **positivism** the modern natural lawyers such as Professor Finnis have no argument and so the old distinction between legal positivists and natural lawyers has somewhat disappeared. St Augustine's centuries old remark that **'an unjust law is not a law' ('lex injusta non est lex')** is no longer a defining mark of the natural law tradition, with modern natural law theorists such as Finnis, **according legal validity to unjust legal directives** but questioning the strength of the moral obligation to obey them that these unjust laws create. For modern natural lawyers such as Finnis an unjust law is still a law but not law in its 'central' or 'focal' sense, which is for Finnis, and Aquinas centuries before him, **'an ordinance of reason for the common good'**.

However, law students and others still try to use labels inappropriately, the most notorious example of that being the work of Professor Dworkin. It is sometimes asked of Dworkin: 'is he a natural lawyer?' because of his anti-positivistic stance and his hostility to the legal positivist 'sources thesis'. There is an error of logic here in those who classify Dworkin 'a natural lawyer'. Although Dworkin is not a legal positivist, he is not in the tradition of natural law thought either. Dworkin's work stands on its own merits and we should resist the temptation to label his work as 'natural law' because it is not in that tradition.

We have seen that there are difficulties of reducing the great variety of legal thought in jurisprudence to simple patterns of traditions, schools, movements, etc. It would be wiser to examine each jurisprudential scholar you come across on their own merits and demerits without trying to lock the legal theorist into some prejudging 'school of thought' or jurisprudential 'movement'.

It is important to be aware that in the final analysis some jurisprudential theories are incompatible with each other: that there is real and persistent disagreement within jurisprudential debate. Two examples will suffice of these irreconcilable differences within legal theory:

(1) natural lawyers such as Finnis in *Natural Law and Natural Rights* (1980) argue for a methodology in jurisprudence which seeks to explain law by reference to an ideal theory of law called the 'central case' of law. This 'central case' of law sees law's inherent function as being to co-ordinate the community for the common good of its members. However as Jules Coleman argues in 'The Architecture of Jurisprudence' (1st conference on Philosophy and Law: Girona May 2010):

> **it is quite contestable whether law has a function in the sense that hearts do. Law serves many social roles, is capable of achieving many desirable and undesirable ends . . . but it does not follow that it has an essential function in virtue of which we understand its nature . . . In fact, most jurisprudence scholars reject the view that law has a distinctive function in this sense.**

So there is an irreconcilable difference within legal theory between those such as Finnis, who argue that law has a 'central case' function of co-ordinating the community for the common good, and those such as Coleman and Professor Hart, who argue that it is fruitless to attribute a function to law beyond guiding conduct by the provision of reasons for action.

(2) Both Dworkin and Raz take the general position that we understand the institution of law through its relationship to morality. However Dworkin and Raz fundamentally disagree with each other as to what the relationship between law and morality exactly is. For Raz the fundamental relationship between law and morality is that of authority. Law serves morality for Raz by replacing the uncertain requirements of morality with the crisp direction of law. For Raz, in order for law to serve the relationship to morality there must be a firewall between law and morality – hence the Razian 'sources thesis': you do not need to engage in a moral argument to work out the content and existence of the law. For Dworkin it is the fact that law makes a claim to justified coercion that stakes out law's relationship to morality. Therefore for Dworkin in order for the law to perform its function of justifying state coercion then law must be permeable or translucent to the influence of morality in the identification of law.

Therefore we have an unbridgeable divide in legal theory between legal positivists, such as Raz, who argue that morality plays no part in the **identification of the content of the law,** and anti-positivists, such as Dworkin, who argue that morality is very much part of the process of identifying the law of a community – at least in the Anglo-American legal cultures.

Whilst some differences in legal theory have been overplayed in the past, such as the alleged division between natural law and legal positivism, there remain genuine disagreements in legal theory which ultimately cannot be reconciled.

A final introductory point to consider is that a major reason why there is a wide range of theories about the nature of law is that law itself is like a prism – it has many sides or facets. Law has multiple aspects which explains why no single jurisprudential theory can capture the essence of law in its entirety. Each important jurisprudential theory such as legal positivism or natural law theory may capture important truths about law but not the whole truth about law. Law certainly involves the following non-exhaustive list:

❖ an historical record of official action both judicial and legislative – this might be termed the law reporters perspective on law;
❖ a system of public reason for the fair and just resolution of disputes – Dworkin's perspective of 'law as Integrity';

❖ an authoritative system of norms for the guidance of human conduct – the perspective of legal positivists notably Hart and Raz;

❖ a permanent official public threat system for the maintenance of civil peace and order – the perspective on law provided by Thomas Hobbes in 'Leviathan' (1651);

❖ the primary and proper means for the co-ordination of society for the common good – the perspective on law provided by the classical natural law tradition as exemplified by Thomas Aquinas and his modern day interpreter John Finnis.

General Aspects of Jurisprudence

INTRODUCTION

This chapter offers only one question, but it is perhaps the most important question in this book. The most important general advice to any new student to the subject of jurisprudence is to identify the viewpoint of the legal theorist. Identifying the legal theorist's viewpoint on law will prevent confusion and many misunderstandings.

QUESTION 1

How does an insight into the 'viewpoint' of a legal theorist concerning law help in understanding the work of the legal theorist?

Answer Plan

The question concerns the general question of the role that a legal theorist's viewpoint has on the understanding of the legal theorist's theory of law. The answer identifies three general viewpoints that a legal theorist might take on the institution we call 'law': (1) the lawyers or participant's perspective where the legal theorist seeks to explain law in terms of a lawyer's understanding of law. Dworkin and Kelsen are the best known examples of this perspective;

(2) the institutional 'engaged' perspective is where the legal theorist goes beyond the lawyer's perspective and examines law in its wider political and social perspective, but this perspective has a strong commitment to a particular type of legal system or an ideal form of law. Finnis, Galligan and MacCormick are all strong examples of this type of approach;

(3) the 'detached' institutional perspective where the legal theorist examines law in its social and political context – the 'institutional setting of law' – but has no express commitment to law or legal systems of any kind. This value-free descriptive jurisprudence is best exemplified by Professor Hart.

A skeleton plan is suggested:

❖ Introduction;
❖ the importance of identifying a legal theorist's perspective on law;
❖ three different types of perspectives on law: the lawyer's perspective, the institutional 'engaged' and the institutional 'detached';
❖ discussion of the legal theory perspectives of Dworkin, Kelsen, Finnis, Galligan, MacCormick, Hart;
❖ conclusion, understanding perspectives on legal theory vital to understanding legal theory.

ANSWER

Jurisprudence can seem bewildering to the new student as a mass of theorists and theories are suddenly thrust upon them and they are expected to absorb, digest and feedback a body of knowledge that seems part philosophy, part sociology and part history, while bearing little relation to traditional law subjects.

One way of imposing order upon the chaos is to try to obtain a sense of where a particular legal theorist stands in relation to the law. Understanding the standpoint of a legal theorist makes understanding that legal theorist easier and allows the construction of a 'mind map' so that important jurisprudential scholars can fit into that 'mind map' schemata.

It is suggested that three broad standpoints could be identified in order to place a range of authors in a 'viewpoint mind map'. These authors include: Dworkin, Kelsen, Galligan, MacCormick, Finnis, Austin, Hart and Raz.

The three viewpoints or standpoint perspectives are:

(1) participant perspectives – Dworkin, Kelsen;
(2) institutional (or 'external') engaged perspective – MacCormick, Galligan, Finnis;
(3) institutional (or 'external') detached perspective – Hart, Austin.

The participant perspective can also be termed the 'lawyer's perspective'. This perspective seeks to give an account of the social institution we call law from the point of view of the court-room or a judge. To a certain extent this perspective is a 'natural' one for a legal theorist to take. As Professor Raz comments in 'The Nature of Law' in *Ethics in the Public Domain* (1994):

most theorists tend to be by education and profession lawyers, and their audience often consists primarily of law students. Quite naturally and imperceptibly they adopted the lawyers perspective on the law.

The problem with the participant or lawyer's perspective on the law is that it can lead the legal theorist who adopts it to neglect important features of law because the lawyer's perspective fails to examine the law in the wider political context in which the law is moored. Two legal theorists who adopted the lawyer's perspective are Hans Kelsen and Ronald Dworkin.

Kelsen took explaining the 'normativity' or authority of the law as the backbone of his theory of law. This in itself is a question which looks at law from the lawyer's perspective – what sense, Kelsen asked, to give to claims of 'ought' in the law? As Kelsen comments in *Introduction to the Problems of Legal Theory* (1934):

> The Pure Theory of Law works with this basic norm as a hypothetical foundation. Given this presupposition that the basic norm is valid, the legal system resting on it is also valid . . . Rooted in the basic norm, ultimately, is the normative import of all the material facts constituting the legal system. The empirical data given to legal interpretation can be interpreted as law, that is, as a system of basic norms, only if a basic norm is presupposed.

Therefore Kelsen, a person who regards a legal order as valid as opposed to a mere coercive order, presupposes a hypothetical 'basic norm' which gives 'normativity' or 'oughtness' to the legal system so interpreted as valid. Kelsen is seeking to explain what lawyers mean when they say 'the law says you ought not to do X or you ought to do X'. Kelsen's persepective is the lawyer's perspective, trying to give sense to 'lawyers' talk' of legal obligation. As Kelsen comments in *Pure Theory of Law* (1967) 'the decisive question' is why the demands of a legal organ are considered valid but not the demands of a gang of robbers. The answer to this question is that only the demands of a legal organ are interpreted as an objectively valid norm because the person viewing the legal order as valid and therefore more than a coercive order from a 'gang of robbers' is presupposing in his own consciousness a basic norm which gives validity and normative force to the legal order.

Kelsen's basic question in legal theory – what sense to give to lawyers' statements of 'legal ought' – is a question from the lawyer's perspective, but this tendency to examine the law from the lawyer's or participant's perspective is reinforced by Kelsen's methodology. Kelsen insisted that his theory was a 'pure theory of law'. He regarded it as doubly pure – pure of all moral argument and pure of all sociological facts. The view of law examined by Kelsen is free of any kind of moral evaluation, such as what moral purposes the law could serve, or sociological enquiry as for example what motivates persons to obey the law. Kelsen merely looks at the raw data of legal experience to be found in the statute books and law reports and asks: what sense to give to legal talk of 'ought'?

For a legal theory to ignore the moral and sociological realities framing the law it must be the case that that legal theory is focusing purely on the lawyer's perspective. Although Kelsen has an interesting and developed theory answering the lawyer's question of what sense to give to lawyers' talk of legal obligation, legal duty and legal 'ought', Kelsen's theory of law has little general explanatory power of the social institution called law. Moreover, by clinging so exclusively to the 'lawyer's perspective' Kelsen makes statements that, from a wider perspective, seem unjustifiable. For example Kelsen comments, in *Introduction to the Problems of Legal Theory* (1934), that:

> the law is a coercive apparatus having in and of itself no political or ethical value.

Kelsen should have considered that the law can have value in itself as a means by which citizens can express loyalty and identification with their community. This point, recognised by modern writers on law such as Raz and Leslie Green, would have been lost on Kelsen – buried as he was in the lawyer's perspective.

Kelsen's theory of law was once termed by the political thinker Harold Laski as 'an exercise in logic not in life' (see H. Laski, *A Grammar of Politics* (1938)). We may interpret this statement by Laski as meaning that although Kelsen tries impressively to answer the question concerning the law's normativity, Kelsen has little of value to say about law as a social phenomenon generally.

The lawyer or participant viewpoint on law can be valuable but it is unreasonable to study the law solely and exclusively from the lawyer's perspective. The law must be examined, in order to get full explanatory power of this important social institution, in the wider perspective of social organizations and political institutions generally. This wider perspective may be termed the 'institutional' or 'external' perspective on law and has been the dominant viewpoint in English jurisprudence from Thomas Hobbes in the seventeenth century to Professor Hart.

However, before we examine the 'institutional' perspective on law we need to examine another famous example of the lawyer's perspective – Professor Ronald Dworkin's theory of law.

Dworkin's preoccupation with his theory of law has been to answer the question: how can law be interpreted so as to provide a sound justification for the use of State coercion involved in forcing the payment of compensation in a civil action at law? This is again a lawyer's question, although a different lawyer's question from Kelsen's preoccupation with the normativity of the law. Dworkin's theory of law is aimed at the justification of State coercion expressed through law. Dworkin has taken appellate case decisions as the testing ground for his theory of law which has involved the controversial proposition that the law of the Anglo-American legal system involves not just the accepted case law and statutes but also the law that includes the best moral interpretation of that law. Therefore there is a greater connection between Dworkin's lawyer's perspective and general legal theory than Kelsen's lawyer's perspective which seemed grounded on the normativity of law only. Dworkin's theory of law at least engages with the debate 'what is law?' or 'what are the grounds of law?' However, despite Dworkin's connection to wider debates in legal theory about the nature of law, Dworkin seeks to answer that question from the lawyer's perspective. Dworkin has defended his preoccupation with the courtroom by observing that it is in the courtroom that the doctrinal question of 'what is law?' is most acutely answered. Dworkin comments in 'Hart and the Concepts of Law' (2006) Harvard Law Review Forum:

> Courtrooms symbolise the practical importance of the doctrinal question and I have often used judicial decisions both as empirical data and illustrations for my doctrinal claims.

Dworkin has often used appellate cases to support his arguments, leading to the charge that he is developing a legal theory out of a theory of adjudication. Dworkin uses the House of Lords appellate case of *McLouglinh v O'Brien* [1982] as the centrepiece for testing various theories of law, including his own theory known as 'law as Integrity' at pp 230–240 of *Law's Empire* – Dworkin's magnum opus on legal theory from 1986. The United States appellate court decisions of the Supreme Court have been used by Dworkin, namely: the 'snail darter' case *Tennessee Valley Authority v Hill* (1978) and *Brown v U.S.* (1954) are both discussed by Dworkin in *Law's Empire* at pp 20–23 and pp 29–30 respectively. A case used by Dworkin in the 1960s to illustrate these arguments about the nature of law – 'Elmer's case' – is used again at pp 15–20 of *Law's Empire*. 'Elmer's case', known properly as *Riggs v Palmer* (1883) is an appellate decision of the New York appeals court.

Dworkin's lawyer's perspective on the law and his tendency to look at the law through the prism of the courtroom has led to criticism that Dworkin has developed a theory of law out of a theory of adjudication. As Professor Raz argues in *Between Authority and Interpretation* (2009):

> [Dworkin's] book is not so much an explanation of the law as a sustained argument about how courts, especially American and British courts should decide cases. It contains a theory of adjudication rather than a theory of the nature of law.

The argument against Dworkin is that his obsession with the courtroom – the lawyer's perspective on law – means that Dworkin can miss, or fail to appreciate, essential features of law that operate in the wider social context beyond the courtroom. For example, Dworkin fails in his legal theory to account for the law's claim to authority which is an important part of the law's method of social organization. Dworkin says a lot about the need for the law to have 'integrity' or 'fairness' but little about the law's authority. Although the integrity or fairness of the law is vital, so is the law's authority. If Dworkin had stepped back from the lawyer's perspective he might have seen this point.

The institutional perspective stands back from the lawyer's perspective, not in order to disregard it, but to examine lawyers and courts in the wider perspective of their place in the social organization and political institutions of a society.

The 'institutional' perspective has had many representatives in the history of legal philosophy. Its influence started with Thomas Hobbes in *Leviathan* (1651) who heavily influenced Bentham (*Of Laws in General* (1782)) and Austin (*The Province of Jurisprudence Determined* (1832)). Hobbes placed law in its wider political context and argued that strong authority was needed to pacify a society, for without a common authority to keep men 'in awe' the natural tendency of man was to war with his fellow men. Once the strong authority – the 'Leviathan' (from the Book of Job, Chapter 41, Old Testament: 'Leviathan' meaning a great sea beast – so the state by analogy is something which should be overwhelmingly powerful and awe-inspiring to people) – was established then the laws were the commands of the sovereign authority designed to maintain civil peace. Hobbes thus provided an account of law in terms of political and social needs. Austin and Bentham continued this tradition. Austin and Bentham first of all identified the sovereign in a society by considering 'habits of obedience' in that society and then in the tradition of Thomas Hobbes, identified the law as the 'commands of the sovereign'. If Austin and Bentham's account of law is too 'thin', i.e. lacks explanatory power, it is not because of the 'institutional' perspective they adopted with regard to law but because the terms they employed in their description of law – 'sovereign', 'habits of obedience', 'sanctions', 'commands' – were too few in number and too simplistic to give an adequate descriptive analysis of law and legal systems.

Austin and Bentham explained the nature of the political system and then proceed to explain the nature of law by placing it within the political system. HLA Hart continued that 'institutional' tradition by examining law against the context of social and political needs. For example, Hart has a famous 'fable' in *The Concept of Law* (1961) to show the general social benefits a system of law might bring to a society governed by social rules only. Those benefits include the ability to change rules quickly through

Parliamentary amendment and procedures to determine the exact scope of a social rule through the setting up of a court structure. Hart also shows how different legal rules help to plan social life out of court through laws on contract, marriages and wills, for example. Hart's approach is to show how the institution of law cannot be understood without considering law against the background of the social and political matrix that the law operates in. Therefore, the 'lawyer's perspective' on law, although valuable for some purposes, is arbitrary as the ultimate viewpoint on law if not for the simple fact that law is a social institution.

With regard to the 'institutional perspective' it is important to make a further sub-division between legal philosophers. There is (a) the 'engaged' institutional perspective and (b) the detached or 'disengaged' perspective.

The 'engaged' institutional perspective is the viewpoint of the legal theorist who seeks to give an account of law from the wide institutional perspective, placing law in its wider political and social context, but who has some sort of commitment to, or endorsement of, a particular legal system or type of legal system. Examples of this type of approach are John Finnis in *Natural Law and Natural Rights* (1980), Dennis Galligan in *Law in Modern Society* (2007) and Neil MacCormick in *Institutions of Law* (2007). Finnis regards 'the central case' of law as being a rationally prescribed ordering by those in authority for the common good of that community. Finnis uses this ideal of law ('ideal' because given human limitations it is not fully realizable) as a standard, or a lens, through which to examine actual legal systems. Indeed Finnis would say that an adequate account of modern Western democratic legal systems (which generally seek to work for the common good) is not possible unless the theorist attends to the moral reasons which cause such legal systems to come into being and be sustained. In an essay entitled 'The Truth in Legal Positivism' (in *The Autonomy of Law*, edited by Robert George) Finnis argues:

> the reasons people have for establishing systems of positive law and for maintaining them include certain moral reasons, on which many of those people often act. And only those moral reasons suffice to explain why such people's undertaking takes the shape it does, giving legal systems the many defining features they have.

Therefore, while Finnis adopts the 'institutional perspective' seeking to examine law in its wider social context he does so with a commitment to an ideal form of law (**'an ordering of reason for the common good'**- the definition of law provided by the father of natural law theory: St Thomas Aquinas in the thirteenth century) and a commitment to the Western style of democratic government under the rule of law, which at least tries to govern for the common good.

In a slightly different way Dennis Galligan has a strong commitment to a certain type of law – not an 'ideal' type favoured by Finnis, but what Galligan calls **'modern legal orders'**. As Galligan notes, such praiseworthy legal systems are few in number: the societies of Western Europe, North America, parts of the British Commonwealth and occasionally elsewhere. Galligan gives a full descriptive account of such legal systems in *Law in Modern Society* (2007). Such societies are governed by a rule of law which is taken seriously by government, and there is also a 'bond of trust' between legal officials, such as police, judges etc, and the public, which is a defining mark of such modern legal orders and is absent in the corruption-soaked officialdom of the rest of the world. Galligan makes it clear in his concluding paragraph that he is writing the book to further the protection of modern legal orders. Galligan writes:

> Legal orders with the features charted and discussed here are of interest and importance compared with other types of legal orders, not for reasons of western truimphalism, but because they have been effective in producing social goods that are valued in western societies and beyond. They are at the same time fragile and unstable, so that if they are to be sustained they must first be understood.

Neil MacCormick, in *Institutions of Law* (2007), focuses on constitutional law-states (Rechstaat in German) and MacCormick is himself committed in his description to the basic values of those, as he calls them, 'institutional normative orders'. MacCormick seeks to uphold the values of those 'law-States', few in number in the world, which are dedicated to the values of realising peace, justice and the common good under the rule of law. MacCormick's enterprise thus resembles Galligan's: to describe the features of a small number of constitutional law states, whilst being wholly committed to the values those few law-States uphold.

There is certainly a place in legal theory for the sort of standpoint that Finnis, MaCormick and Galligan occupy but it should not be the ultimate standpoint of the legal theorist. This is where the third standpoint comes into play – the detached 'institutional' or 'external' perspective.

William Twining notes in 'Institutions of Law from a Global Perspective' (in *Law as Institutional Normative Order* edited by Del Mar and Bankowski 2009) that:

> **pluralism of beliefs and ideologies is a fact and that legal phenomena are immensely varied and complicated**

and as such the legal theorist, if he wants to achieve great generality in his account of law and legal systems, should not become engaged with, or committed to, a particular type of legal system. Professor Hart, in *The Concept of Law*, aimed to develop a descriptive theory of law that involved the standpoint of an external juristic observer and took into account the 'internal point of view' of participants in a legal system but did not claim to approve of or engage with any particular legal system. Hart's external or institutional 'detached' perspective is the most appropriate for an explanation of all legal systems, whether those legal systems are wicked, weak, corrupt, inefficient, incoherent, unjust or just plain indifferent.

For many, Hart's detached perspective will be the correct one to adopt if the observer is a sociologist, a comparative lawyer, an empirical researcher, an historian or if the politics of the observer are anarchistic in outlook. It should always be remembered that even in the most benign constitutional law state, **law is a product of other people's power** and this insight should caution against too ready an endorsement of any legal system.

Hart is sometimes accused of actually endorsing law, whilst at the same time pretending to maintain a detachment from law. The problem arises because of Hart's use of a story to describe the move from a pre-legal society to a society with law, and the benefits that might bring. Some have suggested (e.g. Roger Cotterrell in *The Politics of Jurisprudence* (2003)) that Hart is endorsing and encouraging some version of the rule of law for all societies. This view of Hart is a mistake. John Gardner explains in a 2010 Research paper 'Hart on Legality, Justice and Morality':

In Chapter 5 of 'The Concept of Law' Hart tells his brilliant and seminal fable of the emergence of a legal system (differentiated by its secondary rules of recognition, adjudication, and change) from an imagined pre-legal or proto-legal arrangement of customary primary rules alone. As a way of making such a development rationally intelligible, his narrative emphasises the gains in efficiency and predictability that these secondary norms bring with them. Unfortunately, to the lasting confusion of many readers, he thereby makes it sound like he is extolling the virtues of the transformation from proto-law to law. Not surprisingly, he is therefore taken to task by some critics for attempting to smuggle in a political ideology under cover of his supposedly ideology-neutral explanation of the nature of law. And that political ideology seems to many, not implausibly, to be none other than the ideology of the rule of law ... For all its brilliance, then, Hart's fable is afflicted by severe and damaging presentational flaws. The secondary rules, Hart should have made clear, do not automatically bring with them the rule of law and, even for believers in the rule of law, their arrival is not necessarily to be welcomed. For life without any law at all might well be better than life with law but without the rule of law. The arrival of a legal system makes some forms of oppression possible, and others easier, and there is a further step to be taken to help protect against such law-enabled and law-facilitated oppression, namely the step from having a legal system to having a legal system under the rule of law.

Hart was well aware of the costs, as well as the benefits, of law to a society. In a key passage for understanding Hart in *The Concept of Law* Hart comments of the dangers of law:

> **the cost is the risk that the centrally organized power may well be used for the oppression of numbers with whose support it can dispense, in a way that the simpler regime of primary rules could not.**

Hart's stance towards law was thus one of detachment – aware of the benefits law could bring to a society, but also aware of how law could also allow the more efficient and organised oppression of the population. In other words for Hart law was 'morally risky' and scholastic detachment was the correct intellectual response. Hart maintained, in the Postscript to the second edition of *The Concept of Law*, that it was futile to look for any purpose for law beyond guiding conduct. MacCormick in 'Why Law Makes No Claims' (in *Law, Rights and Discourse*, edited by Pavlakos) claims that:

> **Law is for the securing of civil peace so far as possible.**

This Thomas Hobbes-inspired insight into law's function by MacCormick would perhaps have been too strong for Professor Hart who would go no further with any 'inherent' purpose or function of law than to declare in the 'Postscript' to the second edition of *The Concept of Law* (1994):

> **my theory makes no claim to identify the point or purpose of law or legal practices as such . . . I think it quite vain to seek any more specific purpose which law serves beyond providing guides to human conduct and standards of criticism of such conduct.**

Aim Higher ★

Students can gain extra marks by locating the perspective on law that a particular legal theorist takes. Is the theorist describing law from the perspective of an ideal form of law, or describing law in neutrally descriptive terms, or is the theorist praising in his description of legal systems a particular form of legal ordering such as modern Western legal orders?

NOTES

The best account on 'perspectives in legal theory' is Professor Raz's essay 'The Nature of Law' in *Ethics in the Public Domain* (1994). Professor Hart's account of his own 'general and descriptive' methodology in legal theory can be found in the 'Postscript' of the second edition to *The Concept of Law* (1994), especially at pp 239–241 and pp 248–249. Professor Finnis's legal methodology can be discerned in Chapter 1 of *Natural Law and Natural Rights* (1980). D Galligan's 'engaged' description of modern legal orders can be found in *Law in Modern Society* (2007) and Neil MacCormick's 'engaged' description of modern constitutional 'law-states' can be found in *Institutions of Law* (2007).

2 Precursors of Modern Jurisprudence

INTRODUCTION

The precursors of modern jurisprudence selected as the basis of the questions in this chapter are Cicero (106–43 BC), Hobbes (1588–1679) and Locke (1632–1704). Cicero was concerned with fundamental problems such as the nature of justice and the functions of law. Hobbes and Locke sought, through their theories of 'the social contract', to explain the place of government and law within society. The theories produced by these philosophers formed the basis of many problems which continue to be posed in modern jurisprudence. Questions of the type forming this chapter call for an understanding of the *basic* teachings related to justice, law, state and government. Answers must concentrate on *fundamentals*.

Checklist ✔

The following topics should be revised carefully:

- 'natural rights' according to Locke;
- the social contract viewed by Hobbes;
- Hobbes's 'natural laws';
- Hobbes's 'sovereign';
- Locke's 'state of nature';
- the social contract viewed by Locke and Rousseau;
- Aristotle's view of the state;
- *pacta sunt servanda*.

QUESTION 2

Describe the teachings of Cicero in relation to the basis of the state and the nature of law.

Answer Plan

Cicero (106–43 BC), Roman politician and lawyer, was able, through his teachings, to transmit to his contemporaries, and to posterity, important aspects of Greek (Stoic) philosophy which might otherwise have disappeared. His main interests were in legal and political philosophy and he sought to propagate the virtues of the brotherhood of mankind and a universal law. Cicero's writings have been studied by philosophers, historians and lawyers for many generations; the questions he sought to answer remain on the agenda of our jurisprudence. The following skeleton plan is presented; it should place emphasis on the significance of the natural law, which Cicero saw as of supreme importance for the development of civilisation:

❖   Introduction;
❖   Cicero's life as statesman and jurist;
❖   the essence of the state;
❖   forms of government;
❖   their strengths and weaknesses;
❖   importance of a mixed constitution;
❖   essence of law;
❖   law, God and the nature of man;
❖   justice, good and bad law;
❖   natural law;
❖   conclusion, Cicero as a founder of Western jurisprudence.

ANSWER

Marcus Tullius Cicero (106–43 BC), statesman, lawyer, scholar, writer, and, reputedly, Rome's greatest legal orator, was declared by the legal historian Maitland to have left his ideas 'on every page of Western jurisprudence'. As a jurist, he sought to bring the lessons of Greek philosophy into a consideration of law as the highest reason, implanted in man and providing a universal standard by which justice and injustice might be measured. Born in Arpino, he studied with Philo in Rome and Antiochus in Athens. He became one of Rome's consuls in 63 BC, and participated as a principal figure in the crushing of the insurrection by Catiline. Following exile in 58 BC, he returned to Rome, became an augur in 53 BC, and was promoted to govern Cilicia. He opposed Mark Antony's seizure of power after Caesar's assassination. Antony gave personal orders for the murder of Cicero, which took place in brutal fashion in 43 BC. Cicero's major political and legal tracts were completed during the period 54 to 44 BC; all have been studied extensively by generations of scholars, and reflect his view of the significance of the basis of the state and the essence of law in a manner which gives them relevance for our day.

'If the man lives', he stated, 'who would belittle the study of philosophy, I quite fail to see what in the world he would see fit to praise.' By 'philosophy' Cicero had in mind what we now refer to as 'moral philosophy'. A study of what is meant by 'right' and 'wrong', a search for the essence of justice and an investigation of virtue were fundamental to his view of the place of the law in human affairs. In this investigation, he kept in mind the Stoic belief that virtue is the only good and that the virtuous man is the one who has reached happiness through knowledge. Allied to his acceptance of the primacy of philosophy was a belief that virtue linked man to a divine Providence. All men counted for something; all have an inherent value in themselves; all were linked by a bond of kinship derived from their place in divine Providence; all had the right (which the law must recognise and declare) to be treated well by one another. The Stoic conception of the universe and all creatures therein as sharing a common destiny found expression in Cicero's belief in the essential brotherhood of man. These themes found expression in his legal and political doctrines.

Cicero's views on the nature of the state are set out in *De Republica* (54–52 BC). Human beings should engage in political activity, in the widest sense of the term. Nature has given to mankind a compulsion to do good and a desire to defend the well-being of the community, so that there is a common drive to work for the community's benefit, and this drive will prevail over temptations presented by a life of pleasure and ease. The desire to increase the wealth of the community, to enrich men's life, acts as the spur to unite and work in a common endeavour, to engage in those types of activity which demand the formal framework which only the state can provide.

The state framework can exist in a variety of forms. Cicero chooses, in *De Republica*, to examine three forms of government which can give expression to man's inherent impulse to create societies. Where the supreme authority is vested in one man – a king – the government, known as a 'monarchy', is entrusted with the duty to govern virtuously. When the government is entrusted to a select group, we speak of an 'aristocracy'. When the state is so organised that 'everything depends on the people' we have in mind a 'democracy'. Cicero observes that any of the three types of state may be tolerable though not perfect, but one may, in certain circumstances, be preferable to the others.

The monarchical state can ensure a reasonably stable and secure government, always provided that wickedness and greed are excluded from the work of those who assist the monarch. The problem is that the personal rule of the monarch means that the rest of the population plays only a limited role in state affairs, legislation and debate. Government by an aristocracy, where 'the best' are chosen, has the advantage that nature has decreed that those possessing superiority of ability and character ought to be in charge of those with lesser endowments. Rule by an aristocracy frees the mass of the people from many troubles and anxieties, since grave matters of state are the responsibility of others. The problem of the aristocratic form of government is its tendency to slip into unrestrained rule by a minority, and there is an abandonment, gradually but surely, of the place of reason within the procedures of government.

Democracy is a recognition of equality – all share in the process of government, and all accept a law which recognises and supports systems of duties and rights. Harmony, it is said, can be maintained with relative ease in a state where all have the same basic interests. But Cicero is emphatic in his rejection of the theory of the state based upon the concept of 'so-called equality'. Equality of this nature proves in the event to be highly inequitable: 'For when the same respect is given to the highest and lowest in the community, equity is most unequal . . . this cannot happen where the state is ruled by "the best".' Where no degrees of merit are recognised and acknowledged, equality becomes unequal and degenerates rapidly.

Moderation in all things, including government, must be sought, and Cicero declares himself in favour of a fourth type of government, characterised by a carefully proportioned amalgam of the best features of monarchy, aristocracy and democracy. (He acknowledges, however, that he is personally most attracted to the state ruled by a monarch.) The state should possess 'elements of regal supremacy', 'the best' in the state should be recognised and given tasks and a place in society which acknowledges their talents, and certain affairs ought to be reserved 'for the judgment and wishes of the masses'. A constitution of this nature, in which law will play a role of extreme importance, will confer on citizens a high degree of equality 'without which free men will not endure for long', and provide much stability, 'for there will be little reason to demand change in a society in which all are established firmly in their own places'. The good state will express the virtue and sense of purpose, the harmony and unity under the law which, for Cicero, represent 'the ruling power in the human mind', namely, reason ('for that is the best part of the mind'). *De Legibus* (52–51 BC) is essentially an exposition of the far-reaching doctrine of natural law in which Cicero perceived the plan of divine Providence, which could be realised only when mankind places itself resolutely under the law. *Omnes legum servi sumus ut liberi esse possimus* – 'We must all serve the law if we are to be free'. Law is viewed by Cicero in very wide terms. Its nature must be sought in the very nature of man; all men share in the divine reason and all are brought and bound together by the partnership which characterises justice.

To seek to understand law is to learn the nature of justice and the essence of 'good' and 'bad' law.

The science of law – that which we now speak of as jurisprudence – is derived not from the written law ('not from the Praetor's Edict nor from the Twelve Tables') but from the very deepest recesses of philosophy. Philosophy teaches us to investigate fearlessly, so that we may speak of law as 'the highest reason, inherent in nature, which tells us what should be done and forbids us to act in contrary fashion'.

Indeed, 'law, the function of which is to command right actions and to forbid wrong doing, is wisdom'. But there is a much more profound matter to be recognised: reason is present in God and man so that some kind of partnership exists between them. Those who share reason also share correct reason and, since that is law, men may be perceived as partners with God through the law. Law is, therefore, very much more than 'the Praetor speaking in Rome'. It is an aspect of divine Providence, which 'has placed in our ears a power of judging right and wrong'.

In more precise terms, Cicero teaches that law is not the invention of the intelligence of human beings, nor does it come from resolutions passed by communities. Rather, it is 'an eternal force' which rules the entire world by the excellence of its wisdom in relation to commands and prohibitions. Law is, in truth, an aspect of God's intelligence, for it is God who commands or forbids everything through reason. We may think of the law as representing the intelligence and profound reason of a wise person from whom commands and prohibitions issue forth. Further, reason does not become law when persons have reduced it to writing; it was law when it came into being at the same time as the Supreme Mind. The true, authentic and original law is 'the right reason of Jupiter, the Lord of All'.

The functioning of law demands that man exercise his rational power of choice and learn from nature how to distinguish a 'good law' from a 'bad law'. That which promotes honourable outcomes is good, and is in accordance with nature's teachings; that which is dishonourable is an expression of the rejection of what nature has commanded. Indeed, 'goodness itself is good not because of the opinions of people, but because of nature, the ultimate arbiter'. Every virtue will disappear if nature is ignored so that injustice triumphs. In essence, therefore, justice is necessary if we care to attain the highest good. Cicero describes the concept of 'the highest good' as living by a code of moral excellence, which necessitates following nature, working to her law and not omitting to do those things which nature requires to be done.

Duty is an essential aspect of the law of nature, but how ought citizens to react in the presence of a tyranny? Ought they to obey rules which are clearly contrary to the natural law? In an interesting passage in *De Officiis* (44 BC), Cicero insists that no duties are owed to tyrants. 'Just as certain limbs are amputated if they show signs themselves of jeopardising the health of the other parts of the body, so those fierce and savage monsters in human form [the tyrants] ought to be cut off from what may be called humanity's common body.' This passage has been cited repeatedly as a justification of the removal of tyrants who seek to destroy the common bonds uniting society. Others have interpreted it as a metaphor by which Cicero seeks to proclaim that no man has a right to rule in a fashion that will destroy the unity of the community without being challenged by first being exposed as a destroyer of the social harmony demanded by Providence.

In a style which hints at Cicero's legendary power as a rhetorician, he sums up in *De Legibus* the essence of natural law. 'There is in fact a true law – namely right reason – which is in accordance with nature, applies to all men, and is unchangeable and eternal ... To invalidate this law by human legislation is never morally right, nor is it permissible ever to restrict its operation ... There will be one law, eternal and unchangeable, binding at all times upon all peoples, and there will be, as it were, one common master and ruler of men, namely God, who is the author of this law, its interpreter and sponsor ...' It is the spirit of this formulation which remains central to the theory of natural law, which continues in our time as a potent factor in the jurisprudential thinking of the West.

Stammler, writing of the excellence of the Roman jurists and their universal significance, praises them in terms which apply, in particular, to Cicero. 'They had the courage to raise their glance from the ordinary questions of the day to the whole. And in reflecting on the narrow status of the particular case, they directed their thoughts to the guiding star of all law, namely, the realisation of justice in life.'

NOTES

De Republica and *De Legibus* are translated and discussed by Rudd in a recent edition which provides useful notes on the background to Cicero's work. 'Some reflections on Cicero's naturalism', by Arkes, in *Natural Law Theory*, edited by George, is a valuable commentary on Cicero's interpretation of the theory of law. *Cicero's Social and Political Thought*, by Wood, and *Cicero, the Senior Statesman*, by Mitchell, furnish material relating to Cicero's times and his general theories concerning society. *Law and the Life of Rome*, by Dorey, describes the place of legal theory and procedures in Cicero's day.

QUESTION 3

What are the essential features of Hobbes's theory of the Social Contract?

Answer Plan

The Social Contract (or 'Covenant') theory can be traced back to the ancient Greeks. It enjoyed wide currency in the seventeenth and eighteenth centuries through the writings of Hobbes, Locke and Rousseau, and affected theories of the law concerned with the rights and duties of governments and citizens. The theory involves the fiction of a 'state of nature' in which, according to Hobbes (1588–1679), there were no enforceable criteria of right and wrong; it was a state of perpetual struggle which could be ended only by the surrender of individual liberties into the hands of a sovereign. The question asks for 'essential features'. Attention should be given, therefore, to the 'state of nature', the 'natural laws' and Hobbes's basic remedy for social conflict. A skeleton plan is proposed along the following lines:

❖ Introduction;
❖ Hobbes's 'laws of motion';
❖ *Leviathan*;
❖ analysis of the state of nature;
❖ natural laws;
❖ the Social Contract;
❖ indivisibility of the sovereign power;
❖ law as command of the sovereign;
❖ problem of 'bad law';
❖ conclusion, Hobbes's theories in our time.

ANSWER

Hobbes's legal and political theories are derived from his natural philosophy which is based on his 'law of motion'. All human behaviour, according to this law, mimics the activities of 'bodies in motion'. Just as the natural tendency of moving bodies to follow a line of their original direction will result in their colliding with other moving bodies, so the assertion by some individuals of their rights and freedoms will bring them into conflict with other individuals asserting the same type of rights and freedoms. The result is a continuous collision of wills, and perpetual struggle. In his *Leviathan* (published in 1651, the year in which the future Charles II fled to France after being defeated by Cromwell), Hobbes outlined his views on law, the individual and the state. It pleased no faction: Anglicans and Catholics resented his ideas concerning the role of the church; Royalists objected to his analysis of sovereignty; Cromwellians resented his advocacy of absolute monarchy. The doctrine embodying the fiction of a Social Covenant struck a chord in legal theory which echoes even today.

The condition of men before the emergence of states or civil societies, referred to by Hobbes as 'the state of nature', is analysed closely. In such a state, all men are equal and all have a right to act so as to survive. The 'right of all to all' involves a freedom to possess, use and enjoy all that an individual could obtain for himself. Man was driven by the will to survive and by the fear of violent death. The continuous clash of wills and 'bodies in motion' produced anarchy and a resulting 'war of all against all'. Neither 'good' nor 'evil' was recognised in this conflict: 'good' tended to be equated with 'survival', while 'evil' was associated with 'threats to survival'. In this state, individuals possess no capacity to build an ordered community.

Certain 'natural laws' emerge in the state of nature and attract some support because they are considered as involving concern for individual safety. They are essentially rules of behaviour, the observation of which might assist personal survival. Hobbes considers the first of these laws to be fundamental: 'peace is to be sought after.' This law is 'natural' because it is an obvious extension of concern for individual survival. An individual will have a better chance of survival if he assists in the creation and maintenance of overall conditions of peace. A person will be impelled, naturally, to seek a peaceful environment because of his desire to survive.

From the first law, Hobbes derives a second. Although men have rights to *all* things, these rights ought not to be retained to their full extent; certain rights ought to be 'relinquished or transferred'. A man should be willing, when others are similarly minded, to relinquish his rights to all things 'and be contented with so much liberty against other men as he would allow other men against himself'. To refuse to part with one's rights to all things is to act against the law of nature and 'the reason of peace'. A third law concerns the duty of a man to carry out a contract to which he is a party.

These laws are considered by Hobbes to be immutable and eternal; they have application to all societies and are supplemented by precepts, such as the need to avoid ingratitude, and the using of things in common that cannot be divided.

Without observance of the laws of nature there will be continuous struggle arising from the conflict of individual judgments as to how best to survive. The result will be 'no arts, letters or society ... continual fear and danger of death, and the life of man will be solitary, poor, nasty, brutish and short'. To avoid this necessitates a Social Contract which will bring about a commonwealth or state, and which will create laws distinguishing good and evil (that is, what is contrary to and what is not contrary to the statutes of the realm).

Men will create a civil society only by virtue of a covenant between individuals. (Some jurists have suggested that Hobbes's use of the Biblical term 'covenant' may reflect his acquaintance with the remarks of the Bible translator Tyndale: 'Faith according to the covenants is our salvation . . . Where thou findest a promise, there must thou understand a covenant.' The term is used in the famous declaration of the Pilgrim Fathers in 1620, on the *Mayflower*, where reference is made to a solemn, mutual covenant for combination into a 'civil body politic'.) In Hobbes's words, it is as if men should say to one another: 'I authorise and surrender my right of governing myself to this person or this assembly of persons, but on the vital condition that you, too, will surrender your right to him and authorise all his actions in like manner.' In essence, the Social Contract (or covenant) is absolute and irrevocable. The parties to the Contract are individuals, making promises to transfer their rights to govern themselves to some sovereign. The Contract is *not* made between the individuals and that sovereign. Indeed, the sovereign has an absolute power to govern; there is no point at which he may be considered as subject to those who made the Contract among themselves. Further, it is important to note that Hobbes has in mind, when referring to the sovereign, a 'person' or 'an assembly of persons'. The theory of the Social Covenant does not necessarily demand an absolute monarch (although that would reflect Hobbes's preference); it could have application to an elected assembly.

'Indivisibility of the sovereign power' is an important aspect of the contract theory. The citizens have agreed, in effect, that the totality of their individual wills and judgments will be represented henceforth by the single will and judgment of the sovereign. He acts on behalf of the citizens, and his actions are taken as an affirmation of the identity of their wills with his will. His will is their will; his actions reflect this unity. From this principle follows an extremely important political and legal concept – it is illogical and wrong, according to Hobbes, for a citizen to engage in resisting the sovereign. In doing so, he would be resisting himself and, further, resistance would be a manifestation of the type of independent judgment which characterised the 'state of nature' and is, therefore, undesirable. The sovereign's power must be total and, in effect, absolute.

Without a sovereign, civil law and social contract are not possible. For Hobbes, a law is the command of the sovereign 'to do or to forebear'. Law requires a legal order and a central power of enforcement. In the absence of power to enforce a law, a covenant is mere words. Hobbes suggests, too, that there can be no 'unjust law'. To the care of the sovereign belongs the making of good laws. But 'good law' does not mean 'just law', because a law made by the sovereign cannot be unjust. Justice means, in practice, obedience to the law, and this is why, according to Hobbes, justice comes into existence only *after* a law has been made by the sovereign. Justice cannot itself be the appropriate standard for the law. Further, when the sovereign makes a law, he does so as though the citizens were making it collectively. That upon which they have agreed cannot be 'unjust'. Keeping the contract under which individuals have agreed to obey the sovereign is vital to justice. Because law is the command of the sovereign, and because justice involves obeying that law, an 'unjust law' is impossible.

Hobbes does make clear, however, that there can be 'bad law'. If the sovereign, in making a law, fails to ensure the safety of the people who have entrusted him with appropriate powers, then the law may be considered 'bad'. (Indeed, human sovereigns may command legitimately only those activities that do not constitute contraventions of the law of nature.) Yet this is not a matter for the people to judge lightly, nor should it be used as a justification for disobedience and rebellion. Given that the sovereign alone has the power to judge what has to be done in the interests of the security of the people, he must proceed on the basis of the exercise of that power. To question his judgment, to voice disagreement, is to revert to the anarchy which characterised the undesirable state of nature. This is a part of the price to be paid for the peace which is intended to flow from the surrender of one's individual will. Where a sovereign makes 'bad law' or performs acts which seem contrary to the general interests of the community, it is, says Hobbes, a matter between him and his God, not between him and the citizens. (Hobbes declares that the sovereign is 'obliged by the law of nature, and must render an account thereof to God, the author of that law, and to none but Him'.) But where it is quite clear that the sovereign has lost the capacity to maintain the peace and protect the safety of the citizens, *or* where he has acted in an obvious attempt to destroy the individual's right of self-preservation, citizens may be absolved from their duty of loyalty. There is, therefore, always a check upon the exercise of absolute power exercised by a sovereign who opposes his own interest to the common good.

The fear of anarchy and social violence is ever-present in Hobbes's writings – a sure reflection of the conflicts of his day. Total obedience to an absolute sovereign, to the protector of the community's peace, seemed essential to Hobbes. Indeed, he insisted, in terms which offended the church deeply, on the subordination of church and religion to the state. If circumstances arose in which a Christian were to interpret the actions of his sovereign as a violation of Divine law, then he must continue to give obedience to that sovereign, failing which he may decide 'to go to Christ in martyrdom'. The church itself has the same type of legal status as that enjoyed by any other corporation. As with all corporations, the true head is, according to Hobbes, the sovereign.

Hobbes represents, in Friedmann's words, a jurist who has shaken himself free from medieval society and its ideas and, in so doing, has completed the revolution of the Renaissance. He has removed the authority of Divine law from the church and has challenged its pretensions. The protection of the individual within the community has become a matter of great importance. Law is seen as a means of preventing anarchy and assuring survival in peace. There can be no society distinct from the state. Legal authority is to be vested in a sovereign whose laws will depend upon appropriate sanctions. Hobbes insists that 'governments without the sword are mere words, and of no strength to secure a man at all'. Real law is civil law and that is constituted by the law commanded by the sovereign and enforced by his will.

Almost every aspect of Hobbes's Social Contract theory was reflected in the works of jurists and political theoreticians who were prominent in the eighteenth and nineteenth centuries. Locke built upon Hobbes's individualism, although he opposed his theory of absolutism. Hobbes's utilitarianism, which led him to view the sovereign as 'a utilitarian creature' of individuals who had empowered him to act on their behalf so as to prevent mutual destruction, was linked to Bentham's later view of the law as serving the totality of individuals within a community. The concept of laws espoused by Austin – 'laws properly so called are a species of command . . . all positive law is deduced from a clearly determinable lawgiver as sovereign' – may be likened to Hobbes's view. In our century, the 'enlightened absolutism' favoured by Hobbes has been utilised by some jurists in order to buttress concepts of law at the basis of theories of the collectivist, totalitarian system of government. Others view his analysis of law as a call for the state to concern itself with ensuring the security of citizens' well-being, and for a jurisprudence which will recognise the welfare of individual members of the community as one of the supreme objectives of the law and the legal system.

Aim Higher ★

Students can gain extra marks by noting how Hobbes's absolutist social contract theory was based on his pessimistic and gloomy portrayal of human nature, which was not based on standard Christian theology and the universality of 'original sin' but was based on his observation of human nature and its essentially selfish and self-interested nature. Hobbes believed that without strong central authority human life would be 'nasty, solitary, brutish and short', because of the essentially self-interested nature of human beings who would 'war' against each other unless restrained by 'Leviathan' – the all powerful state. The belief in the moral imperfection of mankind does not necessarily entail belief in the 'original sin' doctrine of orthodox Christianity. Over the centuries Thomas Hobbes, David Hume and Sigmund Freud all understood the moral imperfection of persons from a non-Christian secular perspective.

NOTES

Hobbes's *Leviathan*, edited by Oakeshott, contains an exposition of his views on government, society and law. *The Logic of Leviathan*, by Gautier, is a critical account of Hobbes's theories. Peters gives a useful picture of the man and his work in *Hobbes*. Hampton's *Hobbes and the Social Contract Tradition* examines aspects of social contract theories.

QUESTION 4

'Locke's theory admirably expressed certain ideas which were in the ascendant at his time and about to develop continuously throughout the eighteenth century and most of the nineteenth century': Friedmann (*Legal Theory*).

▶ Give an account of this theory.

Answer Plan

Locke's theory concerning the state and the individual differs radically from that of his predecessor, Hobbes. The 'state of nature' as envisaged by Locke is not that envisaged by Hobbes. This should be emphasised in the answer. Locke's concern for the dangers which could arise from an absolute monarchy should be noted. In particular, the essence of the Social Contract as reflecting the rights of citizens and their power to remove a government in certain extreme circumstances can be seen as a harbinger of the jurisprudential theories which emerged in Europe and America after Locke's day. The following skeleton plan is suggested:

- ❖ Introduction;
- ❖ the *Treatises of Civil Government*, with an emphasis on liberty;
- ❖ man's 'natural state';
- ❖ essence of the Social Contract;
- ❖ preservation of property;
- ❖ division of powers;
- ❖ right of a people to reject tyranny;
- ❖ continuing significance of Locke's views;
- ❖ conclusion, noting the importance of his awareness that tyrannies begin where law ends.

ANSWER

Locke's jurisprudential thought has been characterised as reflecting the doctrines underlying the 'Glorious Revolution' of 1688. His *Treatises of Civil Government* (1699) presented law as a shield against the pretensions of autocracy and despotism and as an instrument for realising and protecting the natural rights of human beings. Where Hobbes had stressed *security*, Locke (1632–1704) placed an emphasis on *liberty*. His writings indicate a reaction against absolutism, a concern for the significance of powers delegated by a people to its government (which prepared the way for later theories of political democracy), an awareness of the importance of the concept of inalienability of individual rights and a sanctioning of the rights of property in particular. These ideas were to flower later in the doctrines which supported the Founding Fathers and the rise of democracy in America.

The 'natural state' of man was, according to Locke, in contrast to that postulated by Hobbes, a situation of total, perfect freedom. Men were able to decide on their activities and to dispose of their persons and possessions as they thought fit 'within the bounds of the law of nature, without asking leave, or depending upon the will of any other man'. It was a state characterised by 'equality', wherein power and jurisdiction were reciprocal. The law of nature allowed men to live together according to reason 'without a common superior on earth with authority to judge between them'. Liberty, not licence, prevailed and, according to the dictates of the law of nature, no one was encouraged to harm another in his life, health, liberty or possessions.

But dangers and inconveniences arose. First, the individual's enjoyment of the natural rights of life, liberty and possessions was uncertain and was exposed to the hostile activities of others. Secondly, there was a lack of impartial judges with authority to determine disputes according to any form of established law. Each man was both judge and executioner in his own cause and each tended to avenge transgressions in intemperate fashion. Thirdly, there was a lack of a commonly accepted power to back up and support sentences where wrongdoing had occurred.

So to end this disorder and insecurity, men found it necessary to enter into a Social Contract. Its object was the preservation of life, liberty and estate against the injuries inflicted by others. Fundamental to the Contract is a *pactum unionis*, whereby men agree 'to unite in one political society', and a *pactum subjectionis*, whereby a majority gives power to a government which will protect the individual. This is in contrast to Hobbes's advocacy of total subjection of the individual to the sovereign. The 'law of nature' stood, for Locke, as an eternal rule made for all men, 'legislators as well as others'. An anticipation of the doctrines of popular democracy, with legislatures accountable to the people, may be discerned here.

It is the *right to enforce* the law of nature which, by virtue of the Social Contract, is given into the hands of the 'body politic', thus creating a 'political, or civil society'. Nothing more is surrendered. Hence Locke rejects the concept of absolute monarchy as a desirable type of government. A government with limited powers is preferable.

(This ideal was to be pursued after Locke's day by jurists and others striving for the 'rule of law' within societies.) Those who have given their 'natural power' of deciding disputes among themselves into the hands of the community are conferring upon that community the role of 'umpire', whereby government is given an authorisation to set up 'a judge on earth' with power to determine controversies and redress injuries. Indeed, without an authorisation of this kind, without a right to enforce the law, men will remain in 'the state of nature' with all its difficulties and perils.

In words that have been echoed in a variety of forms in centuries after Locke (as in the English case of *Entick v Carrington* (1765) and the American case of *Savings and Loan Association v Topeka* (1875)), he emphasised that God had given the earth 'to the use of the industrious and rational . . . not to the fancy or covetousness of the quarrelsome and the contentious', and he enunciated 'the great and chief end of men's uniting into commonwealth and putting themselves under government' as 'the preservation of their property'. The term 'property' is used in a wide sense so as to include 'life, liberty and estate'. Friedmann and other jurists have noted that Locke's views in relation to property ('a combination of noble ideals and acquisitiveness, and the protection of vested interests') underpinned later struggles within democratic societies for a sanctioning of the right to own and dispose freely of the fruits of one's labours.

Locke finds that the institution of private property existed in nature and, therefore, preceded the establishment of civil society. God gave the land to persons in common, commanding them to labour and to use the fruits of the earth. Where men remove parts of the land from the common supply and mix it with their own labour, they are entitled to the objects resulting from their toil. There is a 'natural right', therefore, to appropriate to one's own use land and its produce (the so-called 'theory of unilateral acquisition'). Indeed, says Locke, land values arise largely from the labour expended on the land. Private ownership is enlarged, as a result of the use of money as a means of exchange, well beyond those boundaries authorised by a simple act of appropriation. The call for extended rights of private ownership of the land and other types of property became important in moves in the eighteenth and nineteenth centuries towards an extension of general political rights when it was realised that the ownership of land conferred economic and political power. Locke's influence on this area of thought remains powerful. Gray, writing in 1991, speaks of the 'brooding omnipresence of Locke' as a pervasive influence on all philosophical thinking on property, even today.

Because of the significance of property rights in Locke's pattern of liberty, he was obliged to maintain that no part of a person's property ought to be taken from him by the government without his consent. Such an improper exercise of government power should be considered as a violation of the Social Contract by virtue of which power is exercised. The community as a whole must ensure that its governing body does not move beyond the powers bestowed on it. The legislative authority may not assume to itself any power to rule 'by extemporary arbitrary decrees; it is bound to dispense justice and decide the rights of citizens by promulgating laws'. Nor should these laws be varied so as to have 'one rule for the rich and poor, for the favourite at Court, and the countryman at plough'. Locke is enunciating an ideal which was to be advocated repeatedly in the writings of later jurists who called for equality of all before the law.

The supreme power within a community has no other end, according to Locke, but 'preservation'; it can never have a right to 'destroy, enslave or designedly to impoverish subjects'. This necessitates a 'division of powers' within the state: a legislative power to create rules, an executive power to enforce them, and a 'federative power' to control the state's external relations. Where the legislative and executive powers are concentrated in the same hands, a breach of the desired ends of the Social Contract is likely. But this danger was not viewed by Locke as an argument for removing the prerogative of the executive to use its general discretion for the good of the community. Where appropriate laws have not been promulgated by the legislature, where no general directions have been given to the executive, and where unusual stress and emergency demand swift action, the executive may act for the public advantage. But separation of powers (a concept which Montesquieu (1689–1755) and jurists in our day see as essential to the rule of law) remains for Locke an important guarantee of the preservation of a commonwealth and its individual members.

Even where powers are separated, abuse and violation of individual rights may occur. There is needed, therefore, a final guarantor of the law of nature. Fundamentally, Locke rejects the 'rights' of a 'tyrant'. The people as a whole, acting in the name of the liberties which have been entrusted to the supreme power under the Social Contract, may remove a legislature which, deliberately or otherwise, forgets the purpose and nature of its trust. Locke, who had experienced the practice of absolute government under the Stuarts, urged that the power of the state must 'never be supposed to extend further than the common good', so that where a legislature moves beyond its powers, as understood by the community, the people may apply appropriate checks. He argues that nobody can transfer to another more power than he has in himself, and nobody has an arbitrary power over himself or over any other person to destroy his own life or take away the life or property of another. The final resort by the people to an 'appeal to Heaven' which, in practice, may take the form of resistance or revolution, is seen by Locke as necessary if the law of nature is to be upheld against oppressive laws which seem to deny its validity.

Locke's appeal to 'natural rights' as the true guarantee against a regime which seems to abuse its powers, so that the community has the right to resume a trust which is in danger of betrayal, is yet another theme which came to dominate advances in the eighteenth and nineteenth centuries towards the rule of law and the extension of democracy. The American Declaration of Independence (1776) embodies the essence of Locke's doctrine relating to the fundamental right of a people to 'alter or abolish' a form of government which becomes destructive of the ends perceived by the people as constituting the very purpose of the state. The Declaration suggests the concept which Locke had stressed, but in a novel manner – the idea of a government resting upon trust, upon a *fiduciary relationship* of government and governed, rather than upon the mere duties flowing from a Social Contract. But Locke must not be considered as advocating rebellion in all cases of an abuse of governmental powers. The justification of popular resistance must be sought in a long series of abuses and a very clear threat to the 'lives, liberties and estates' of citizens. Nor does resistance imply revenge; it is an activity aimed at the restoration of an order violated by an oppressor.

The political and legal ferment within societies of the eighteenth and nineteenth centuries was often within the context of circumstances envisaged by Locke. His warnings that *whenever laws end, tyrannies will begin*, and that 'what duty is, cannot be understood without a law' were utilised by jurists who sought to express theories resting on the need for a widening of the basis of law. His cautions concerning the consequences of unbridled governmental powers were remembered in calls for the creation of popular power and an extension of the franchise. Although doubt was cast in increasing measure upon the veracity of Locke's 'state of nature' (thus, Hamilton, writing in this century, speaks of this 'state' as being 'a curious affair, peopled with Indians of North America and run by the scientific principles of [Locke's] friend, Sir Isaac Newton'), his contribution to political and legal theory is profound. Keeton reminds us that it is from Locke that we derive today 'the principle of democratic government, resting upon the consent of the governed' – an extraordinarily valuable legacy of the *Treatises of Civil Government* and the subsequent jurisprudential and political thinking which they engendered.

Common Pitfalls

Students can avoid the common pitfall of contrasting the difference between Hobbes and Locke whilst ignoring the similarities between Hobbes and Locke. The good student will observe that both thinkers were secular and rationalistic in their political philosophy and that Locke was profoundly influenced by Hobbes's *Leviathan*. However, in the final analysis Hobbes was 'totalitarian' in his belief in absolute sovereign power, whereas Locke was much more in line with the tradition of modern western democratic thought in believing in limited government which could be replaced if the government violated citizen's property rights.

NOTES

Locke's *Two Treatises of Civil Government* is available in an edition by Laslett. Comments on Locke's theory of property may be found in 'Property according to Locke', by Hamilton, in (1932) 41 Yale LJ and 'Property in thin air', by Gray, in [1991] CLJ 293. *John Locke: a Biography*, by Cranston, explains the nature of the society in which Locke lived.

3 Natural Law

INTRODUCTION

Natural law, which is the subject of the questions in this chapter, is an enduring concept in jurisprudence, ranging from Aristotle, who held that there is a natural law which 'everywhere possesses the same authority and is no mere matter of opinion', through Cicero, who taught that 'Nature herself has placed in our ears a power of judging', and Aquinas for whom the natural law was 'the participation of the eternal law in the rational creature', to today's natural lawyers such as John Finnis who view law from the perspective of its ultimate moral function which is taken to be the ability of law to co-ordinate human activity for the common good. Natural law is often contrasted with the 'positive law', namely, the legal rules promulgated in formal fashion by the state and enforced through defined sanctions. A problem for students is to decide which 'type' of natural law is being referred to, since the term has been used in so many different senses. It is essential, therefore, to *check the precise historical and juristic context* of the term, particularly when answering questions on this topic.

Checklist ✔

Ensure that you understand the following topics:

- natural and positive law contrasted;
- natural law as an aspect of Divine providence;
- Aquinas's divisions of law;
- the link between natural law and modern legal systems (the 'common good' view of law);
- Finnis's self-evident human goods.

QUESTION 5

What is Aquinas's theory of law?

Answer Plan

Thomas Aquinas (1225–74) was concerned with systematising knowledge, on the basis of Catholic doctrine, so that the cosmos might be understood as a vast unit in which everything had a place and a meaning. Within this system of knowledge, God's plans for mankind occupied a special place, and the law was to be comprehended as a part of those plans. Aquinas propounded a theory of law based on his conception of 'reason'; this resulted in a fourfold division of law in which so-called 'natural law' is of much significance. The answer given below is based on the following skeleton plan:

- ❖ Introduction;
- ❖ background of Aquinas;
- ❖ influence of Aristotelian thought;
- ❖ fourfold division of law;
- ❖ problem of morality;
- ❖ violation of the natural law and its consequences;
- ❖ conclusion, stressing the work of Aquinas as a synthesiser of philosophy and religious thought in his interpretation of law.

ANSWER

St Thomas Aquinas occupies an important place in the history of the development of natural law doctrine. He had studied as a Dominican monk under Albertus Magnus and, in later years, produced works of lasting significance in which he effected a synthesis of the logic of Aristotle, the religious thought of the early Christian Fathers, and some of the patterns of classical Roman law. In his celebrated *Summa Theologica* (c 1266) he set out a fully systematised approach to law which, even today, dominates the thinking of many Catholic jurists, as evidenced by the growing neo-Scholastic school of jurisprudence. Law is to be understood as part of God's plan for mankind – this is the belief which is central to the concepts mentioned below.

It is important to remember the context within which Aquinas worked. The authority of the Catholic Church was expanding, and those whose task it was to explain doctrine were guided by a strict pattern of thought. Interpretation of the Scriptures had produced two principles which were of direct relation to attempts at explaining the nature of law. First, the principle of *unity* (based on 'one God, one Church') was reflected in the wish for 'one Church believing in one law'. Secondly, the principle of supremacy of law, which was seen as an aspect of the unity of the world, taught that all persons, including rulers, were under the law's dominion. Aquinas's general approach to law was fashioned with these principles in mind.

At this time, a study of the works of Aristotle was not always welcomed by the dominant church hierarchy, which viewed his 'scientific rationalism' as a potential threat to church dogma. Aquinas did not share this attitude. He was deeply impressed by Aristotle's emphasis on reason and the primacy of intelligence. He made a deep study of Aristotle's works, lectured publicly on their significance, and was affected profoundly by their elucidation of the part that could be played by reason in the understanding of phenomena such as law.

In the Summa Theologica Aquinas seeks to establish the framework of a systematised 'science of theology'. He employs the highly formalised style of argument which was common in his day (and which was to be found in the procedures of the civil courts in those parts of Europe where the inquisitorial style of trial was common). Questions are posed, sub-questions emerge and are answered, and further argument leads to attempted refutation until an outline of proof and a final enunciation of an answer to the original question appear. The exposition of law associated with Aquinas is derived from his answers to Questions 90 to 97 in the Summa. Law is perceived always as God's instrument for assisting man in the lifelong process leading to the perfection of his nature.

Aquinas begins his examination and interpretation of law by considering 'morality'. The very basis of moral obligation is to be discovered within man's nature. Built into his nature is a group of God-given 'inclinations'. They include self-preservation, propagation of the species and (reflecting man's rationality) an inclination towards a search for truth. Man is guided by a simple and basic moral truth – to do good and to avoid evil. Because man is rational, he is under a natural obligation to protect himself and to live peacefully within society. A peaceful, ordered society demands human laws, fashioned for the direction of social behaviour. These human laws will arise from man's rational capacity to discern correct patterns of 'good conduct'. The rules underlying human laws will derive from a moral system which ought to be taken into account by all mankind – a sort of 'natural law'.

Law must be thought of, according to Aquinas, as being linked essentially with reason. A law may be considered as a 'rule' and also as 'a measure' of the nature of human activities. He reminds us that the word lex is derived from ligare (to bind) and that law 'binds us' to act in particular ways. The rules and measures of human acts are to be thought of in terms of law and also in terms of our reason. Reason directs us to the fulfilment of 'our ends' (an Aristotelian concept). Man's laws should go hand in hand with reason. Indeed, man's laws may be thought of as *'ordinances of reason for the common good, made by those who have care of the community, and are promulgated'*. The natural law is 'promulgated' by the very fact that God has instilled it into man's mind so that it can be known 'naturally'. The natural law is the product of God's wisdom. We can better comprehend that wisdom by studying human nature and the natural law. Theology *and* philosophy together will help in this quest for comprehension of the truth. Aquinas is suggesting that a synthetic approach to a study of the law, in which Christian dogma and Aristotelian philosophy will assist, will produce a clear understanding of the nature and power of God's law.

A *fourfold division of law* is put forward by Aquinas. The first type of law is *lex aeterna* – 'eternal law': all laws, in so far as they participate in 'right reason', are derived from the eternal law. This is the Divine Intellect and Will of God directing *all things*. God's rational guidance is not subject to constraints of time – it is eternal. Not to know eternal law – God's plan for his creatures – is to be without direction, so that one's true ends can never be achieved; but awareness of the eternal law is imprinted on us. God alone knows the eternal law in its totality, but those few 'blessed persons' who have been able to know God in His essence may perceive its truth.

'Divine law' – *lex divina* – is the eternal law governing man and may be known by him through direct revelation, as in the Scriptures, for example, The Ten Commandments. Man requires a type of law that can direct him to his end, namely, eternal happiness; such law contains no errors, and forbids all sins, allowing no evil to go unpunished. Aristotle had argued that man had a natural purpose and an end, so that natural law, known through human reason, could provide an adequate guide. Aquinas distances himself from Aristotle at this point. Because man's eternal happiness is related to God's plans, man needs direction from God's law in addition to human law and natural law. Natural law comes from man's rational knowledge of 'the good', but that knowledge is, by its nature, limited. Divine law comes, through revelation, directly from God. Revelation is the guide for man's reason, allowing his highest nature to be perfected by Divine grace. Here is an interesting example of Aquinas giving a 'Christian gloss' to the views of the 'pagan Greeks' and achieving an imaginative synthesis.

The third type of law is 'natural law' – *lex naturalis*, which is man's participation in the eternal cosmic law, as it is known through reason. Because of man's possession of God-given reason, he may enjoy a share in Divine reason itself and may derive from it 'a natural inclination to such actions and ends as are fitting', such as the search for good and the avoidance of evil. Where man exercises his reason correctly he will understand the fundamental principles of God's plan. Basic principles for human guidance will emerge, such as that 'good' ('that which all things seek after') is to be done and evil is to be shunned. But, because of bad customs and habits, some humans will ignore the natural laws; the result is a division of their energies from those tasks of a life-fulfilling kind.

The fourth type of law is 'human law' – *lex humana*, involving the particular application of the natural law and resulting in legislation by governments. Just as men draw conclusions in the various sciences from naturally known, but indemonstrable, principles, so, declares Aquinas, human beings must draw from the precepts of the natural law answers to problems which emerge when they live together in society. Where human law conforms to the law of reason, it conforms to the law of God and advances human development. A significant aspect of Aquinas's concept of human law, which has overtones of relevance for the present day, is the relationship he perceives between human law and its moral dimensions. He repudiates the thesis that a law is a law merely because it has been decreed by a sovereign. He suggests that a rule takes on the character of 'a law' only where it has appropriate moral dimensions. Certain questions must be asked: does the rule exist in conformity to the precepts of the natural law, and does it suggest agreement with the basis of the moral law? 'That which is not just seems no law at all', he declares. Where a human law diverges from the law of nature, it is no longer a law, but a mere perversion of the law. *Such a law cannot bind in conscience.* This is not to say, however, that it must not, therefore, be obeyed; obedience to it might be essential so as to prevent an even greater evil, such as the spread of lawlessness, scandal or great harm. Aquinas takes a further step forward. Laws which are opposed to the Divine plan, such as the laws of tyrants inducing to 'idolatry', must not be observed: our duty is to obey God rather than man. *A law which is a violation of the natural law should not, in general, be obeyed.*

There are many jurists, inside and outside the Catholic Church, who see Aquinas as a divinely-inspired genius, able to synthesise a variety of approaches and capable of bringing system into an unwieldy group of theories. In moving beyond his predecessors and contemporaries, he was able to produce a unified set of principles in relation to the law. Natural law is envisaged as a source of *general principles* rather than detailed jurisprudential rules. Above all, perhaps, is *the elevation of human reason* in the service of comprehension of the law. God's law is the 'reason of Divine wisdom'; Christianity is reason; human institutions, including those related to law, required the exercise of reason if they are to be built in enduring fashion. The Thomist view of law is, fundamentally, that of Cicero, writing in *De Republica* (52 BC): '... true law is right reason in agreement with Nature ... God is the author of this law, its promulgator and its enforcing judge.' In essence: 'The proper effect of the law is to make men good ... it should lead men to their proper virtue.'

NOTES

A classic account of the work of Aquinas is given by D'Arcy in *Thomas Aquinas*. Gilson's *The Philosophy of Aquinas* gives the setting of Aquinas's legal thought. Bloch relates the theory of Aquinas to contemporary problems in 'The relative natural law of Aquinas' in his book, *Natural Law and Human Dignity*. Lisska's *Aquinas' Theory of Natural Law* contains an account of the principles of the *Summa Theologica*.

QUESTION 6

What is the relevance of natural law theory today?

Answer Plan

The tradition of 'natural law' theory is often misunderstood as having little in common with the mainstream of jurisprudence or being concerned with crass slogans, such as 'An unjust law is not a law'. However, properly understood, the tradition of natural law going back to Thomas Aquinas has much to offer legal theory by providing a moral basis for the criticism and guidance of the activities of judges, legislators and citizens. The 'big picture' perspective of natural law thought, as exemplified by Professor Finnis in *Natural Law and Natural Rights* (1980), offers an antidote to the 'narrowness' of some legal theory dominated by, for example, what happens in the courtroom. It is perfectly possible to grasp the essence of natural law theory without subscribing to the theological underpinnings of much natural law thought. Therefore, in a secular 'post religious' society, natural law theory can have continued relevance today. A skeleton plan is presented as follows:

- ❖ Introduction;
- ❖ the relevance of natural law theory today;
- ❖ the purposes of traditional 'natural law' thought;
- ❖ the 'common good' view of law;
- ❖ the distinction between 'central' and 'peripheral' cases in concepts such as 'friendship' and 'law';
- ❖ criticisms of natural law theory: natural law gives a distorted benign view of law, the 'common good' is a problematic concept;
- ❖ conclusion, natural law is not concerned centrally with the slogan *lex injusta non est lex* but with working out the relationship between law and morality.

ANSWER

The tradition of natural law theory can appear to be somewhat detached from the mainstream of analytical jurisprudence – represented by legal positivism and Ronald Dworkin's theory of law – which asks questions concerning the nature of a legal system or the nature of common law adjudication. Natural law theory appears at times to be remote from such issues as its concerns seem much more high flown, relating to the connections between the cosmic order, divine will, human reason and law.

However, natural law theory does have a significant contribution to make to mainstream jurisprudence. As Brian Bix comments (in an essay entitled 'Natural law: the modern tradition', in *The Oxford Handbook of Jurisprudence and Philosophy of Law* (2002)) perhaps the most important idea brought to jurisprudence by modern natural law theorists is that a view of law that recognises law's higher moral aspirations gives a fuller understanding of the institution of law than legal theories which are merely content to describe law (for example, legal positivism – see Hart, *The Concept of Law* (1961)) or to focus on one important feature of law (for example, Dworkin's account of common law adjudication – see *Law's Empire* (1986)).

The insight that modern natural law theory offers to contemporary legal theory is that the human institution of law can only be fully understood if we understand the ultimate moral value of law to human society. In the words of the central figure in natural law theory, Thomas Aquinas (1225–1273): 'Law is an ordinance of reason for the common good.' This basic insight is lost if we merely focus on describing the crucial elements of law and a legal system or concentrate too fully on common law adjudication. As Aquinas pointed out, there is an intimate connection between the institution of law and the proper (as in the sense of morally correct) governance of society: 'Law is the primary proper means of co-ordinating civil society.' This view of the 'bigger picture' than that provided for by mainstream jurisprudence is perhaps the greatest contribution natural law theory can make to legal theory today. As Professor Finnis comments (in his modern restatement of natural law theory, *Natural Law and Natural Rights*), the true tradition of natural law theory is not about the rather obvious insight that morality often affects the law but, instead, is about pointing out the true requirements of morality to provide a rational basis for the activities of legislators, judges and citizens. This is linked to the ultimate purpose of natural law theory which is to show, according to Finnis, how law and legal institutions can be justified – on what conditions, and to criticise those legal institutions by showing the ways in which they are defective. The natural law theory of Professor Finnis is not then merely descriptive of law (as in the tradition of legal positivism) but is normative (guidance giving), similar to Dworkin's legal theory, although the theory of Finnis looks at the whole institution of law rather than the narrow issue of 'a judge in a hard case' that has preoccupied Dworkin's legal theorising for, as Finnis comments, the tradition of natural law theorising is not characterised by any particular answer to the question of what a judge should do in a 'hard case'.

The 'natural law tradition' has been around for thousands of years and can be traced to Ancient Greece (Aristotle) and Rome (Cicero). St Augustine, in the fifth century, was an important figure in the development of a specifically Christian natural law doctrine, but the key historical figure was Thomas Aquinas in the thirteenth century. As Mark Murphy comments (in 'The natural law tradition in ethics' in *Stanford Encyclopedia of Philosophy* (2008)) we should take Aquinas's natural law theory as the central case of a natural law theory, given his influence at the time (for example, Pope John XXII in the fourteenth century was a canon lawyer and devotee of Aquinas) and in the present day (Professor Finnis wrote a commentary on the moral, legal and political thought of Aquinas in 1998). Indeed, the continuing influence of the thought of Aquinas can be seen in a recent work, *St Thomas Aquinas and the Natural Law Tradition* (edited by Goyette, Latkovic, and Myers (2004)) where, in the introduction, the authors comment that we are in the midst of a great revival of interest in natural law. Much of this thinking, say the authors, is traced in one degree or another to the thoughts of St Thomas Aquinas.

For Aquinas there are two key features of the natural law, as discerned in his work, *Summa Theologica*. The first feature looks at God's role as the giver of the natural law; the natural law discovered by the reason of man is just one aspect of divine providence. The second feature looks at things from the human perspective as the human recipient of the natural law. The 'natural law' constitutes the principles of practical rationality – those principles by which human action is to be judged as reasonable or unreasonable. From God's point of view, natural law is seen through its place in the scheme of divine providence and, from the human point of view, the natural law constitutes a set of naturally binding and knowable rules of reason.

There is a crucial point to be made. The natural law is discernible without divine revelation but purely through human reason. As Thomas Aquinas pointed out, the first principles of natural law are self-evident to the human mind but knowledge of the existence of God is not self-evident to the human mind and is only known through supernatural grace. 'Original sin' (a key 'natural law' doctrine), inherited by all persons from birth, has so clouded man's reason that knowledge of the divine creator can only come through divine revelation. Given that the natural law and natural law theory can be understood, assented to and analysed without considering the question of God's ultimate existence, it may be tempting to ask in a secular 'post Christian' age whether natural law theory really needs to argue for the existence of God at all. The central point of the theory of Finnis in *Natural Law and Natural Rights*, that the law is a specific and social human institution for the maintenance, protection and realisation of the 'common good' of society, can be grasped and assented to by even the most militant atheist or secularist or humanist. However, the ultimate connection between 'natural law theory' and the existence of God cannot be broken for the following reasons: first, just because natural law theory can be understood, analysed and applied without referring to the question of the existence of God it does not mean that no further explanation of the origin of natural law is available or that the existence and nature of God is not that explanation. Second, the founders of Christian natural law theory – in particular, St Augustine (*The City of God*) and St Thomas Aquinas (*Summa Theologica*) – would not have regarded as intelligible a theory of natural law without the existence of divine providence for mankind. The 'internal point of view' of St Augustine, St Thomas Aquinas, and even modern writers such as Finnis who see an unbreakable link between the existence of God and the natural law, must be considered when assessing natural law theory. However, Finnis dismisses as a 'phantom' the view of Kai Nielsen (in 'The myth of natural law', in *Law and Philosophy*, edited by Hook (1964)) that natural law concepts are totally dependent for intelligibility on the view that God exists. Natural law theory can be understood in terms acceptable to an atheist even if many natural law theorists posit God as the ultimate origin of natural law.

Exactly how modern natural law theory relates to modern society will now be sketched. Professor Finnis, in his groundbreaking work *Natural Law and Natural Rights*, rescued the natural law tradition from many misconceptions that had grown up over the centuries, such as the slogan *lex injusta non est lex* ('an unjust law is not a law') which does not represent the natural law tradition according to Finnis.

Finnis identified a number of self-evident 'human goods' which are self-evident to human reason. The integration into life and ordering of these basic goods over a lifetime is an important aspect of human well-being. These goods are seven in number: life, knowledge, play, friendship, religion, practical reasonableness and aesthetic experience (enjoyment of nature or art). It may be observed that some of these 'self-evident' goods are rather 'bourgeois' in character and their supposed 'universality' can be questioned.

The law, for Professor Finnis, comes in the following way to regulate human society: when many human beings as exist in a society try to pursue these 'self-evident' goods there will be inevitable conflicts and co-ordination problems which only practical authority can resolve. The law is the expression of the judgments and decisions of that practical authority. The point or function of human law is to facilitate the common good as connected to the realisation of the self-evident goods in human life by providing authoritative rules (laws) that solve the conflicts and co-ordination problems that arise in connection with many persons pursuing the 'self-evident' goods. Finnis comments in *Natural Law and Natural Rights* that the term 'law' refers to rules made by an effective authority for a community and supported by sanctions in accordance with the rule-guided courts. These legal rules and legal institutions are directed to the reasonable resolving of the community's co-ordination problems for the common good of that community. In order to effectively solve co-ordination problems, the law must be clearly and certainly identified by legal officials, civil servants and officials. Therefore, the natural lawyer, Professor Finnis, defends the legal positivist thesis that the law is identified from social sources. The argument is this: to perform the moral function of solving society's co-ordination problems for the benefit of the common good, the law must be clearly ascertained from human sources and no moral argument should cloud the identification of the law.

Therefore, the identification of the law independent of a moral argument is necessary for the central moral function of law: to co-ordinate human behaviour for the common good. The adoption of the legal positivist 'sources thesis' by the leading contemporary natural lawyer, Professor Finnis, supports the observation by the legal positivist, Raz (in his article 'About morality and the nature of law' (2006)), that it is a mistake to make the division between 'legal positivists' and 'natural lawyers' the basic division in legal philosophy. In distinction to Professor Hart's analysis in *The Concept of Law*, Professor Finnis goes beyond an analysis which purports only to describe law as a social phenomenon and social institution. Professor Finnis seeks to give an account of law from the central or focal case of law as a human institution designed to further the common good. This technique of seeking an explanation of a concept by focusing on the 'central' or 'focal' example of that concept rather than seeking a definition which will include 'peripheral' examples of that concept can be traced back to Aristotle (384–322 BC). So there are central cases, as Aristotle insisted, of friendship (lifelong friends, for example) and more or less peripheral cases (such as business friendships, casual or work friendships). There are central cases of constitutional government (such as the United Kingdom) and there are peripheral cases (such as Hitler's Germany). As Finnis, following Aristotle, points out, there is no point in restricting one's explanation of the central cases to those features present also in the peripheral cases. The description of the 'central cases' should be as conceptually rich and complex as is required to answer all relevant questions about these central cases. Therefore, Finnis, in *Natural Law and Natural Rights*, takes as his perspective for description the central case of law: the morally just legal system working for the common good. Finnis believes that a fully complex and adequate description of the concept of law cannot be given without analysing law through the prism of the ultimate function of law: to order civil society for the common good.

Professor Hart, in *Essays in Jurisprudence and Philosophy* (1983), criticises Finnis for believing that the 'central' case or 'focal' case of law is that which is for the 'common good'. Professor Hart comments that, in view of the horrors of human history and the evil use of law, then to say that the central meaning of law is that which is for the common good is an unbalanced perspective and as great a distortion of reality as the opposite Marxist identification of the central case of law with the pursuit of the interests of a dominant economic class. However, to defend Finnis against this trenchant criticism by Professor Hart, the interest of Finnis is in the ideal form of law, the potential of the idea of law to unlock and further the common good. Finnis is interested in the idea of law as a moral ideal, not the historical reality of the use of law which, as Hart correctly points out, has often been used for evil ends. Only by living in an ordered community under the rule of law can the common good be properly realised.

As Finnis comments in the very first sentence of *Natural Law and Natural Rights*, there are human goods that can be secured only through the institution of human law. For example, a taxation system which is fair and efficient, and is necessary to provide social services for the old and vulnerable in society, is one obvious advantage of a society under law. Natural law theory does not dictate what the precise level of taxation shall be in a particular society as this will depend on many changing economic and social factors, but natural law theory does stipulate adequate social service provision through an effective and fair taxation system. As Finnis comments, if material goods are to be used efficiently for human well-being there must normally be a regime of private property. However, the precise rules of such a regime of private property are not settled by natural law theory. Those in lawful authority must choose the particular rules of taxation, private property and contract, for example, but once the choice is made it becomes authoritative for officials and citizens alike. For Finnis, in a morally just legal order, the law represents the choices (the determination-concretisation by rational choice) of lawful authority to further the common good. The rulers' choice from a range of reasonable options determines what thereafter is just for those subject to their authority. There arises a moral obligation on citizens to obey the law. The citizens' obligation to obey is a duty not, strictly speaking, owed to the rulers themselves but rather to, if anyone, their fellow citizens in fairness since the law of a just state represents a seamless web of social co-ordination and fairness (see Finnis's article, 'Law as co-ordination' (1989)).

Finnis comments, in his commentary on Aquinas (*Aquinas: Moral, Political and Legal Theory* (1998)), that the central case of law is co-ordination of willing subjects by law which, by its fully public character, its clarity, generality, stability and predictability, treats them as partners in public reason. Aquinas, according to Finnis, understands the state precisely as the type of community fitted to securing goods which are only well secured by general and published laws employed with impartiality and coercive force. Aquinas holds that governments themselves are not above the law but are appropriately regulated and limited by law. This is reflected in two important moral truths: (1) that government is for the common good, not for the advantage of the rulers, and (2) that no-one has any 'natural right to govern'.

Aquinas originally based his argument for authority on the superiority in wisdom and intelligence that some would have, compared with others in their society. Whilst this is an important consideration in his later works, Aquinas added the more fundamental consideration that social life needs common policy and common action which cannot be achieved in a group whose members have many ideas about priorities – proper co-ordination requires authoritative choice and that can only come from proper authority. We have already considered the criticism of Professor Hart, that in the light of the horrors of human history the identification of the 'central case' of law with the co-ordination of society for the common good is an historical distortion. Further criticism can be made of the natural law 'common good' concept of law – namely, that in our conflict-ridden societies there is too much observable conflict to identify the 'common good'. This is the thrust of the criticism by Leslie Green, in *The Authority of the State* (1988), of the 'common good' conception of law. Green comments that there is 'zero-sum' conflict between individuals and classes over power, status and other goods in which there is no 'common good', but merely winners and losers. Also, there are areas of less sharp but still conflicting interests over such public goods as clean air. The combined result over all this inevitable conflict in society is to leave little room for the 'common good'. Natural law theory's 'common good' view of law can be criticised as utopian and unrealistic in the light of the many real conflicts which beset all modern democracies. Government should be seen on the model of 'managing grievances' within society rather than the high flown concept of the common good. The utopianism of natural law theory should be set against the harsh realities of politics, for as Benjamin Disraeli, Lord Beaconsfield (1804–1881), the nineteenth century Prime Minister of Britain once said: 'Politics is the art of the possible.' The pursuit of the 'common good' by government through law is much more impinged upon by social, political and economic factors than 'natural law theory' would have us believe.

This discussion of natural law theory will conclude by examining a supposed central tenet of natural law theory – namely, that *lex injusta non est lex* (an unjust law is not law). St Augustine comments in one of his dialogues that 'a law that was unjust would not seem to be a law'.

St Thomas Aquinas rather more carefully commented that morally bad laws are not law in the 'focal' or 'central' sense but are still 'law since they have the character of law in one important respect – they are the command of a superior to his subordinates'. Therefore, Aquinas carefully avoids saying that 'an unjust law is not a law'. Professor Finnis, in *Natural Law and Natural Rights*, adopts the formulation of Aquinas on this issue. Finnis does not deny legal validity to unjust laws but argues that they are not law (an ordinance of reason for the 'common good') in the central 'focal' or flourishing sense of the word 'law'. Indeed, Finnis argues that the main focus of natural law theory, properly understood, has never been the false slogan 'unjust laws are not laws' but rather that the main concern of a proper theory of natural law has been to explore the requirements of natural reason for a community under the rule of law.

Aim Higher ★

Students can gain extra marks by pointing out that there may be an inescapable connection between law and the pursuit of the common good, in that given the essential selfishness of human nature then the institution of law is a necessity to act as a restraint on destructive human impulses. Students can avoid the pitfall of thinking that natural law theory endorses the principle 'an unjust law is not a law' because modern natural law theorists, such as Professor Finnis, do not endorse the view of St Augustine that an unjust law is not a law, but rather argue that an unjust law is still a law but that the moral obligation to obey that unjust law may be severely affected by its unjustness. Finnis, in *Natural Law and Natural Rights*, denied that the proverb 'an unjust law is not a law' in any way characterised the tradition of natural law thought.

NOTES

The modern *locus classicus* of natural law thought remains *Natural Law and Natural Rights* (1980) by Professor John Finnis. Finnis wrote a detailed commentary on the thought of the father of natural law theory, St Thomas Aquinas (1225–1273) in 1998, *Aquinas: Moral, Political and Legal Theory*. A good commentary on natural law thought can be found in the online and free *Stanford Encyclopaedia of Philosophy* with the entry on 'The natural law tradition in ethics' being written by Mark Murphy (http://plato.stanford.edu/). Criticisms of 'natural law theory' can be found in Hart's *Essays in Jurisprudence and Philosophy* (1983) and L Green, 'Law, co-ordination and the common good' (Oxford Journal of Legal Studies (1983)) and also in Green's *The Authority of the State* (1988). Essays on 'Natural law' in *The Oxford Handbook of*

Jurisprudence and Philosophy of Law (2002), edited by Coleman and Shapiro, should be consulted. The first essay in that collection is by John Finnis: 'Natural law: the classical tradition.' The following essay is by Brian Bix: 'Natural law: the modern tradition.' Professor Finnis has also written a useful entry on 'Natural law theories' (2007) in the online and free *Stanford Encyclopaedia of Philosophy*.

QUESTION 7

MacCormick, commenting on Finnis's *Natural Law and Natural Rights*, states that the text necessitates our abandoning 'our caricature version of what a natural law theory is'.

▶ Do you agree?

Answer Plan

Finnis has attempted in recent years to restate the natural law in terms acceptable to contemporary society. This has involved him in an enumeration of 'human goods' – that is, fundamental values of man's existence that are 'self-evident', the securing of which requires a system of law. The 'human goods' must be discussed in the answer. Consideration should be given to the claim that Finnis has restored 'meaning' to the true natural law which has been discredited because of distorted versions of its pretensions. Criticisms of Finnis ought to be mentioned. A skeleton plan is presented as follows:

- ❖ Introduction;
- ❖ the caricature of natural law;
- ❖ essence of Finnis's restatement of natural law;
- ❖ the seven 'human goods';
- ❖ law's end as the common good;
- ❖ criticism of Finnis's catalogue;
- ❖ imprecision of his categories;
- ❖ problem of the 'self-evident' nature of the goods;
- ❖ conclusion, misgivings remain.

ANSWER

'Natural law' is seen here as the system of jurisprudential thought which asserts the existence in nature of a rational order from which we can derive universal and eternal value statements, allowing us to evaluate the legal structure with objectivity. The 'caricature' version which MacCormick has in mind is, presumably, sketched from the claims of those jurists who see natural law as based rigidly upon a unique revelation of truth, as flaunting the principle that 'ought' cannot be derived from 'is', and as proclaiming a set of immutable principles, including the assertion that unjust laws cannot be law. Some of Finnis's attempts to remove distortions of the image are considered below. It will be suggested that his attempts create their own problems.

Natural Law and Natural Rights (1980) is, in essence, a restatement of natural law in novel and contemporary terms. Finnis's central thesis consists of two major propositions. First, there are certain 'human goods' – that is, *basic values of human existence* that are self-evident and that can be secured only through the law. Second, these goods may be achieved through 'practical reasonableness' and this, too, necessitates law. The human goods constitute a catalogue of forms of 'human flourishing', exemplifying the conditions required by individuals if they are to attain their full potential (an end which was reiterated in earlier versions of the natural law). 'Practical reasonableness' involves use of the word 'practical' in an Aristotelian sense as meaning 'with a view to decision and action'; it is an aspect of 'human flourishing'. Finnis is seeking, in his categorisation of human goods, to provide a rational basis for morality and a justification for law.

The forms of human goods that are 'irreducibly basic' are seven in number: life, knowledge, play, aesthetic experience, sociability (friendship), practical reasonableness and religion. These constitute 'human well-being', and any real understanding of law or justice must rest on a comprehension of the nature of these 'goods'. Although there may be innumerable forms of human goods, Finnis claims that those outside his list are merely ways, or combinations of ways, of attaining any of the seven enumerated. By 'life', he has in mind the drive for self-preservation. The term signifies every aspect of vitality, including anything done by mankind to further its preservation. 'Knowledge' corresponds to man's basic drive of 'curiosity'. It is knowledge for its own sake, and ranges widely from scientific and philosophical speculation to mundane questions. 'Play' involves engaging in performances which have no point beyond the performances themselves.

'Aesthetic experience' – perception and enjoyment of 'dance or song or football', for example – may involve actions of one's own, or mere contemplation. 'Sociability' necessitates being in a relationship of friendship with at least one other person. 'Practical reasonableness' refers to freedom and reason, integrity and authenticity. It relates to bringing one's own intelligence to bear effectively on the problems of choosing one's actions and lifestyle and shaping one's character. Finnis uses the term 'religion' in an unusual sense as referring to a concern for an order of things 'beyond' each and every individual.

These human goods are, according to Finnis, 'basic' in that they are not derived from other goods and any other values will be seen as merely subordinate to them, and 'objective', which may be evidenced from a survey of anthropological research which reveals that 'all human societies show a concern for the value of human life'. Each constitutes a principle for 'practical reasoning'. They are also 'self-evident': thus, the 'good' of 'knowledge' is self-evident in that it cannot be demonstrated, but, equally, it needs no demonstration, no further argument; it has the quality of 'ultimacy'. Finnis insists that all self-evident principles are not validated by individual feelings and that in every field of human inquiry there is, and must be at some point, an end to derivation and inference. At that point, we find ourselves 'in face of the self-evident'. The goods are also equally 'fundamental': none can be *shown* to be more fundamental than any of the others and, therefore, there is no objective priority of values among them. They possess the property of 'incommensurability'.

'Practical reasonableness', which is a human good, is also a proposition in Finnis's overall scheme. It comprises ten principles which allow the individual to distinguish the social from the unsocial type of thinking, thereby enabling him to distinguish between morally right and wrong actions. First, an individual should have a rational plan of life, reflecting a harmonious set of purposes and effective commitments. He should pay equal regard to all the human goods and should not neglect the significance of others' participation in those goods. He should have a certain detachment from the projects he undertakes and should not abandon his commitments lightly. Opportunities ought not to be wasted by using needlessly inefficient methods and there must be respect for the human good in any act performed. *One should foster the common good and act according to one's conscience.* (In a later work, Finnis added a further principle, namely, that one should not choose 'apparent goods', knowing them to be a mere simulation of real goods.) It should be observed that Finnis, in his articulation of a scheme of common goods and values, is moving beyond any particular set of religious tenets. His view of the natural law suggests the *objective nature* of the values he enunciates; these values are not the exclusive property of Catholic believers. His emphasis on the need to reason about moral matters (and that necessitates decisions on which goods are worth pursuing) goes beyond a purely religious approach to 'the good life'.

Finnis views the law as involving rules made by 'a determinate and effective authority' for a 'complete community', strengthened by appropriate sanctions, and directed at the reasonable resolution of the community's problems of co-ordination. *Law is a means to an end*: its end is 'the community's good', and its manner and form should be adapted to that good by specificity, minimisation of arbitrariness and 'maintenance of a quality of reciprocity between the subjects of the law' among themselves and in their relations with the authorities. (The common good is defined by Finnis as 'a set of conditions which enables members of a community to attain for themselves reasonable objectives, or to realise reasonably for themselves the values for the sake of which they have reason to collaborate with each other . . . in a community'.)

The maxim *lex injusta non est lex* is viewed by Finnis as pure nonsense. He denies the correctness of its attribution to Aquinas and stresses that in natural law tradition wicked laws may have legal validity where they are enacted constitutionally and where accepted by the courts as guides to judicial decisions. One may have, according to natural law tradition, a 'collateral obligation' to conform to some iniquitous laws so as to uphold respect for the legal system as a whole.

A perusal of Finnis's views suggests to many critics a number of unsolved problems. Thus, the list of 'human goods' may be no more than a subjective addition to the long list of similar catalogues, such as the ancient Chinese Six Virtues and Eight Happinesses. Such catalogues tend to reflect, in a highly subjective manner, personal preferences, class and social mores and religious principles, indicating reactions to compelling, but often temporary, crises within society. Finnis, it is argued, may be reflecting little more than attitudes held desirable by a small group. His list of human goods is value laden and in no sense universal. There is evidence to suggest that some of the goods might be rejected as desirable ends by some sections of the community. What measure of agreement could be hoped for among nihilists, liberals and Marxists on matters of 'play' or 'aesthetic experience'?

Some of Finnis's categories are presented in wide and imprecise terms, making their significance difficult to grasp. 'Knowledge', in his words, embraces a spectrum from 'the intellectual cathedrals of science and philosophy' to 'everyday mundane gossip'. This is a very wide heading for activities of such a disparate nature. Also, it has been pointed out that the pursuit of knowledge 'for its own sake' is forbidden to some sects and religious orders for whom the very questioning of fundamentals may constitute an undesirable practice, if not a heresy. Further, Finnis's category of 'religion' has a meaning which is so wide as to rob it of any significance for wide groups of persons searching for a guide to thought and action.

The problem of the 'self-evident nature' of the 'human goods' is an obstacle for those jurists who search for a rationale behind the catalogue. The history of much endeavour in the realm of speculation is a story of a refusal to accept any statement as 'self-evident'. Indeed, according to critics, the term is an abnegation of the individual's duty to seek continuously for verification of theories. The same critics express doubts as to the 'self-evident' nature of, say, 'play' (in Finnis's sense) as a basic 'human good'. Weinreb, in a trenchant criticism of Finnis, notes that the text states, or suggests repeatedly, that those who are against the 'human goods theses' have not thought out their position carefully, or are 'blinded by bias', whereas, in fact, each of Finnis's conclusions has been contested by many thoughtful, morally committed persons.

Finnis's view of the law in terms of what it achieves, rather than what it is, has been considered less than helpful. It suggests a mere instrumental view of law and fails to examine the question – vital for advocates of the natural law – of the fundamental significance of law in our society. His argument concerning *lex injusta* has been criticised as resting on casuistry and as providing no guide for action to individuals within a community in which the law is perceived as oppressive.

There is doubt as to Finnis's general attitude to 'the good' and 'the just'. It has been suggested that his exposition is far too abstract to be of use in the resolution of day-to-day problems relating to disputes and the law. Yet there is a powerful attraction in his restatement of natural law doctrine: it is a carefully argued investigation of common good, moral choice and the place of the law in the co-ordination of human activity, and it is far removed from the 'caricature version' of natural law which emphasises an authoritative view of the common good and the means of its realisation. It calls for a fundamental examination of the place of the individual within society. In the tradition of the natural law, he urges for emphasis to be placed on the human condition and on the ways in which man may fulfil himself. His greatest achievement, in the eyes of some jurists, may be, in Weinreb's words, that he has called attention to principles which he claims to possess eternal validity and to transcend mere historical discourse, and that 'he has helped us to recognise the level of agreement about human ends and how to achieve them, and he has provided a shelter from the wind of moral relativism' – an accomplishment in itself.

NOTES

Extracts from Finnis, and a useful commentary, are to be found in Davies and Holdcroft, pp 186–204. A criticism of Finnis is contained in *Natural Law and Justice*, by Weinreb.

MacCormick writes on 'Natural law reconsidered' in (1981) OJLS. A detailed examination of Finnis's views appears in Westerman's *The Disintegration of Natural Law Theory*.

QUESTION 8

Is Professor Dworkin a 'natural lawyer?'

Answer Plan

Professor Dworkin is noted in his legal theory for his hostility to the central idea of legal positivism – that the existence and content of law can be worked out without a moral argument. Dworkin argues the contrary position, namely that:

'people who argue about the content of law draw on moral considerations in a way that positivism cannot explain' – see *Justice in Robes* (2006) at p 187.

Dworkin's hostility to legal positivism's 'sources thesis', through his insistence that morality forms part of the grounds of law (the identification of law), have led some people to assert that Dworkin is a 'natural lawyer', or at least a 'weak natural lawyer'. However on true reflection Dworkin's work in legal theory should not be placed within the tradition of natural law thought, with its emphasis on a universal moral law discerned by reason which Dworkin has never subscribed to, let alone the theological underpinnings of the natural law tradition. Dworkin's work on common law appellate court reasoning places him instead in the tradition of classical common law thought, and in many ways Dworkin is a 'common law romantic' for he views the common law as providing from within itself, through the process of constructive interpretation by the judge, nearly all right answers to hard questions that need decision by the appellate courts.

The following skeleton plan is suggested:

- ❖ Introduction;
- ❖ Dworkin not a 'natural lawyer' merely because he opposes the legal positivist 'sources thesis';
- ❖ natural lawyers such as Finnis do not oppose the legal positivist 'sources thesis';
- ❖ Dworkin is best located within the classical common law tradition;
- ❖ Dworkin's pre-occupation with common law reasoning is at odds with the modern domination of legislation as a legal source in the Anglo-American legal system;
- ❖ Dworkin's theory of appellate court adjudication has more resonance in the United States given the pivotal role of the Supreme Court in that jurisdiction.

ANSWER

Professor Dworkin has sometimes been termed 'a natural lawyer', perhaps because of his jurisprudential hostility to the central tenet of legal positivism – namely the 'sources thesis' that law is identified by reference to social sources alone and that therefore a moral argument is not required to work out the content of the law. There seems to be an assumption that because Dworkin, in his legal theory, makes the identification of law depend on a moral reading of existing law, therefore Dworkin is anti-positivist and ergo a natural lawyer. There is a fundamental fallacy in this argument. First of all some natural lawyers actually subscribe to the legal positivist 'sources thesis'. Professor Finnis, who breathed new life into the 'natural law tradition' in 1980 with the publication of *Natural Law and Natural Rights*, has given his powerful assent to the legal positivist 'sources thesis' since, in order to perform its essential task of defending, maintaining and promoting the common good of society, the law must be crisply identified from social sources such as legislation, common law or custom. As Finnis writes in 'The Truth in Legal Positivism' in *The Autonomy of Law: Essays on Legal Positivism* (1996):

> since the whole of a human community's existing law . . . custom, legislation, judgments – can all be identified by lawyerly historical methods, without 'moral argument.

The implications of this are that Finnis, the natural lawyer, is at one with legal positivists from Hobbes in the seventeenth century to Raz in the twenty-first century in holding that the judge must exercise a law-making function when the legal sources run out. As Finnis argues:

> when the sources yield no determinate solution all concerned have the responsibility of supplementing the sources to fill the gap by a choice guided by standards of fairness and other morally true principles and norms . . .

Therefore Dworkin is very much on his own amongst present day leading legal theorists in asserting that the common law itself can find the solution to any novel legal problem by the constructive moral interpretation by the judge of existing law. There is nothing particularly tied to the natural law tradition in Dworkin's theory, indeed Finnis writes in *Natural Law and Natural Rights* that the natural law tradition has not been characterised by the answer as to what a judge should do in a 'hard case', when the legal rules do not provide a definite answer. It is strange that Dworkin should ever have been considered a 'natural lawyer' merely on the ground that he disputed the legal positivist 'sources thesis'. However Kent Greenawalt, in the collection of essays edited by Robert P. George, referred to above, comments:

> **weak natural law is the term I attach to Dworkin's views . . . Dworkin has consistently maintained that judges deciding difficult cases must rely on principles that have a sort of mixed moral and legal status. These principles do**

**not owe their status as law to having been authoritatively posited on any
particular occasion ...**

However, as we have seen assenting to the legal positivist 'sources thesis' is not
inconsistent with the natural law tradition, and indeed Dworkin's professed liberalism
seems somewhat out of kilter with mainstream natural law views that abortion,
pornography and homosexuality are 'sins' that the state ought to discourage. Indeed
Dworkin has defended a right to pornography (see *A Matter of Principle* (1985)),
asserted the rights of homosexuals and a right to abortion. Also, natural lawyers
dating back to Thomas Aquinas in the thirteenth century have traditionally asserted a
realm of natural law or natural reason which is not human in origin and from which
positive human law is derived or, in the terminology of natural lawyers, human law is
a 'determination' of the natural law – a concretization or determination of the natural
law. Dworkin in his legal writings over forty years has never written of his support for
the view that there is a universal and eternal natural law to be discovered by the use
of reason, which applies to all persons in all ages, let alone the traditional natural law
belief that the natural law is the product of transcendent authority (i.e. God).

Therefore it is a serious mistake to categorise Dworkin as a 'natural lawyer', whether
weak or otherwise. Dworkin, in his liberal atheistic beliefs, cannot be assimilated to
the natural law tradition and the only foothold that can be made to place Dworkin in
the 'natural law' camp is due to Dworkin's jurisprudential belief that the identification
of law depends on moral evaluation of that law. However this foothold is tenuous
because, as previously argued, whether law is identified purely by social sources or
partly by morality is not part of the natural law tradition. As Robert P George argues in
In Defense of Natural Law (1999):

> the role of the judge as law-creator reasonably varies from jurisdiction to
> jurisdiction according to each jurisdiction's determinationes ...

and George comments:

> Some people who are loyal to the tradition of natural law theorizing are tempted
> to suppose that Professor Dworkin's position is the one more faithful to the
> tradition. This temptation should, however, be resisted ... natural law theory
> treats the role of the judge as fundamentally a matter for determinatio
> (determination or concretization), not for direct translation from the natural law.

Professor Dworkin is best characterised not as some adjudicative version of a natural
lawyer but rather as being a subtle, persuasively argued modern representative of the
classical common law tradition. Dworkin, in support of his theory of adjudication

called 'law as integrity', has drawn a parallel between the incrementalist approaches of judges at common law and the development of, what Dworkin calls, 'the chain novel'. In the 'chain novel' a different writer writes a different chapter of the same book with the aim of producing a readable coherent product. The 'chain novel' is a kind of literary 'parlour game' and is meant to mirror the development of the common law over generations of different judges. Each writer (judge) must take the preceding chapters (decided cases) and develop the story (the common law) to make his own contribution the best it can be, consistent with the other chapters. In this metaphor Dworkin seeks to mirror how judges develop principle out of earlier decisions, in much the same way as Lord Atkin did in *Donoghue v Stevenson* (1932).

As Dworkin comments in *A Matter of Principle* (1985), aiming his fire at judges who, in their common law decisions, seek to ignore previous legal decisions in the search for justice or policy:

> A judge's duty is to interpret the legal history he finds, not to invent a better history.

Dworkin uses the case of *McLoughlin v O'Brien* (1982) to support his arguments for a theory of the common law driven by judicial adherence to principle not policy. Indeed in *McLoughlin v O'Brien* Lord Scarman gives a statement of the common law method which strongly echoes Professor Dworkin's theory of the common law. Lord Scarman commented:

> whatever the court decides to do, it starts from a baseline of existing principle and seeks a solution consistent with or analogous to a principle or principles already recognised ... The distinguishing feature of the common law is this judicial development and formation of principle ... By concentrating on principle the judges can keep the common law alive, flexible and consistent, and can keep the legal system clear of policy problems which neither they, nor the forensic process which is their duty to operate, are equipped to resolve. If principle leads to results which are thought to be socially unacceptable, Parliament can legislate to draw a line or map out a new path.

Professor Dworkin, consistent with this judicial view of the common law method expounded by Lord Scarman, has always denied judges the legitimate power to make law in the name of 'policy' and has maintained that the richness of the common law gives the judge in a 'hard case' the resources to find the 'right answer' located within the existing legal history – if that legal history of cases is subject to 'constructive interpretation' by the judge. However, the fact that Lord Scarman was in a minority of judges and that most English judges think that policy has a role to play in the determination of cases suggests that Dworkin's theory of adjudication is a theory of how judges ought to decide cases, rather than a correct descriptive account of how they actually do decide cases.

Dworkin has called his theory of adjudication 'law as Integrity' which can be summarised by quoting from *Law's Empire* (1986):

> Law as integrity asks judges to assume, so far as this is possible, that the law is structured by a coherent set of principles about justice and fairness and procedural due process and it asks them to enforce these in the fresh cases that come before them, so that each person's situation is fair and just according to the same standards.

Dworkin should be viewed as part of the classical common law tradition that elevates the common law as part of, and a driver of, a community's morality and also sees the common law as rich enough to find a 'legal' solution to any issue that comes before the courts for adjudication. Indeed Dworkin's implicit affinity with classical 'common law' thought is made explicit in *Law's Empire* where Dworkin refers with great approval to Lord Mansfield's celebration of the common law that: 'the law works itself pure' (see *Omychund v Barker* (1744)). The connection between Dworkin's conception of the common law and Lord Mansfield's view that the common law works itself pure is explained by Dworkin in *Law's Empire*:

> Sentimental lawyers cherish an old trope: they say that the law works itself pure. The figure imagines two forms or stages of the same system of law, the nobler form latent in the less noble, the impure, present law gradually transforming itself into its own purer ambition . . . never worked finally pure, but better in each generation than the last. There is matter in this mysterious image, and it adds to both the complexity and the power of law as integrity.

Having allied himself with classic common law thought it is hardly surprising that Dworkin has been termed a 'common law romantic' by D. Dyzenhaus and M. Taggart in *Common Law Theory* (edited by D. Edlin, 2007). Certainly Dworkin has always seemed focused in his legal theory on common law adjudication. Indeed the very first sentence of *Law's Empire* (1986) starts:

> 'It matters how judges decide cases.' Four hundred pages later in the same book comes the statement:

> 'The courts are the capitals of law's empire, and the judges are its princes.'

For Dworkin the common law, if viewed as a coherent sytem of rights and duties, can provide the solution to any novel problem at law, i.e. through the constructive interpretation by the judge of previous common law decisions the common law works itself pure – it develops more 'integrity' over time through the successive efforts of generations of judges.

As a result of viewing the law through the prism of common law appellate adjudication Dworkin has been criticised for developing a theory of law from a theory of adjudication. As Professor Raz comments in *Between Authority and Interpretation* (2009):

> his book (Law's Empire) is not so much an explanation of the law as a sustained argument about how courts, especially American and British courts should decide cases. It contains a theory of adjudication rather than a theory of the nature of law.

Raz would argue that since law is an important social institution and a cultural phenomenon, it should be examined from the 'institutional' perspective – how law operates in the context of its societal and political setting. The 'lawyer's' perspective of Dworkin, looking at law from what goes on in the courtroom or more specifically what goes on in an appellate judge's mind, is getting things the wrong way round. A theory of law should be developed, followed by a theory of adjudication, not the other way round as Dworkin implies. Indeed Dworkin makes a double mistake in his focus on the common law's courtroom adjudication for (1) law as a social institution should be studied by standing back from the lawyer's perspective and (2) common law is in the present era very much subordinated to legislation as a legal source, although judicial adjudication has a special resonance in the United States where the Supreme Court acts as a guardian of the United States Constitution.

In England at least Dworkin's preoccupation with common law adjudication seems at odds with the domination of legislation as a legal source, as Roger Cotterrell comments in *Living Law* (2008):

> The old common law image of law distilled from community experience and morality, brought to the court in litigation, has to co-exist with the modern and in many ways much more powerful image of enacted positive law, handed down "from above" in the form of statutes and other law produced from non-judicial sources.

Cotterrell is keen to make clear 'the considerable tension between the modern concept of enacted positive and the older idea of common law as found by judges.

English law has seen a long 'cold war' between these two conceptions, in which common law thought has fought a lengthy rearguard action in a battle of ideas'.

Dworkin may best be characterised as a jurist who has given a modern and subtle interpretation to classical common law thought, but at a time when legislation, not the common law, in England is the much more dominant legal source. However Dworkin's focus on appellate court reasoning as his focus for a theory of law may have much more resonance in the United States where the Supreme Court regularly adjudicates on great moral-political questions and where the United States Supreme Court (unlike the Supreme Court in the United Kingdom) has the final authoritative say to settle controversial moral-legal questions.

Aim Higher ★

Students can gain extra marks by pointing out that Professor Dworkin has little in common with the classical natural law tradition but has much in common with classical common law thought where Dworkin shares the view of old writers, such as Lord Coke, that the common law is a rich enough resource to provide sound answers to any novel legal question if the judge is skilful enough in his search. Students can avoid the common pitfall which argues that because Dworkin is 'anti-positivistic' and makes morality part of the grounds for identifying law that therefore Dworkin is a 'natural lawyer'.

NOTES

Kent Greenawalt discusses his view that Dworkin is 'a weak natural lawyer' in 'Too Thin and Too Rich: Distinguishing Features of Legal Positivism' in *The Autonomy of Law*, edited by Robert P George (1996) at p 5. Dworkin defends his own legal theory in *Justice in Robes* (2006), see pp 187–188 and pp 234–239. Dworkin comments: 'I want to oppose the idea that 'law' is a fixed set of standards of any sort.' Roger Cotterrell discusses Dworkin's theory of law in *The Politics of Jurisprudence* (2003, 2nd edition) at pp 160–174.

Common Law and Statute

INTRODUCTION

Common law and statute law are the two most important sources of law in the Anglo-American legal systems so this topic should have an inherent appeal for students of jurisprudence. However the common law and statutory law are also a useful lens through which to view legal theorists, as different legal theorists tend to focus on common law or statute law, depending on the focus of their own theory of law. For example, Bentham was implacably hostile to the common law but saw his ideal form of law in the comprehensive codification of law. Modern legal positivists such as Professor Raz and Professor John Gardner view the essence of law as being an exercise of authority to change the normative position of others, so there is an emphasis on the finality of legislation as a legal source. Professor Dworkin has concentrated in his legal theory on judicial adjudication so the common law tends to be the focus of his legal theory.

Checklist ✔

Ensure that you are acquainted with the following topics:

- Bentham's hostile attitude towards the common law;
- the theory of classical common law;
- the role of experience in the formation of the common law;
- the reasons for the domination of legislation as the primary legal source in the Anglo-American legal systems.

QUESTION 9

Discuss Bentham's attack on the common law.

Answer Plan

Bentham was rigorously hostile towards the common law of England, which he saw as serving the sinister interests of lawyers. Bentham argued for the systematic codification of the law, which would mean the extinguishing of the common law although judges would still be needed to apply and interpret the codes. A judge could override the codes where utility demanded that course, but no judicial decision would have precedent value – a judicial decision would be like a bus ticket valid for only one journey. If there were gaps in the code the judges should refer the case back to the legislature for decision. This extremely utopian scheme of Bentham never saw its realization, but some law was codified in the nineteenth century, e.g. the Sale of Goods Act 1893 and statute became the dominant legal source over the common law in the twentieth century. It was John Austin, Bentham's friend and student who became the 'voice' of early legal positivism in the nineteenth century, partly because Austin 'depoliticised' Bentham's legal theory by leaving out the radical law reform measures and therefore Austin was a more palatable legal theorist than Bentham in the eyes of nineteenth century lawyers.

A skeleton plan is sketched below:

- ❖ Introduction;
- ❖ the views of classical common lawyers such as Lord Coke and Lord Mansfield on the superiority of common law over legislation;
- ❖ Bentham's attack on the common law and common law theory especially Bentham's attack on Sir William Blackstone's 'Commentaries' which first made Bentham's reputation as a philosopher;
- ❖ Bentham's plan for wholesale codification of the law: 'the death of the common law';
- ❖ the more sympathetic views of John Austin (to whom Bentham was a mentor) to the common law;
- ❖ the emergence in the twentieth century of statute as the primary legal source and the 'eclipse of the common law'.

ANSWER

Jeremy Bentham is known as one of the originators of 'the command theory of law', a descriptive account of the nature of law and legal systems – see Bentham's *Of Laws in General* (1782).

However, Bentham also had a normative side to his jurisprudence – a clear view of what the law ought to be – and in this plan the old common law of England was to be squeezed out of existence by the widespread codification of law.

Bentham was writing at a time when the common law was a much more potent force than in the present era, which is 'an age of statutes' where legislation is used to obtain broad social goals and the common law is relegated to 'interstitial' gap filling in the pattern of law woven by legislation.

Although we are now living in an era which can be characterised as 'the eclipse of the common law', back in the eighteenth century (when Bentham was forming his views) there was a view that the common law was a superior form of law-making to statute. In a phrase attributed to the great eighteenth century judge Lord Mansfield, the common law was thought 'to work itself pure'. This image meant that by its incremental, step by step development from underlying principles of justice the common law could be relied upon to cover all cases that came before the courts with justice and fairness.

Legislation – statute law – in contrast was considered by Lord Mansfield to be a clumsy tool, lacking precision to achieve justice in all cases. Legislation is very much the **product of the moment** and lacks the accumulated wisdom of the common law. In the case of *Omychund v Barker* (1744) Lord Mansfield held the opinion:

> **a statute very seldom can take in all cases, therefore the common law, that works itself pure by rules drawn from the fountain of justice, is for this reason superior to an Act of Parliament.**

As Thomas argues in *The House of Commons in the Eighteenth Century* (1971):

> the old idea that the common law rendered new legislation unnecessary died hard.

As Conrad Russell argued in 'Topsy and the King: the English common law' the common law enjoyed a limitless capacity for growth:

> It was in, Sir John Davies's vivid phrase, **"like a silk-worm that formeth all her web out of her self only."**

The common law, in the classical common law thought of men such as Sir Edward Coke (1552–1634) and Sir Matthew Hale (1609–1676), was considered to be based on the collective wisdom of generations of judges, a wisdom which far surpassed the wisdom of any individual judge – no matter how brilliant. The common law was considered to be a vast reservoir of legal experience of the life of the nation which derived its great authority from its persistence and continuity over the centuries. The great late eighteenth century exponent of the common law, Sir William Blackstone (1723–1780), praised the common law in almost extreme terms:

> the fundamental maxims and rules of the law ... have been and are everyday improving, and are frought with the accumulated wisdom of ages.

The mantra of the classical common lawyers was that 'the common law is no other than common reason' and from this close connection to reason itself, as well as its antiquity, the common law derived its status and authority.

Judge Learned Hand famously said in 1922 that the common law:

> **stands as a monument slowly raised, like a coral reef, from the minute accretions of past individuals, of whom each built upon the relics which his predecessor left, and in his turn left a foundation upon which his successors might work.**

The authority of the judges at common law then rested upon the authority of the past, upon the idea that, in the words of Lord Simonds in *Chapman v Chapman* (1954):

> **It is even possible that we are not wiser than our ancestors.**

The authority of judges at common law being based on the past record of judicial decisions was well explained by the great American judge Learned Hand – speaking of the common law judge he said:

> **His authority and immunity depend upon the assumption that he speaks from the mouths of others, he must present his authority by cloaking himself in the majesty of an overshadowing past.**

However, Sir William Blackstone was not content to argue only that the common law was the accumulated wisdom of the ages or the perfection of natural reason but also that the common law's reason derived from God's reason – in other words that the common law of England, according to Blackstone, had a direct link to God himself.

Such outlandish claims about the status and authority of the common law was bound to attract disapproving attention when the 'age of reason' we call 'The Enlightenment' dawned in the eighteenth century. One such child of 'The Enlightenment' was Jeremy Bentham (himself a personal friend of a central Enlightenment figure, Voltaire) for whom the common law of England, with its archaic procedures and grandiose claims of 'natural' or even 'Divine' authority, was a standing target for contempt and ridicule. Indeed Bentham first made his reputation by attacking Blackstone's *Commentaries on the Laws of England* which was in fact the first textbook of law in England for students, as well as a paean of praise for the common law. Bentham said that, even at the age of sixteen as a student at Oxford University, he heard Blackstone's lectures on the common law with 'rebel ears'.

Bentham, according to Gerald Postema in *Bentham and the common law tradition* (1986), attempted to shift the paradigm of law, as then understood in England, from the common law to the sharper lines of statute law and its idealization, the code. Bentham regarded his attack on the common law as being part of the great Enlightenment tradition of raising rational and rationalist challenge to established institutions and the dark forces of religion, superstition and traditional custom.

Bentham commented of his 'plan' to abolish the common law by the wholesale codification of the law:

> **It is evident that the plan as far as it went could in a certain sense be the destruction of the common law; since whatever goes at present under that name would be abrogated . . . that is expressed in assignable authoritative terms and thereby converted into the forms of statute law.**

Under Bentham's plan for codification of English law judicial decisions would have no precedent value but would be good only for that particular case under decision. Disputed questions of interpretation of the codes would be referred back to the legislature for decision, but judges could disapply the codes if utility in a particular case demanded that.

As Postema argues, by the mid-eighteenth century English common law had grown into a complex thicket of technical rules, antiquated concepts and mysterious procedures. For Bentham, the disciple of rationalist utilitarian thought, it was a standing insult that the common law, a major part of the law at that time, was inaccessible except to a professional elite of lawyers and judges who used the mysteriousness of the common law to the ordinary man to further their own sinister professional and financial interests. Bentham wanted to make the law accessible to the common man through written codes, so that the law on any subject could be discerned by merely opening the pages of a book.

Statute law for Bentham was far superior to common law as Bentham said:

'as a system of general rules the common law is a thing merely imaginary'. Not only did the common law lack systematic form or shape, but its vagueness was such that according to Bentham:

> a law is to be extracted by every man who can fancy that he is able: by each man perhaps a different law.

For Bentham statute law had a clarity which the haphazard common law could never have. For Bentham statute law 'marks out the line of the subject's conduct by visible directions, instead of turning him loose into the wilds of perpetual conjecture'.

Bentham downgraded the common law, but in much greater detail than the earlier criticisms of Thomas Hobbes in the seventeenth century. Hobbes commented of the common law, contrasting it with statute:

'It is not Wisdom, but Authority that makes a law.' For Hobbes as well as John Locke and Bentham, law properly called was a result of sovereign will expressed through statute.

Bentham was on firmer ground than Hobbes in the championing of legislation since the enormous growth of legislation and its understanding as a source of law from the beginning of the nineteenth century made Bentham's paradigm identification of law with statute seem in touch with the historical flow. As Nobles and Schiff comment in *A Sociology of Jurisprudence* (2006):

> **to understand how positivist legal theory became an accepted self-description of the legal system one needs to consider the generative effects of a constant outflow of particular legislation.**

As statute law began its long process of overwhelming domination as a source of law from the nineteenth century it is hardly surprising that 'command theories' of law propagated by Austin and Bentham, with the emphasis on legislation handed down from sovereign power, became the paradigm legal theories until their replacement by the subtler 'rule governed' theories of Herbert Hart and later legal positivists who argued that law was not best understand as a series of commands from a sovereign but as an institutionalised system of norms.

It might be thought that Bentham's project for the elimination of the common law has been partly realised by the overwhelming use of legislation as a source of law in the modern age. Indeed Galligan, in *Law in Modern Society* (2007), claims Bentham should be the 'icon' of modern Western legal orders since there is in modern English law overwhelming use of legislation to achieve mighty social goals. As Frederick Schauer comments in *The Autonomy of Law* (edited by Robert George, 1996) we live in a law-soaked world : **'everywhere we turn there are directives emanating from authority.'**

However, the experience of legislation in the modern Western legal era of rushed, ill-considered and transient statutes is very different from Bentham's vision of legislation as codification: codes which would be carefully thought out, have some permanence and be systematically coherent. Perhaps then Bentham should not be considered the 'icon' of modern Western legal orders.

It is well known that Bentham scorned judicial law-making but that his disciple John Austin was more sympathetic to the common law which Austin thought could be accommodated within the 'command theory'. However it is noticeable that when Austin writes about the common law he assimilates it to the model of legislation. For Austin the common law decisions of judges were the tacit commands of the sovereign who would endorse the decisions of judges at common law by not overturning them with statute. Common law on the Austinian model partook then of the same authority as legislation, there was no understanding of the common law as standing somehow outside state authority through the common law's alleged close relation to natural reason. For Sir Frederick Pollock (1845–1937), Professor of Jurisprudence at Oxford University and an outspoken nineteenth and early twentieth century critic of Austin's jurisprudence, the common law's strength was such that it could not be assimilated to state authority as Austin had tried to reduce the common law with his theory of the common law as the 'tacit' commands of the sovereign. Pollock in a letter of 1918 to the writer Lytton Strachey commented that:

> **the common law is older than our political institutions and not being tied to dogmas will live to see them transformed.**

For Frederick Pollock the English common law could never be reduced to an aspect of state authority, no matter what Austin argued in *The Province of Jurisprudence Determined* (1832). The common law for Pollock was not part of the political apparatus, but was rather the product of a special legal mindset – the way in which lawyers and judges think and work. The common law was thus a kind of 'supermind' independent of, although ultimately subject to, state authority through repeal by statute. Indeed, on the 'independence' of the common law from politics, Jeremy Waldron writes in *The Dignity of Legislation* (1999) of:

> the appealing anonymity of (common) law, its apparent neutrality . . . its distance from or independence of politics. . . . If we don't like an emerging

doctrine of common law, we can blame it on the heritage. But if we don't like a statute, we tend to see it as a piece of Tory legislation, or a socialist measure....

Although Austin was more sympathetic to judicial legislation than his mentor Bentham, Austin moved in Bentham's direction in this matter over time. In 1832 in *The Province of Jurisprudence Determined* Austin describes judge-made law as 'highly beneficial and even absolutely necessary'.

However Frederick Schauer, in a paper entitled 'Positivism before Hart' (University of Virginia School of Law January 2010), comments that later on in his career Austin wrote extensively in support of legislative codification generally, especially in the light of what Austin called the 'evils inherent in judiciary law'. Austin believed that judicial legislation could and should be diminished were Parliament to legislate more clearly, precisely and comprehensively. Unlike Bentham, Austin did not believe that judicial legislation was not really law or that it could be eliminated entirely. History has shown that on the subject of judicial law-making Austin has been closer to legal reality than Bentham's utopian and unrealistic views which argued for the complete abolition of the common law.

Aim Higher ★

Students can gain extra marks by putting Bentham's attack on the common law of England in its social and historical context as part of the general Enlightenment attack on established institutions and old habits of thought such as the Christian religion. Students can avoid the common pitfall of thinking that Bentham's theory of law was identical to Austin's by pointing out Bentham's more subtle account of law than Austin's theory of law, such as the recognition by Bentham of the different functions of different laws in that some laws allow the exercise of legal powers which Austin overlooked in his simplification of the theory of Bentham (Austin's mentor). Bentham, unlike Austin, had an extensive agenda for law reform which included plans for the wholescale codification of English law.

NOTES

Bentham's views on the common law are extensively treated in *Bentham and the Common Law Tradition* (1986) edited by Gerald J Postema. Bentham's views on law are considered by R Cotterrell in *The Politics of Jurisprudence* (2003) at pp 51–54.

Nobles and Schiff in *A Sociology of Jurisprudence* (2006) discuss Bentham's views on law at pp 75–86. A useful paper on Bentham and Austin to download from the internet is 'Positivism Before Hart' by Frederick Schauer University of Virginia School of Law: http://ssrn.com/abstract=1512646 (Social Science Research Network Electronic Paper Collection).

QUESTION 10

'The life of the law has not been logic: it has been experience.' Oliver Wendell Holmes. Discuss.

Answer Plan

This question involves discussion of the strengths of the common law as a source of law.

The great advantage of the common law is that it presents a vast reservoir of human wisdom as contained within judicial precedent. Given the conservative belief concerning the radical intellectual imperfection of the human individual (see Anthony Quinton, *The Politics of Imperfection* (1978)) then judges should trust the historically accumulated wisdom of the community as expressed in the common law rather than their own imperfect judgment. This is the essence of Holmes's dictum that 'the life of the law has not been logic: it has been experience'. The message of the common law is that where logic points one way for the law to go, and experience points in another direction for the law then the law should rather follow experience. There is a discussion of the common law method of reasoning, which is the slow incremental development of the law rather than sudden breaks and turns in the law which characterises much legislation.

A skeleton plan is suggested:

- ❖ Introduction;
- ❖ the general strengths of the common law as opposed to legislation as a legal source;
- ❖ common law as a vast deposit of sound judgment and practical wisdom;
- ❖ the radical intellectual imperfection of mankind necessitates the common law. The radical moral imperfection of mankind necessitates the criminal law;
- ❖ the incremental reasoning of the common law, the slow step by step extension of the law;
- ❖ the life of the common law has been experience, but experience recognises the place of logic in the law.

ANSWER

However much the common law has taken a back seat to statute in the present era there is still something to be said for the view that the common law represents a form of collective wisdom to be set against the tide of often rushed, ill-considered legislative measures. Roger Cotterrell in *Living Law* (2008) writes of modern statute law's 'transience, disposability and moral emptiness' and 'the endlessly pragmatic adjustment of regulation to increasing social complexity'. Compared to this gloomy vision of modern statute law, the common law, built upon incremental steps laid down by generations of judges, seems positively attractive.

The great strength of the common law is that it is a repository of the collective experience and wisdom of a nation's judiciary over centuries. Statute law, on the other hand, is 'of the moment' – the result often of temporary political expediency. The great American jurist and future Supreme Court judge Oliver Wendell Holmes put the point succinctly about the strength of the common law when he wrote in his 1880 work *The Common Law*: 'The life of the law has not been logic: it has been experience.'

Holmes used the above saying to demonstrate the limitations of using 'logic' as a guide to the doctrines of the common law. Holmes commented:

> The law embodies the story of a nation's development through many centuries, and it cannot be dealt with as if it contained only the axioms and corollaries of a book of mathematics.

Holmes reflected further on the common law in his article 'The Path of the Law' (1897 Harvard Law Review), drawing an analogy between the growth of a plant and the organic growth of the common law based on experience:

> The development of our law has gone on for nearly a thousand years, like the development of a plant, each generation taking the inevitable next step, mind, like matter, simply obeying a law of spontaneous growth.

Specifically on the law of contract as part of common law doctrine Holmes writes in *The Common Law*:

> the distinctions of the law are founded on experience, not on logic.

Perhaps Holmes overstated the point about the role of experience in the formation of the common law for the life of the law has a place for logic as well as experience: the common law should be a result of logic tempered by experience and experience checked by logic. However, the strength of the common law resides in the fact that when it is considered necessary to follow experience then logic must give way to experience. Two famous common law cases *Ibrahim v R* (1914) and *R v Howe* (1987) will illustrate the point mentioned in the previous sentence.

In the Privy Council case of *Ibrahim v R*, the great judge of the First World War period, Lord Sumner (described as the 'benevolent malevolence' by Lord Goddard) considered the common law rule that a confession was inadmissible as evidence if obtained by a person in authority who held out the fear of prejudice or hope of advantage to the suspect. Lord Sumner commented that 'logically' the fact that a confession was obtained under circumstances of hope or fear induced in the suspect by those in authority should go to the weight of the confession before the jury and not its admissibility. Lord Sumner in *Ibrahim* commented that in an action for tort such as false imprisonment heard before a civil jury the fact that a defendant had made a confession as a result of threats or promises would not make the confession inadmissible in the tort action. As Lord Sumner commented:

> in action of tort, evidence of this kind could not be excluded when tendered against a tort-feasor, though a jury might well be told as prudent men to think little of it.

Given this civil law position what then justified the rule in criminal cases that a confession obtained by threats or promises by those in authority was inadmissible at trial? Logic said admit the confession for the jury's consideration, as in civil cases, but experience in criminal cases pointed another way. Judicial experience over the centuries considered that in criminal cases where the prospects of an innocent man being imprisoned (or, before 1965, hanged to death for murder) on the basis of dubious confessions was too great a risk to take and therefore, since 1783 the common law had erected a rule in criminal cases preventing the jury from hearing evidence of a confession obtained by threats or promises of those in authority. The Eleventh Report of the Criminal Law Revision Committee in 1972 was composed of some eminent judges such as Lord Justice Lawton, Lord Edmund-Davies and Mr Justice James who justified an exclusionary rule for some confessions obtained by the police. Drawing on judicial experience the Report concluded:

> Persons who are subjected to threats, inducements or oppression may confess falsely; juries are particularly apt to attach weight to such a confession even though the evidence of the threat, inducement or oppression is before them; consequently they must be prevented from knowing of the confession.

In the case of *R v Howe* (1987), House of Lords logic pointed one way but judicial experience pointed in a different direction for the law. The case concerned the dramatic legal and moral issue as to whether the common law defence of duress was available on a charge of murder. The defence of duress was available at common law for many offences, such as manslaughter and causing grievous bodily harm with intent to do so, an offence that is only a heartbeat away from murder. Logic would therefore argue that duress should be available on a murder charge. Lord Hailsham in *R v Howe* (1987) successfully resisted the argument from logic by insisting that judicial experience, dating back to Hale in the seventeenth century and Blackstone in the eighteenth century, had always maintained that a man should sacrifice his own life when threatened with death rather than taking the life of an innocent to save his own life. Lord Hailsham commented of the arguments on the other side for allowing duress as a defence to murder:

> First, among these is the argument from logic and consistency. A long line of cases, it is said, carefully researched and closely analysed, establish duress as an available defence in a wide range of crimes . . .

and therefore logic pointed to the availability of duress as a defence to murder.

However, despite this argument from 'logic and consistency' Lord Hailsham denied that logic should have the last word in shaping the common law and said of the common law, especially that branch concerned with the deterrence of criminal conduct:

> Consistency and logic, although inherently desirable, are not always prime characteristics of a penal code based like the common law on custom and precedent. Law so based is not an exact science.

Lord Hailsham quoting long judicial experience going back to Lord Hale and Sir William Blackstone – 'an unbroken tradition of authority' said that duress was not available at common law to murder since, in the words of Sir William Blackstone:

> a man under duress ought rather to die himself than escape by the murder of an innocent.

Judicial experience suffused with Christian morality, as expressed in the common law, did not allow the murder of an innocent in order for a man to escape with his own life.

Indeed the very nerve of the common law is judicial experience given the incremental organic development of the common law refracted through case law over the centuries. Legislation, statute law often brings in sudden breaks and new starts in the law (e.g. the smoking ban in public places introduced in July 2007) but the common law method is one of careful, slow incremental growth.

In an essay entitled 'Judicial Legislation' (1989) Lord Oliver outlined the traditional common law method of judicial law-making by examining Lord Atkin's formulation of a general principle of liability in the tort of negligence in the very famous case of *Donoghue v Stevenson* (1932):

> The way in which he arrived at his decision was by a careful review of previous cases, the extraction from them of a number of propositions and an extrapolation from those propositions to the broad general proposition of the foundation of liability . . . The case is an excellent example of the way in which English judges develop the law by extension from what has gone before, each decided principle being used as the stepping stone to a further step forward by way of what at least is claimed to be a logical progression. *Donoghue v Stevenson* certainly resulted in the establishment of a joint broad general proposition, but it was not one which, at any rate in the intention of its author, was conceived as a massive step forward in the legal development.

Lord Oliver, building on his theme of the inherent 'incrementalism' of the common law, comments of the general common law method:

> The process is essentially an incremental one built up from case to case, the conclusion being reached by deduction from what has gone before. Lord Atkin was not inventing a principle. He was merely stating in terms which had not previously been universally perceived, the principle which he was able to deduce from the previously decided cases.

The common law is like a carpet weaved by many hands and it is only when the carpet reaches a certain stage of development that certain motifs can be discerned, as Lord Atkin discerned a general principle of tort liability in *Donoghue v Stevenson*. In the weave of the carpet can be discerned reason and logic but also the guiding hand of experience.

Aim Higher ★

Students can gain extra marks by noting that the strength of the common law is that it relies on the collective wisdom of the past, set against the intellectual imperfections of people of any given human era. Given the intellectual imperfections of any individual the common law's strength is as the accumulated wisdom of the community. Respect for the common law is therefore a feature of 'conservative' thought which emphasises attachment to or reverence for established customs and institutions. Given man's moral and intellectual imperfections conservatives place their trust in the social wisdom of established institutions such as the common law.

NOTES

Roger Cotterell in *Politics of Jurisprudence* (2003) discusses the common law and the theory of classical common law thought at pp 21–48. The common law is also extensively discussed in *Common Law Theory* (2007) edited by Douglas Edlin. The most comprehensive discussion of the thought of Oliver Wendell Holmes is to be found in *The Path of the Law and its influence: The Legacy of Oliver Wendell Holmes* (2000) edited by Steven J Burton.

QUESTION 11

Explain the dominance of legislation as the primary source of modern law.

Answer Plan

This question seeks to explore the reasons why legislation, statute law has become the dominant legal source leading to the subordination of common law. The circumspection of the modern judiciary, with regard to their law-making powers (with exceptions, most notably Lord Denning) compared to the golden age of the common law under Lord Mansfield in the late eighteenth century, partly explains the rise of the statute but legislation itself offers many advantages to the modern policy maker in terms of rapid response, finality and the ability of legislation through extremely detailed Codes of Practice to minutely regulate areas of social life, such as police work (see **The Police and Criminal Evidence Act 1984** and its ever updated complex codes of practice) or health and safety.

A skeleton plan is suggested:

- ❖ Introduction;
- ❖ the growth in importance of legislation as a legal source;
- ❖ the reasons why modern judges are cautious with regard to their law-making powers;
- ❖ the advantages of legislation as a legal source;
- ❖ the relation of legal positivists, such as Professor Raz, to legislation as a legal source.

ANSWER

In his biographical note for Lord Scarman in the *Oxford Dictionary of National Biography* Stephen Sedley comments:

One of the long term processes which the twentieth century witnessed in the legal system of England and Wales was the transition from the common law dominated system of the nineteenth century to the statute dominated system of the twenty-first.

Perhaps the eclipse of the common law as a legal source and the rise of the statute owes something to the democratic impulse. The unaccountable law-making power of unelected judges raises a democratic legitimacy deficit in contrast to the inherent democratic legitimacy of Parliamentary produced statute law. The legitimacy of European Union derived legislation raises whole new areas of democratic concern which we will not examine.

Certainly judges in the present era are more careful in their use of their law-making powers than in previous eras and overly activist judges such as Lord Denning are frowned upon; indeed Lord Denning positively gloried in the judicial law-making role.

Lord Bingham, the former senior Law Lord, in an essay entitled 'The Judge as Lawmaker: An English perspective' outlines the many restrictions that a judge in England should recognise as impinging upon his law-making powers:

(1) where reasonable and right-minded citizens have legitimately ordered their affairs on the basis of a certain understanding of the law. As Lord Reid put it:

> People rely on the certainty of the law in settling their affairs, in particular in making contracts or settlements. It would be very wrong if judges were to disregard or innovate on what can fairly be regarded as settled law in matters of that kind.

(2) where, although a rule of law is seen to be defective, its amendment calls for a detailed legislative code, with qualifications, exceptions and safeguards which cannot be feasibly be introduced by judicial decisions. Such cases call for a rule of judicial abstinence, particularly where wise and effective reform of the law calls for research and consultation of a kind which no court of law is fitted to undertake;

(3) where the question involves an issue of current social policy on which there is no consensus in the community;

(4) where an issue is the subject of current legislative activity. If Parliament is actually engaging in deciding what the rule should be in a given legal situation, the courts are generally wise to await the outcome of that deliberation rather than to pre-empt the result by judicial decision;

(5) where the issue arises in a field far removed from ordinary judicial experience.

Lord Bingham, having outlined these major general reasons why a judge should be circumspect in her use of her law-making powers, offers some further reasons which should act as a check on judicial law-making:

(a) On the whole, the law advances in small steps, not by giant bounds ... If judges make too free with existing law, or are too neglectful of precedent, the law becomes reprehensibly uncertain and unpredictable.

(b) Lord Denning's glorification of judicial law-making is dangerous because then too much of the law depends on the temperament and predilections of individual judges.

(c) A judge who works to a pre-determined law reform agenda necessarily deprives himself of the capacity to respond to the merits of the particular case as it unfolds before him.

(d) Judges are, by and large, not fitted to be law reformers but are trained to interpret and apply the law.

The courts are unlikely to change the law where the change in a particular area does not cohere with the law generally, as was said by McHugh J. in *Burnie Port Authority v General Jones Pty Ltd* (1994):

> A judge-made rule is legitimate only when it can be effectively integrated into the mass of principles, rules and standards which constitute the common law and equity. A rule which will not "fit" into the general body of the established law cannot be the subject of judge-made law.

Legislation can ride roughshod over existing legal principle and forge out a new direction for the law, such as bringing in a ban to stop smoking in public places, but the common law does not progress in so aggressive a fashion – it builds slowly upon a 'reef' of existing legal principle.

This judicial caution of the present era with regard to their law-making powers would not in itself explain the modern domination of legislation as a legal source. There must be powerful reasons why statute law has become such a powerful agent for the Governmental steering of society. The following reasons are suggested for the fact that we now live in the 'age of statutes':

(1) Legislation is the deliberate production of law, the presentation of new legal norms as a direct exercise of authority. The common law, judge made law, is in a sense accidentally produced through the chance occurrences of litigation. If the essence of law is that it involves an exercise of authority to change another's normative position then it is hardly surprising that legislation rather than common law has become the primary legal source. As the state has expanded

and deepened into the social fabric in the massive growth in the state in England since the Second World War, then **it is not surprising that legislation has grown in importance in parallel, as the state seeks to penetrate deeper into and regulate the social fabric**. As the philosopher Anthony Quinton notes in *The Politics of Imperfection* (1978) the state has expanded its reach into areas formerly occupied by other social institutions:

> **it has seemed not merely convenient, but imperative, for government to take on itself all sorts of functions that were previously discharged by other institutions, such as the Church or the family, or in a private, non-institutional way.**

(2) Legislation is proactive, identifying social problems and addressing them directly, whereas judicial decisions are reactive dependent on legal problems being brought forward for decision.

(3) Legislation is seen in contrast to judicial common law as an explicitly political process, statute law is the result of overt political conflict or debate. Statute law thus embodies policy, defined collective goals for the management of complex modern societies. Common law judges often defer to Parliament on policy matters for the forensic process is ill-equipped for the broad consultation and debate process required to deliver policy-driven law.

(4) Legislation can be viewed of as a process aiming at a certain finality – a conclusive clarity in legal expression. Judge made law is provisional in a way that legislation is not. The common law is always 'work in progress', by its very nature 'a barrier reef' in which deletions and additions are continually made by the surge of the common law wave. Of course legislation can be repealed by other legislation but at least in intention legislation is meant to enjoy some permanence. Case law is always being restated in updated form, by contrast legislation aims at finality and even code-like comprehensiveness in an area of law. Legislation, by aiming at finality, fits with the essence of law as perceived by thinkers from Thomas Hobbes in *Leviathan* (1651) to Raz in *Between Authority and Interpretation* (2009). For Raz:

> it is in the nature of law that it claims authority ie that it claims to be authoritative, and that means that it claims to have settled moral and other social issues.

The law then is an exercise of authority to achieve finality in disputed social or moral matters or to achieve finality where there is no controversy but a decision is still required as to some matter. Legislation is, on this model of law, the paradigm of law-making with the common law a secondary source of law. Raz has commented on why legislation is so important given the nature of modern, pluralistic democratic societies. In 'The Politics of the Rule of Law' in *Ethics in the Public Domain* (1994) Raz comments:

> The reason for the importance of legislation in modern societies is that democratic legislation seems essential for the adequate government of a pluralistic society in a continuous process of social and economic change . . . Only democratic politics can be sufficiently sensitive to the results of change, and only democratic politics can respond adequately to the different interests and perspectives of different subcultures.

Raz adds that although legislation is the primary legal source in today's society:

> Mine is not the theory that courts should have no share in making and developing the law. I am an advocate, not an opponent, of both judicial discretion and judicial power to set precedents, which between them give the courts considerable law-making power.

NOTES

An excellent account of the reasons why modern English judges are very cautious about using their law-making powers at common law is given by Lord Bingham (who held the three top judicial posts in the English legal system: Lord Chief Justice, Master of the Rolls, Senior Law Lord) in an essay entitled 'The Judge as Lawmaker: An English perspective' in a collection of essays called *The Business of Judging: Selected Essays and Speeches* (2000).

The reasons as to why legislation has become the dominant legal source are examined by Roger Cotterrell in *Living Law* (2008) at pp 344–349.

Utilitarianism

INTRODUCTION

This chapter is made up of questions concerning the doctrine of utilitarianism associated with Jeremy Bentham (1748–1832), John Stuart Mill (1806–73), and related criticisms of the doctrine by Nozick (1938–2002) and Rawls (1921–2002) and others. The principles of utilitarianism made a direct impact on jurisprudence, particularly in areas involving the criminal law. Utilitarians perceived the 'true good' as *happiness* and argued that each person always pursues what he considers to be his personal happiness. The legislator's task is to effect a balance of public and private interests. Hence, the criminal law may be viewed as a mode of producing *a coincidence of the interests of the community and of the individual*. Bentham was concerned, in particular, with influencing legislation and policy along utilitarian lines. Mill was less dogmatic. His major interest was in the liberty of the individual and the consequent need to set limits to government action. Questions in this area of jurisprudential thought require an understanding of the general principles of utilitarianism, the arguments used by Bentham and Mill and the views of critics of utilitarianism, such as Nozick and Rawls.

Checklist ✔

Ensure that you are acquainted with the following topics:

- the principles of utilitarianism;
- Mill's fundamentals of liberty;
- Bentham's views on punishment;
- the legitimate role of government;
- the appeal of utilitarianism (eg egalitarianism);
- criticism of utilitarianism that it ignores the 'separateness of persons' and cannot satisfactorily account for fundamental human rights.

QUESTION 12

To what extent might a modern legislator find JS Mill's views on the limits of toleration and government powers in relation to the individual to be of relevance to contemporary problems?

Answer Plan

The eloquent plea on behalf of freedom of speech by Mill (1806–1873), contained in his essay, *On Liberty* (1859), contemplates a society in which interference with individual rights is kept to a minimum. Freedom will flourish only where there is respect for citizens and where conditions prevail allowing for the recognition of points of view, no matter how unpopular they may be. An answer to this question should seek to consider some of the many ways in which Mill's conclusions on matters concerning the fundamental freedom of the individual might be relevant to problems of our own day. A skeleton plan along the following lines is suggested:

- ❖ Introduction;
- ❖ Mill's insistence on a synthesis of justice and utility;
- ❖ liberty as a 'good' and as a means to an end;
- ❖ freedom of expression;
- ❖ 'paternalistic' legislation;
- ❖ duties towards others;
- ❖ principles of government interference;
- ❖ conclusion, relevance of Mill's analysis.

ANSWER

The views of Mill (1806–1873), set out in his essay *On Liberty* (1859), constitute a statement as to the fundamentals of a desirable balance of interests between the state and the individual citizen. His powerful plea for individual liberty emerges from an analysis of relationships of individual and general interests, of 'justice' and 'utility'. The philosophy of utilitarianism suffuses the essay: liberty, for Mill, rests on no 'natural law' or other metaphysical doctrine, but on a synthesis of the essential features of justice and the concept of utility. A modern legislator would be interested, for example, in Mill's warning of the dangers of the oppression of minorities by majorities, in his insistence on the need for safeguards against those forces that might deny an individual's free and full self-development, and in the intensity of his concern for the preservation of liberty by imposing limits to government action. The legislator will find no detailed instructions for legal and governmental action, but rather a basic appraisal of principles in the area of state intervention designed 'for the good of the people'.

What better can be said of any condition of human affairs, asked Mill, than that it brings human beings nearer to 'the best thing they can be'? Mill's interest in state, law and society centres on their ability to provide the circumstances in which individuals might flourish. Liberty, which in itself is 'a good', is also a means to an end: the end is man's attaining his optimum development, including his full freedom. Mill is reminding legislators and others that in arranging a social and legal framework, they have to keep in mind the long-term goals of justice and human development. Further, asks Mill, when should society enact legislation which interferes with an individual's liberty of action? Our legislator might understand the import of Mill's question in relation, say, to the **Regulation of Investigatory Powers Act 2000** or the **Care Standards Act 2000**: what *right* (apart from its democratic mandate) has a government to enact legislation of this nature?

Mill's answers to the questions he poses form a key to an understanding of his concept of liberty as essential for the development of society. There is only one purpose, according to Mill, for which a government can rightfully exercise power over a citizen *against his will*, and that is to prevent harm to others. The citizen's own physical or moral good will not, on its own, constitute a sufficient warrant. Legislators are urged by Mill to consider the thesis that they may not *compel* a citizen against his will 'to do or forbear' because it is better for him to do so or because his happiness will be intensified as a result; they may remonstrate or reason with him, but they may not force him. The overriding exception is where harm may be caused to others. Conduct which is calculated to produce evil to some other person provides a sufficient reason for the exercise of power against the person who intends such a course of action.

Legislators contemplating current problems relating to liberty of thought and expression would find Mill's views to be highly relevant. He is emphatic in his insistence that a society in which this liberty is not respected cannot be 'free', and that such freedom must be absolute and unqualified. Indeed, he argues, if all mankind minus one individual shared one opinion, mankind would be no more justified in silencing that individual than he, if he had the power, would be justified in silencing mankind. To silence the expression of opinion is to rob the human race of the opportunity of exchanging error for truth or of the opportunity of acquiring a clearer perception of truth as produced when it collides with error.

Mill stresses this theme by stating a case for the free expression of opinion. A contemporary legislator, under pressure to support or oppose enactments relating to the suppression of a highly unpopular type of opinion, might wish to contemplate this case. First, says Mill, if an opinion is silenced, that opinion, for aught we know, may be true; if we deny this, we are assuming our infallibility. Secondly, even though the silenced opinion be erroneous, it may contain a portion of truth ('truth often comes on the scene riding on the back of error'); but since current opinion on any matter is rarely the *whole* truth, it is only through the collision of contrary opinions that the remainder of a truth might emerge. Thirdly, unless received opinion is subjected to vigorous and earnest challenge, it may be held with little comprehension and may take on the character of mere prejudice. Finally, if the opinion is unchallenged and degenerates into dogma, it prevents the growth of any real conviction from reason or personal experience.

The modern legislator will probably respond that this line of reasoning ignores practical necessity. What of the demands of the community for protection against the expression of opinion in circumstances which might inflame sentiment and lead to public disorder? Was it 'wrong' to enact, for example, s 23 of the **Public Order Act 1986** (dealing with possession of racially inflammatory material)? Is freedom of expression to be allowed to overt racism or the encouragement of terrorism?

Mill would reply in measured terms. No one claims that men should be free to act upon all their opinions; no one claims that actions should be as free as opinions. Quite to the contrary, opinions should lose their immunity when the very circumstances of their expression constitute a mischievous act. Mill gives as an example of an intolerable expression of opinion a speech in which corn dealers are accused of starving the poor, delivered to a mob gathered before a corn dealer's home. The liberty of an individual must be limited to the extent that he may not make himself a nuisance to other people. However, if a person merely acts according to his opinion in matters *which concern himself*, he should be allowed to carry his opinions into practice at his own cost. In matters which do not primarily concern others, individuality may be permitted to assert itself; but where there is a chance of injury to others, a person may be restrained.

The modern legislator may respond further by questioning the relevance of this thesis in the face of a growing tendency to 'paternalistic legislation'. Mill's reply would be based on his belief that, in general, it is the privilege of an individual who has arrived 'at the maturity of his faculties' to use and interpret experience in his own way. Mill intends that his principles shall be applicable only to *mature persons* (he excludes, for example, minors). Today's legislators might consider the relevance of Mill's thesis to the contemporary theory of 'the least restrictive alternative', which suggests that if there is an alternative way of accomplishing some desired end without restricting an individual's liberty, then, although it will probably involve considerable inconvenience and expense, it should be adopted.

To an individual, says Mill, should belong that part of his life in which he is largely interested, and to society the part which largely interests society. A modern legislator may consider this thesis relevant to today's problems only if it casts light on the basic problem – where does society's (that is, government's) authority begin? The problem might be posed thus: what are the 'rightful' limits to an individual's sovereignty over himself?

Mill's answer begins with an assertion that society is not founded on any type of 'contract' and there is no purpose in inventing one so as to deduce social obligations from it. All persons who receive the protection of society owe some return; the fact that one lives in society makes it necessary that each individual should be obliged to observe a specific mode of conduct towards others. That conduct involves not hurting the interests of others (that is, those interests which by express enactment and tacit understanding are classified as 'rights'). Further, each individual must bear a share of the efforts incurred in protecting society from injury. Wherever and whenever a person behaves in a way which affects the interests of others in a prejudicial manner, society, through its legal institutions, must have and exercise jurisdiction. But where it is obvious that the interests of no person apart from himself will be affected by an action, that person must have the freedom (legal and social) to perform the action and accept its consequences.

This is not to suggest that members of society, or its representatives in government, ought not to be concerned with individuals' conduct of their own lives. There is, Mill claims, need of 'disinterested exertion' intended to promote the good of others. But that benevolence, he insists, can and must find other methods of persuading people to their good rather than 'whips and scourges either of the literal or metaphorical sort'. Nor must it be forgotten that no individual, no group, no government has a *right* to say to an individual 'of ripe years' that he shall not do with his life for his own benefit what he chooses to do with it. In the same vein, Mill emphasises that whenever there is a definite risk of damage to an individual or to the public, the case must be removed from 'the province of liberty' and must be considered as falling within the area of morality or law.

Given that there is a legitimate role for government to play in the affairs of individuals, Mill advocates three important principles to be kept in mind by legislators. First, government interference which does not involve the infringement of liberty should be considered very carefully when that which has to be done is likely to be better done by individuals than by the government. Mill is suggesting that legislators ought to remember that there are no better persons to determine how or by whom an undertaking should be conducted than those who are personally interested in it. Secondly, although individuals may not perform some types of administrative task as competently as government officials, nevertheless, they should be allowed, as a mode of furthering their development and social education, to carry them out. Thirdly – and

Mill sees this as a most cogent reason for restricting government interference – there is the 'great evil' of a government adding unnecessarily to its powers by creating a bureaucracy. Large-scale ownership by the state might seriously diminish freedom. Not all the freedom of the press and the existence of a popular constitution would make free a country dominated by a government bureaucracy, otherwise than in name. A modern legislator may find, indeed, that the problems which Mill posed and attempted to answer are of particular relevance to him and to those who administer the law. Today's problems may be outwardly different from those which confronted Mill, but, fundamentally, many of the problems are based on precisely the same tensions which arise in any society committed to individual liberty, social order and cohesion.

In our day, the coming into force (in October 2000) of the **Human Rights Act 1998**, and the decisions of the European Court of Human Rights, have led – as was expected – to a reconsideration by wide sections of the community, including jurists and legislators, of the problems inherent in processes of government related to areas of intervention in the lives of citizens.

Mill's thought can be interpreted as possessing a particular relevance. Some areas of human behaviour ought to be accepted, he argues, as being outside the proper sphere of communal control – they are:

> The inward domain of consciousness, demanding liberty of conscience in the most comprehensive sense; liberty of thought and feeling; absolute freedom of opinion and sentiment on all subjects, practical or speculative, scientific, moral or theological; liberty of tastes and pursuits and liberty of combination among individuals; freedom to unite for any purpose not involving harm to others.

Valuable words of guidance, indeed, for today's legislators.

NOTES

Mill's On Liberty appears in a variety of editions. His theories are considered in Riddall, Chapter 14; Bodenheimer, Chapter 6; Friedmann, Chapter 26; Ryan's Mill; and Himmelfarb's On Liberty and Liberalism. Dworkin examines government paternalism in Morality and the Law, edited by Wasserstrom. Mill's background is analysed in John Stuart Mill, by Britton, and John Stuart Mill: Critical Assessments, by Wood.

QUESTION 13

Is utilitarianism an acceptable foundation for justice and human rights?

Answer Plan

Utilitarianism has been a very influential theory since its origins with David Hume (1711–1776) and Jeremy Bentham (1748–1832). However, serious doubts persist as to whether even sophisticated versions of utilitarianism can account for the importance, persistence and absolute quality of fundamental human rights in Western societies. The appeal of utilitarianism has rested on its egalitarian and consequentialist features but the theory has been accused, with some justification, of ignoring 'the separateness of persons'. The two most influential modern attacks on utilitarianism as a moral and political theory have been by John Rawls in *A Theory of Justice* (1971) and Robert Nozick in *Anarchy, State and Utopia* (1974). These two anti-utilitarian masterpieces seek to develop principles of justice for the organisation of the state that are totally independent of any 'utilitarian' calculation. A skeleton plan is given:

❖   Introduction;
❖   the historical importance of utilitarianism;
❖   the factors giving utilitarianism appeal;
❖   the inability of even sophisticated 'rule utilitarians' to account for fundamental human rights;
❖   the critique of utilitarianism given by Professor Bernard Williams;
❖   the anti-utilitarian theory of justice of Rawls;
❖   the critique of utilitarianism given by Nozick;
❖   conclusion, despite its influence utilitarianism is seriously flawed as a foundation for fundamental human rights.

ANSWER

Until about 1970 the governing theory of political philosophy in the Western world was some version of utilitarianism. In 1971 John Rawls published his anti-utilitarian masterpiece, *A Theory of Justice*, which rejected utilitarianism as an acceptable foundation for principles of justice. The early 1970s saw further insightful assaults on utilitarianism as a political philosophy in the form of Bernard Williams's anti-utilitarian essay published in 1973 in *Utilitarianism: For and Against* and, most critical of all, in Robert Nozick's 1974 *Anarchy, State and Utopia*, which claimed that utilitarianism ignored the basic fact of human life – namely, our 'separate existences'.

However, utilitarianism as a form of political theory had a remarkably long shelf life and, therefore, the theory must have some form of intuitive appeal. The core idea behind utilitarianism is that political arrangements are sound when they are organised so as to produce the greatest happiness or satisfaction of the greatest number of persons. Indeed, this is the rough and ready rule of thumb which is the background justification of most government policy in liberal democracies concerning education, social services and health policies, for example. However, the question is not whether a utilitarian calculus should play some part in government calculations, but whether the pursuit of utilitarian goals by government should be qualified by 'side-constraints' in the form of fundamental non-negotiable human rights which should block the pursuit of utilitarian policies where these infringe individual human rights. So utilitarianism cannot be dismissed out of hand as a political philosophy; it has a legitimate space in government calculations. The crucial question is whether it occupies all the space in political philosophy and political decisions.

Utilitarianism has two central appealing features: (1) it aims to maximise human satisfaction or happiness; and (2) it is fundamentally egalitarian in structure in that in the utilitarian calculation 'everybody to count for one, nobody for more than one' (see this utilitarian slogan mentioned in John Stuart Mill's *Utilitarianism* (1863) taken from Bentham's *Rationale of Judicial Evidence*). There is no recognition or bias in utilitarian philosophy for caste, class, race or religion. The 'democratic' nature of utilitarianism, as opposed to 'aristocratic' or 'hereditary' forms of political organisation, may account for the long-term appeal of utilitarianism as ideas of democracy and egalitarianism grew in the West from the late eighteenth century (the French Revolution, for example, in 1789 whose slogan was 'liberty, equality, fraternity'). Indeed, in 1776 the English lawyer–philosopher, Jeremy Bentham, had written that both government and the limits of government were to be justified by reference to the greatest happiness of the greatest number of citizens (see Bentham's *A Fragment on Government* (1776)). This, at first sight, seems to be an intuitively attractive theory: for the promotion of the well-being of as many citizens as possible within the constraints of reality would seem to be a natural aim of government. Indeed, as a background theory of government, utilitarianism has been and continues to be influential. Utilitarianism can be viewed most favourably as a version of 'a common good' (*commune bonum*) theory of political theory. However, government must have much more in mind than utilitarianism to be politically acceptable. Yet the principle of utility formulated by Bentham claims to be the only principle which can provide an objective foundation for morals and legislation as opposed to other principles, such as the law of nature, law of reason, natural justice and natural equity, for example.

Utilitarianism has mutated into many different forms as sympathetic philosophers have tried to defend the theory against attack from hostile philosophers, exemplified by Rawls (1921–2002) and Nozick (1938–2002). The main criticism directed against utilitarianism is that it fails to provide a sufficiently secure foundation of human rights. However, some sophisticated versions of utilitarianism do claim, with some if not complete persuasiveness, that utilitarianism can account for the existence, extent and fundamental importance of human rights in modern liberal democracies. Indeed, the lack of 'fit' between utilitarianism and the persistence and importance of human rights in the Western world has been used to discredit utilitarianism as an acceptable political theory. Sophisticated utilitarians, such as the British philosopher, RM Hare (see *Moral Thinking* (1981)), argue that refined versions of utilitarianism can justify and support many of the basic human rights valued and protected in the West. For example, protecting freedom of speech and freedom of the press is very likely in fact to lead to the maximisation of human happiness through (a) a better informed and educated population which, in turn, will lead to the election of more competent political leaders and (b) the scrutiny and 'watchdog' effect of the media on government, which is likely to lead to better and more honest government.

Therefore, a 'rule of utility' supporting freedom of speech and the Press, even when that is inconvenient to utility in individual cases, can explain the persistence and importance of the human right of free speech in the West. Indeed, the 'rule utilitarian' can argue that his justification for human rights – to promote utility in the long run – is a much more stable and understandable justification for 'human rights' than anti-utilitarian justifications of human rights based on such nebulous, and arguably empty, concepts such as 'equality' (Dworkin – see *Taking Rights Seriously* (1977)), 'the separateness of persons' (see Nozick) or 'fairness' (see Rawls's *Justice as Fairness*).

Another example of rule utilitarianism at work justifying fundamental human rights concerns the universal prohibition in liberal democracies on the use of torture by the police to obtain evidence or intelligence. The rule utilitarian would say that an absolute ban on the legitimate use of torture by the police would serve utilitarian aims of promoting the greatest happiness of the greatest number in the following ways : (a) prohibiting torture by the police is likely to maximise utility because citizens will not suffer anxiety in case they or their family members are arrested and may suffer torture at the hands of the police; (b) the police will use more reliable methods in solving crime rather than rely on the unreliable fruits of torture; and (c) the morale and self-respect of the police as an organisation will be improved by a rule prohibiting the torture of suspects.

Therefore, for these compelling reasons based on utility, the state should adopt a strict rule prohibiting the torture of suspects by the police. However, despite the persuasive nature of these subtle arguments, the 'rule utilitarian' fails to account for the following strong counter-arguments:

(a) The torture of suspects by the police is wrong in itself independent of any argument based on utilitarian consequences. Torture of suspects by the state is intuitively a moral wrong in itself independent of the utilitarian calculus. Of course, a utilitarian such as Bentham would denounce such an argument as 'nonsense upon stilts', but the utilitarian has no convincing explanation of our deep intuition that torture is wrong in itself other than to deny our intuitions as valid.

(b) It may be that in certain cases the torture of suspects would improve utility, such as where a terrorist could be tortured by police to find out the location of a bomb that would kill thousands of innocent persons. Many reasonable persons would believe torture to be justifiable in such circumstances and agree with the utilitarian to carve out an exception to the prohibition on torture in such 'ticking bomb' situations. However, the utilitarian cannot therefore adequately account for the absolute and non-derogable nature of many prohibitions on torture in many liberal democratic states (see, for example, **Article 3** of the **European Convention on Human Rights** which allows for non-derogation on the absolute prohibition on torture).

The ultimate failure of even sophisticated versions of utilitarianism, such as 'rule utilitarianism', to account for our intuitions about the moral wrongness of violations of rights such as the state torture of suspects has led political philosophers to develop non-utilitarian theories of rights and justice, the two most celebrated being *A Theory of Justice* (1971) by John Rawls and *Anarchy, State and Utopia* (1974) by Robert Nozick. The contingent or 'everything depends on the circumstances' feature of utilitarianism has been a too slippery slope for the foundation of fundamental human rights. Before we examine the political philosophy of the twin American giants, Rawls and Nozick, we should consider the devastating critique of utilitarianism given by the English philosopher Bernard Williams (1929–2003) in the 1973 work *Utilitarianism: For and Against*, Williams gave the following graphic illustration of the deficiencies of utilitarianism as a moral theory by using the imaginary account of 'Jim in the jungle'.

'Jim in the jungle' has become a standard stock phrase and example for critics of utilitarianism. The story is as follows. Jim finds himself in the central square of a small South American town at a time in the early 1970s when dictatorship blighted that continent. Tied up against the wall is a row of twenty native Indians, most terrified, a few defiant, and in front of them several armed men in uniform. A heavy man turns out to be the captain in charge and, after establishing that Jim is not a spy but an innocent tourist, the captain explains that the captured Indians are from an area where there has been a revolt against the government. The twenty captured Indians are to be executed by firing squad so as to deter further revolts against government by the native Indian population. However, the captain of the execution squad informs Jim that, since he is an 'honourable foreign guest', the captain will spare the lives of nineteen of the Indians if Jim himself shoots dead one of the captives. If Jim refuses his grisly task then, says the captain, all twenty Indians must be executed immediately. This dilemma facing Jim confronts us with the limitations of utilitarianism as a moral theory, for the utilitarian would reply to the dilemma by urging Jim to kill one lone Indian captive in order to save nineteen lives. The calculus of utility would demand that Jim carries out the captain's offer and himself kill one Indian in order to save nineteen Indians from certain death. Utilitarianism would always prefer one dead to twenty dead. However, the moral equation is more complex than utilitarianism would allow.

As Professor Williams argues, it is not obvious that Jim should kill the one Indian in order to save the other nineteen Indians from certain death at the hands of the captain and his troops, for utilitarianism cannot account for the moral point that each one of us is especially responsible for what he does rather than for what other persons do. This is, says Professor Williams, an idea closely connected with the value of integrity. Utilitarianism makes the moral value called integrity unintelligible. The crucial point overlooked by utilitarianism is that by shooting one captive Indian in order to save nineteen Jim becomes a murderer and, as a result, his moral character in the eyes of himself, other persons and God is changed forever. His view of himself and what is important to himself is changed forever even though he was trying through the murder of one innocent to save nineteen other innocents. If Jim refuses the captain's offer to kill and then the captain orders his troops to kill twenty Indians, Jim has not himself killed anyone, he has merely refused an immoral offer. It is the captain's choice to kill twenty and the captain had the power to choose mercy or to kill. Jim's decision to refuse to kill one is indeed a cause of the deaths of twenty but it is not the significant or substantial cause which is, in fact, the captain's order to his troops to execute the twenty Indians.

Utilitarianism fails as a moral theory because it has the effect of depriving human life of all that makes it worthwhile, failing sufficiently to take account of each person's integrity, the projects central to their lives, and the especial obligations and loyalty owed to family and friends. By judging human actions in terms of their consequences for utility only, utilitarianism makes human agency of only secondary and derivative importance whereas, for example, deontological (duty based) moral theories, such as expounded by Kant (1724–1804), make human agency the central aspect of morality. For Immanuel Kant, the morality of an action is to be judged not by the consequences of that action as utilitarianism does, but by the intention or will which motivates that human action. The idea of personal integrity and personal responsibility is a 'golden thread' that runs through the Judaeo-Christian tradition and which cannot be accounted for in utilitarian moral theory. As is reported by St Paul in the Epistle to the Philippians, Chapter 2 verse 12: 'Work out your own salvation with fear and trembling.'

The American philosopher Thomas Nagel has another telling point to make against utilitarianism. Nagel writes in *Equality and Partiality* (1991):

> moral rules by which murder and torture are always wrong, confer a certain status on persons which they do not have in a moral or legal system in which murder and torture are regarded merely as great evils – so that sometimes it may be permissible to commit them in order to prevent even more of the same. Faced with the question whether to murder one to save five from murder, one may be convinced that fewer people will be murdered if one does it; but one would thereby be accepting the principle that anyone is legitimately murderable, given the right circumstances. This is a subtle but definite alteration for the worse in everyone's moral status. Whereas if one refuses, one is saying that all murders are illegitimate, including of course the five that one will have refused to prevent. To preserve the status of every person as someone that it is never legitimate to murder . . . is vitally important, and its recognition by a society is an enormous good in itself, apart from its consequences.

The pervasive 'moral blindness' of utilitarianism has led some political philosophers to develop sophisticated non-utilitarian theories of justice. It is proposed to sketch briefly the non-utilitarian based theories of justice developed by John Rawls and Robert Nozick.

The political philosophy of Rawls is driven by certain facts – historical facts about modern Western liberal democratic states. In a 1987 article called 'The idea of an overlapping consensus' (in *Oxford Journal of Legal Studies*) Rawls asks, given that modern society is made up of deep divisions between religious, social and political groups, what political principles to organise civil society could be formulated which could be given the assent of reasonable persons who otherwise fundamentally disagree about religion, morality or politics? The Rawlsian 'overlapping consensus' represents those fundamental principles to organise society which could be agreed upon by persons who disagree with each other about much else in life. The need to achieve social stability and unity over fundamental political principle in deeply divided societies in the Western world has been a major theme of the more recent work of Rawls who has said: 'The problem of stability is fundamental to political philosophy.' (See Rawls, *Political Liberalism* (1993).)

'Political liberalism', as Rawls terms his most recent theory, accepts, as it must, the existence of reasonable but incompatible doctrines in society (for example, Roman Catholicism and atheism) which do not reject the essentials of a liberal democratic regime (society, for example, contains democratic persons who do and who do not believe in God). Of course, society may contain unreasonable, irrational or even mad elements (such as political or religious terrorists) and Rawls says that the issue for society here is one of containment and suppression of such groups, for as Rawls comments: 'In their case the problem is to contain them so that they do not undermine the unity and justice of society.'

The basic idea of Rawls is to devise principles of justice that govern the constitutional structure of the state which can obtain the consent of the differing reasonable groups in society (that is, an 'overlapping consensus'). How to discover these basic principles which will form the basis of the 'overlapping consensus' and so obtain the 'holy grail' of political philosophy – namely, social stability in a liberal democracy? Rawls has a version of 'social contract' theory to discover the basic constitutional principles. Rawls, in his original work in 1971, *A Theory of Justice*, asked the reader to imagine a situation in which rational individuals do not know how rich or poor they are, where they do not know where they come in the socio-economic index of society. Behind this 'veil of ignorance' (as Rawls terms this position of 'blind choice') rational individuals choose what principles of justice should govern society. The 'original position' is meant to model conditions of fairness as the rational individuals will not be able to choose those principles of justice which reflect their actual position in society – hence, the self-description of Rawls of his own theory as 'justice as fairness'. It should be noted that no consideration of any utilitarian calculations enter the theory and therefore Rawls's theory is a non-utilitarian theory of justice. At the outset of *A Theory of Justice* Rawls explains why he calls the theory 'justice as fairness' by reference to the hypothetical social contract, 'the original position' which is the foundation of Rawls's theory. Rawls comments:

> the original position is, one might say, the appropriate initial status quo, and thus the fundamental agreements reached in it are fair. This explains the propriety of the name "justice as fairness": it conveys the idea that the principles of justice are agreed to in an initial situation that is fair.

The initial 'original position' is fair since the rational choosers of the 'principles of justice' are screened from any information about themselves which might unfairly influence their choice of principles for society. Rawls claims that a rational person in the 'original position' would choose the following two principles of justice, given that it could turn out that the rational chooser was at the bottom, middle or top of the socio-economic index of society. Those two principles of justice are:

(a) Each person has an equal claim to a fully adequate scheme of equal basic rights and liberties, which scheme is compatible with the same scheme for all persons in society.

(b) Social and economic inequalities in society (and so Rawls is neither a socialist nor Marxist) are to satisfy two conditions: (i) all positions and offices are open to all persons under conditions of fair equality of opportunity, and (ii) the inequalities in society are to be justified if those inequalities work for the benefit of the least advantaged members of society.

The American philosopher, Thomas Nagel, in an article in 1997, 'Justice and Nature' (in *Oxford Journal of Legal Studies*), comments that the complete absence of distinguishing information under the veil of ignorance of the choosers in Rawls's theory in the 'original position' would require that all inequalities in society be justified by reference to their contribution to everyone's interest. This is because no chooser could not guarantee that he would be at the bottom of the socio-economic index in society. So 'justice as fairness' would allow for socio-economic inequalities so long as that system worked for the benefit of the worst off in society. Indeed, it is possible to make too much of the principle of equality which, although justifying the important value of equality of opportunity, can be taken to absurd extremes. As Nagel points out, it seems a mindless abuse of the ideal of equality that advocates for the physically handicapped have blocked the installation of free-standing pay toilets on Manhattan streets in New York (of the kind that are common in Europe) unless they could all be large enough for wheelchair access.

Much ink has been spilt by philosophers as to whether the two principles of justice which Rawls says would be chosen in the 'original position' would in fact be chosen behind 'the veil of ignorance' (see, for example, the criticisms of the 'original position' by Thomas Nagel in *The Philosophical Review* (1973)). In more recent writings (such as his restatement of his views in his 1993 book, *Political Liberalism*), Rawls argues primarily not that his two principles of justice would be chosen in the 'original position' (as he argued in 1971) but rather that his two principles of justice are most likely to gain acceptance, the sought-after 'overlapping consensus', in conflict-ridden modern Western liberal democratic societies such as the United States of America. The hypothetical 'original position' in the more recent Rawlsian writings has taken a back seat to the more pressing problem of achieving consensus in actual liberal democratic Western societies. It is important to note that Rawls's 'principles of justice' are not formulated as 'universal' principles of justice aimed at all societies whatever the historical period or geographical location. Rawls is explicit that his 'theory of justice' is aimed at the modern Western state with its respect for and tradition of democracy, the rule of law and equality of opportunity for all citizens. Rawls can be criticised, therefore, for holding up merely a 'mirror' to liberal democratic states since the Rawlsian two principles of justice are likely to gain acceptance as reflections of current ideals in those liberal democratic states.

Rawls comments in *Political Liberalism*:

the aim of "justice as fairness" then is practical: it presents itself as a conception of justice that may be shared by citizens as a basis of a reasoned, informed and willing political agreement. It expresses their shared and public political reason. It should be independent of the opposing and conflicting philosophical and religious doctrines that citizens affirm.

Rawls, in his writings in the 1980s and 1990s, is keen to stress 'the idea of society as a fair system of co-operation' (*Political Liberalism*). This 'fair system of co-operation' crucially depends on principles of political arrangement that each reasonable participant can accept provided that, likewise, everyone else accepts them. Rawls has a noble dream for Western liberal democracies: the idea of a well-ordered society as a society effectively regulated by a public political conception of justice. Whether in the light of factors such as pervasive human evil manifesting in rising crime rates and civil disorder, religious and political terrorism, and factors such as global warming, food shortages and energy crises, the 'well ordered' liberal political society of Rawls's imagination can be maintained in the long run only history will tell.

However, Rawls is insistent that his two principles of justice are practicably realisable and that they are not utopian:

the most reasonable political conception of justice for a democratic regime will be liberal. It will protect the familiar basic rights and assigns them a special priority; it also includes measures to ensure that all persons in society have sufficient material means to make effective use of those basic rights. Faced with the fact of pluralism, a liberal view removes from the political agenda the most divisive issues (such as religion or morality), reduces serious contention and conflict which must undermine the bases of social co-operation.

For Rawls, his liberalism is 'political' only in that his 'two principles of justice' can be supported by a wide range of persons with conflicting religious, moral and ideological viewpoints. Rawls's 'two principles of justice' form the 'overlapping consensus' which is realisable in otherwise deeply divided liberal democratic societies.

Robert Nozick published his *Anarchy, State and Utopia* (1974) partly as a response to Rawls's *A Theory of Justice* and also to refute utilitarianism as any acceptable theory for government. Nozick is even more hostile to utilitarianism than Rawls was in *A Theory of Justice*. Nozick seriously doubts the intelligibility of the utilitarian calculation balancing the happiness and pains of all persons in society. Nozick comments that there is no social entity with a good that undergoes some sacrifice for its own good. There are only individual people, different individual people, with their own individual lives. Nozick continues that using one of these persons for the benefit of others, as utilitarianism allows, uses that person and benefits the others. Nothing more. What happens is that something is done to him for the sake of others. Talk of an overall social good covers this up. To use a person in this way does not sufficiently respect and take account of the fact that he is a separate person, that his is the only life he has. Nozick, therefore, doubts whether utilitarianism is intelligible as a moral theory and that the existence of fundamental human rights reflects the crucial metaphysical and sociological fact of our separate existences from each other. This root idea for Nozick – namely, that there are different individuals with separate lives and so no one may be sacrificed for others – underlies the existence of the fundamental human rights and leads to the rejection of utilitarianism as a moral theory with its talk of 'balancing' the pleasures and pains of different persons so as to produce a 'utilitarian' calculation. The individual rights that we enjoy (indeed, the very first sentence of *Anarchy, State and Utopia* states: 'Individuals have rights, and there are things no person or group may do to them without violating their rights') reflect the basic insight that persons have 'separate existences' (as Nozick comments, we should remind ourselves 'of how different people are' from each other).

From this metaphysical and psychological fact about our separate existences Nozick savages utilitarianism as a political and moral philosophy and builds his own 'theory of the state' which does respect individual persons and their rights – namely, the 'minimal state'. Nozick argues that only the minimal state is morally legitimate as it treats us as inviolate individuals who may not be used in certain ways by others as means or tools or instruments or resources: the 'minimal state' treats us as persons having individual rights with the dignity this constitutes. Treating us with respect, says Nozick, by respecting our rights, the 'minimal state' allows us, individually or with whom we choose, to choose our life and to realise ends and our conception of ourselves aided by the voluntary co-operation of other individuals possessing the same dignity. The 'minimal state' of Nozick's imagination would be different from the USA and UK in important respects. Nozick is not an anarchist, he believes in the legitimacy and necessity of a central authority with a monopoly on the use of legitimate coercion. This central authority is necessary to protect individuals against the violence and theft of others. No individual, no matter how wealthy, can match the crime-fighting resources of a modern state. Therefore, some taxation to support the 'minimal state' is necessary.

However, Nozick is insistent that any redistributive taxation to support the poor and needy is impermissible as it treats the wealthy as a resource to be used to support others and, therefore, violates the sanctity of the cardinal principle for Nozick, 'the separateness of persons'. As Nozick comments, every person is entitled to all that they have acquired provided they gained their possessions justly. The state must do no more than enforce contracts, prevent crime and safeguard the country from external attack. It is for individuals, through charitable donations and voluntary bequests, to help the poor and needy. Enforced taxation of the rich to help the poor is not legitimate for Nozick. The state is too dangerous an entity to be trusted with power beyond that which is required by the 'minimal state'. Nozick can be viewed as the father of right-wing free market and anti-welfarism political philosophy, which denies utilitarianism as both a dangerous egalitarian and potentially socialistic philosophy and which threatens, in its treatment of persons as 'units' of utility, the sacred rights of inviolable individuals.

However, Nozick's views can be criticised in the light of Professor Hart's criticisms in an essay entitled 'Between utility and rights' (in *Essays in Jurisprudence and Philosophy* (1983)). Hart comments that it is a distortion of language to suggest that some taxation of the rich to help the poor and needy is inevitably a violation of the rights of the rich. As Hart comments: 'Can one man's relief from great suffering not outweigh a small loss of income imposed on another to provide it?' Therefore, as a fair society we accept some redistributive taxation so long as the level of taxation on the rich is reasonable and fair. Nozick wants to shield the rich from any redistributive taxation to relieve the poor. This seems intuitively unreasonable and no serious politician today would assert such an extreme position. Moreover, Nozick's concern for freedom seems to extend only to those who have the resources to exercise it. As Hart comments: 'It is, of course, an ancient insight that for a meaningful life not only the protection of freedom from deliberate restriction but opportunities and resources for its exercise are needed. Except for a few privileged and lucky persons, the ability to shape life for oneself and lead a meaningful life is something to be constructed by positive marshalling of social and economic resources . . . Nothing is more likely to bring freedom into contempt and so endanger it than failure to support those who lack, through no fault of their own, the material and social conditions and opportunities which are needed if a man's freedom is to contribute to his welfare.'

The consequences of the 'minimal state' envisaged by Nozick could well lead to social and economic resentment from the mass of individuals denied economic help through redistributive taxation, leading possibly to civil disorder and revolution and disturbing the security of the rich which Nozick was so keen to protect. The key point which Professor Hart makes in his criticism of Nozick is that, in constructing his theory, he sought to derive too much from the idea of the 'separateness of persons' and that other values are relevant to a moral and political theory. As Hart comments: 'Why should there not be included a basic right to the positive service of the relief of great needs or suffering or the provision of basic education and skills and why should property rights have an absolute, permanent, exclusive and unmodifiable character?'

It is arguable that Nozick has made in *Anarchy, State and Utopia* as much a false idol of the idea of 'the separateness of persons' as utilitarianism made of the slogan 'the greatest happiness of the greatest number'. Perhaps, to use a phrase coined by Professor Hart, the truth in political philosophy lies 'between utility and absolute rights'.

Common Pitfalls

Students can avoid the pitfall of thinking that utilitarianism cannot provide a theory of human rights. Sophisticated utilitarians, such as RM Hare, argue that utility is nearly always served by strict adherence to fundamental human rights: therefore there can be a 'utility of rights'. Students can gain extra marks by arguing that even the most sophisticated versions of utilitarianism cannot account for the absolute and persisting nature of fundamental human rights.

NOTES

The section on utilitarianism by Rawls in *A Theory of Justice* (1971) is the best starting point for learning about the criticisms of utilitarianism. Heavier reading is provided by Nozick in *Anarchy, State and Utopia* (1974), but the reader should refer also to Professor Bernard Williams's critique of utilitarianism in *Utilitarianism: For and Against* (1973) with JJC Smart. Nozick's extreme anti-utilitarian theory is itself critiqued by Professor Hart in 'Between utility and rights' in *Essays in Jurisprudence and Philosophy* (1983).

Punishment

6

INTRODUCTION

The question concerning the sound justification of punishment of an individual criminal by the state has preoccupied philosophers of the stature of Kant, Bentham and Professor Hart.

The deliberate infliction of pain and humiliation on an individual by the state through the judicial system requires strong justification and the two main contenders for the justification of state punishment, namely 'retribution' and 'deterrence', have persisted in the philosophical literature on punishment.

Checklist ✔

Ensure that you are acquainted with the following topics:

- the main philosophical justifications for punishment: 'retribution', 'deterrence';
- the minor justifications for punishment: 'rehabilitation', 'incapacitation';
- the view of major philosophical thinkers on punishment such as Kant and Professor Hart;
- the views of Bentham on the punishment of offenders from the standpoint of utilitarianism.

QUESTION 14

What are the main justifications for imposing state punishment on an individual?

Answer Plan

This question involves discussion of the thorny issue of how the punishment of the individual offender is to be justified. The discussion should mention the views of important philosophers such as Kant and Bentham and the main philosophical basis of punishment. There are four general justifications for punishment that vary in weight: retribution, deterrence, rehabilitation and incapacitation. The soundest theory of punishment may involve an amalgam of two or more principles of punishment.

A skeleton plan is suggested:

- ❖ Introduction;
- ❖ the need to justify state punishment of an individual offender;
- ❖ the views of major philosophers on punishment such as Kant and Bentham;
- ❖ the general principles of punishment: their advantages and disadvantages;
- ❖ conclusion, a 'mixed theory' of punishment may be the soundest justification of state punishment of an offender.

ANSWER

The central issue involved in the justification for state punishment is this: the state has legitimacy partly because it is an organised entity with the resources to co-ordinate society for the common good – the well-being of citizens within the state. When the state, through the judiciary, orders that a person be punished then this is the deliberate infliction of loss and pain on an individual. This deliberate infliction of state-licensed coercion stands in need of justification. Professor Dworkin has spent most of his academic career arguing how the coercive activity of the state in the civil law, forcing someone to pay compensation, can be justified, but this is a separate question of how criminal punishment by the state can be justified. Philosophers have wrestled with this issue for centuries.

Immanuel Kant, the famous German philosopher in 1797 in his work *The Metaphysics of Morals* argued that the only justification for punishment was strict retribution – the idea that a person 'deserved' the punishment inflicted upon them. Kant said:

> The right to punish is the right a ruler has against a subject to inflict pain upon him because of his having committed a crime.

Kant's 'retributivist' philosophy of punishment was so severe that he argued the following:

> Even if a civil society were to be dissolved by the consent of all its members (e.g. if a people inhabiting an island decided to separate and disperse throughout the

world) the last murderer remaining in prison would first have to be executed, so that each has done to him what his deeds deserve and blood guilt does not cling to the people for not having insisted upon this punishment.

Kant was influenced in his 'retributivist' or 'desert' philosophy of punishment by the Bible, especially The Old Testament and the 'lex talionis' or 'the law of retribution laid down in The Book of Exodus, Chapter 21, verses 23–25. Exodus says at this point: 'Wherever hurt is done, you shall give life for life, eye for eye.'

The actual infliction of 'an eye for an eye' has few supporters, but the notion of punishing criminals because they 'deserve' such treatment has widespread intuitive appeal and this popular intuition that criminals 'deserve' punishment cannot be reduced to some philosophical formula that retribution is all about the 'satisfying of grievances' as Ted Honderich argued. See T. Honderich, 'Punishment, the New Retributivism and Political Philosophy' in 'Philosophy and Practice' 1985 edited by A. Phillips Griffiths, Royal Institute of Philosophy Lecture Series: 18. Although the grievances of victims and the public are satisfied when someone is punished for a notorious crime they perpetrated the desire for retribution has a deep intuitive basis that goes beyond 'grievance satisfaction'.

The archdisciple of rationalist utilitarian thought, Jeremy Bentham, had no time for any argument for punishment based on 'desert' or 'retribution'. As Professor Hart comments in *Essays on Bentham* (1982):

> desert and retribution were to Bentham mere mystifying superstitions: not reasons for punishment but emotional reactions posing as reasons.

However, despite Bentham's ridicule of retribution, retributivist arguments still have a potent hold in the world today, for example in the widespread support for the death penalty for those guilty of certain murders in the United States of America.

Bentham argued that punishment was justified by the need to deter – the deterrence of the individual from repeating his crime and deterrence of would-be offenders by the example of the punished offenders. So deterrence as a justification for punishment can be separated into individual deterrence (the person punished will hopefully not repeat his crime) and general deterrence (the punishment of some will deter others from violating the law). Individual deterrence can be seen in the remarks of Lord Justice Lawton in *R v Sargeant* (1974):

> It is his memory of the clanging of prison gates which is likely to keep him from crime in the future.

Professor Hart, in *Punishment and Responsibility* (1968), has arguably the most potent theory for the justification of punishment, which combines deterrence and retributivist theories – hence Hart's theory has been called a 'mixed theory' of punishment. For Professor Hart the general aim of punishment is deterrence, however the general aim of deterrence is qualified by the side constraint that only those convicted of crime should be used by the state to deter others. Therefore for Professor Hart retribution (desert) qualifies deterrence. Professor Hart's 'mixed theory' of punishment answers two questions aimed at pure retribution and pure deterrence theories of punishment: (1) Professor Hart's theory would rule out the punishment of an innocent man if the authorities thought by punishing him crime might be deterred. Hart insists that only the guilty can be used as an example for deterrence. (2) Pure retributivist theories, such as Kant's, have to answer the question – what social benefit does punishment bring under your theory? Kant may say that the social consequences of punishment are irrelevant and what matters is 'justice', but the point sticks: why inflict pain on an individual just to satisfy some mysterious notion such as 'desert' or 'justice'?

Professor Hart's 'mixed theory' of deterrence qualified by retribution seems fairly watertight and a modern turn on Hart's 'mixed' theory is given by Ted Honderich in *The Oxford Companion to Philosophy* (1995):

> some recent theories justify punishment by dividing the issue in a manner reflecting the different competencies of an ideal legislature or judge. Thus, the primary concern amounts to answering a legislative question: Why is anyone punished, or made liable to punishment in the first place? The secondary issue is in effect the judicial question: Why is this person being punished?

> The former question can be answered best by citing the benefits conferred on a society by the institution of punishment as a permanent, public threat system that provides an indispensable incentive to obey the law. In so far as the justification of punishment is conceived in this manner, it is inescapably forward looking and consequentialist in nature.

So, in this Hart-like 'mixed theory', at a legislative level the institution of punishment is justified as 'a deterrence system' – 'a permanent public threat system'. However, when it comes to justifying punishment of a particular offender at court or judicial level we ask the retributivist question: has the defendant been found guilty by correct procedures? Such a justification for punishment is retributivist and based on 'desert' – the 'desert' of the particular offender. Retribution accommodated in this 'mixed theory' falls far short of Kant's full blown retributivist theory which seeks to use retribution for the general justification of the institution of punishment and punishment of actual individual offenders.

Retribution and deterrence are generally considered the main contenders to justify state punishment and, as we have seen, a 'mixed theory', famously propounded by Professor Hart, combining the two principles seems the best way of justifying punishment. However two other subsidiary principles need passing mention as both have been used as at least as partial justifications of punishment. Those two subsidiary principles are: (1) rehabilitation and (2) incapacitation.

Rehabilitation is an approach to punishment where the purpose of punishment is to make the offender a fit person to be re-integrated into society. Indeed Rule 1 of the Prison Rules 1964 of England and Wales states that an aim of punishment is to reform the offender so as he can **'lead a good and useful life'**. However rehabilitation has generally been considered an important but subsidiary aim of punishment and indeed if rehabilitation was the main aim of punishment then it is arguable that no offender except the dangerous should be sent to prison at all, given the corrosive effects of imprisonment on the individual: prison is an expensive way of making bad persons worse.

Incapacitation is necessary to take out of society, sometimes permanently, a small but significant number of dangerous offenders who pose an ongoing risk to the life and limb of the public such as psychopathic killers. Obviously incapacitation, although important for the dangerous few, cannot be used as the main justification for punishment since most offenders do not pose that kind of serious risk to the public.

Aim Higher ★

Students can gain extra marks by noting that 'pure' theories of punishment, such as 'retribution' or 'deterrence', are not satisfactory in themselves as justifications of punishment but that 'mixed theories', combining retribution and deterrence principles, are much more stable and satisfactory as justifications of punishment. Students can avoid the pitfall of thinking that 'rehabilitation' is itself the justification for punishment, but rather merely a part of a theory of punishment.

NOTES

Discussion of the topic of punishment can be found in Brian Bix, *Jurisprudence: Theory and Context* (2009) at pp 123–128. A thorough discussion (with extensive extracts) of punishment theory can be found in *Jurisprudence and Legal Theory: Commentary and Materials* (2005) edited by Penner et al at pp 539–594. A good discussion of the problem of justifying state punishment is to be found in Nicola Lacey's *State Punishment* (1988).

QUESTION 15

How did Bentham apply the general principles of utilitarianism to the specific problem of punishment for criminal offences?

Answer Plan

The general principles of utilitarianism should be set out, together with a brief indication of Bentham's view of the criminal law. It is in this setting that the question of punishment has to be considered. The following skeleton plan is suggested:

* Introduction;
* Bentham's general views;
* essence of utilitarianism;
* aim of legislation;
* essence of the criminal law;
* fundamentals of punishment and its rationale;
* criticism of Bentham's concepts;
* conclusion, positive features of Bentham's approach.

ANSWER

Philosopher, economist, jurist and legal reformer, Bentham (1748–1832) was able to spin from the thread of the 'principle of utility' a vast tapestry of ethics and jurisprudential doctrine, known as 'utilitarianism', which sought an answer to the question 'What ought an individual to do'? Bentham's answer was that he should act so as to produce 'the best consequences possible'. 'Consequences' include all that is produced by an act, whether arising during or after its performance. A summary of the main principles of utilitarianism is given below, together with details concerning Bentham's application of those principles to the problem of punishment for criminals – a matter with which he was closely involved in his campaigns for a revision of the criminal law, and in which he had been influenced by the Italian jurist, Beccaria (1738–1794). Central to Beccaria's theory of punishment was his belief that an act, and not an offender's intention, constituted the measure of actual harm done, and that the prevention of further offences was the sole justification for imprisonment.

The 'principle of utility' was set out by Bentham in his *Introduction to the Principles of Morals and Legislation* (1789). He defined it as 'that property in any object whereby it tends to produce pleasure, good or happiness, or to prevent the happening of mischief, pain or evil and unhappiness to the party whose interest is considered'. Nature had placed mankind 'under the governance of two sovereign masters, pain and pleasure'; they indicate what we *ought* to do and determine what we *shall* do. The principle that we desire pleasure and wish to avoid pain is utilised by Bentham so as to make the judgment that we *ought* to pursue pleasure. The principle of utility cannot be demonstrated because it is not susceptible to proof; indeed, says Bentham, it is needless even to attempt a demonstration.

Bentham attempted to give the theory some measure of mathematical precision. A thing will promote the interest of an individual when it tends to add to the *sum total* of his pleasure, or to diminish the *sum total* of his pains. It was possible, he argued, to make a *quantitative comparison* of the pleasure and pain likely to result as the consequences of alternative courses of action. A person should sum up the likely pleasures and pains so as to arrive at the 'good' or 'bad' tendency of the act in question – the 'felicific calculus'. An account of the number of persons whose interests appear to be involved should be taken, and the calculus applied to each. The result would be an estimate of the good or evil likely to be produced within the community as a whole.

The aim of the legislator, according to Bentham, should be to produce *the greatest happiness of the greatest number*. 'Community interest' was no more than the sum of the interests of those who compose a society. The art of legislation involves the discovery of the means to realise 'the good'. The legislator considering the ambit and content of the criminal law must take into account the fact that the acts he desires to prevent are 'evils' and that they are greater evils than the laws (which are infractions of liberty) to be used to prevent them. Legislation ought to aim at four goals: subsistence, abundance, security (the protection of status and property) and the diminution of inequality. The laws that a legislator should seek to promote should be seen in relation to desirable conduct to be expected from persons or classes of persons.

In considering the criminal law, Bentham applied the principle of utility in rigorous fashion. First, the mischief of an act should be measured. 'Mischief' consisted of the pain or evil inflicted by the act. If an act tended to produce evil, it must be discouraged. 'Evil' could be 'primary' or 'secondary'. If X steals from Y, this is 'primary' evil. 'Secondary' evil arises where X's theft weakens the general respect for property. Bentham stresses that secondary evils may often outweigh primary evils.

Because the legislator is concerned to increase the total happiness of the community, he must discourage acts likely to produce evil consequences. A criminal act is one which is obviously detrimental to the happiness of the community; hence, the law should be concerned solely with acts that diminish the pleasure of persons by the infliction of pain. The criminal law is intended to assist in the active promotion of the community's total happiness by punishing those who commit offences characterised as 'evil' according to the principle of utility.

Bentham would not accept a division of offences into *mala in se* (acts wrong in themselves) and *mala prohibita* (acts wrong because the law prohibits them). The principle of utility insists that an act cannot be wrong 'in itself'; whether it is right or wrong depends on its *consequences*. If it is highly probable that an act will produce harm, it should be prohibited; if it is unlikely to produce harm, its prohibition is unjustified. We prohibit murder and theft and punish those responsible, not because the acts are wrong in themselves but because of the evil consequences for others. For precisely the same reasons, we punish also those who commit minor offences.

Punishment, said Bentham, is in itself an evil: it necessarily inflicts suffering on the offender. But the object of the criminal law is the augmentation of the community's happiness; hence, if punishment is to be administered, it must be shown that the pain to be inflicted on offenders will prevent or exclude some greater pain. The 'usefulness' of punishment emerges only if its infliction achieves a greater measure of happiness for the community. It has no value if it merely adds more units of pain to the community as a whole. Mere retribution is valueless because it only adds to the total quantum of pain caused by the offences.

Bentham insisted on an examination of *why* society ought to punish offenders. There is no value in inflicting punishment where it is 'groundless'; hence, an offence which admits of compensation, and which can be followed by such compensation, ought not to be punished. Punishment which is too expensive ought not to be inflicted. The 'proportion' between punishment and the offence must be kept in mind. Punishment should be great enough to outweigh profit derived by the criminal. The greater the offence, the greater should be the punishment.

Punishment ought to be variable and adapted to suit circumstances, but the same punishment should be given for the same type of offence. The quantum of punishment should never exceed the amount required to make it effective, so that extravagant punishment should be rejected as wasteful. The more uncertain it is that a criminal will be caught, the greater should be the punishment when he is apprehended and convicted. Punishment should act as a deterrent, it should be reformatory where that is possible and should have wide popular support – hence, Bentham's acceptance of the need for capital punishment which, he believed, did provide a deterrent. It is interesting to note the support for capital punishment shown by Bentham's disciple, John Stuart Mill. On one of the rare occasions on which Mill spoke in the House of Commons, in 1868, he advocated the retention of the death penalty (and underlined the need to preserve severe punishments, such as flogging).

Bentham's utilitarian principles, as applied to the criminal law and punishment, led him to prepare practical schemes for the 'rational punishment' of offenders. Among a large number of such plans, which were often worked out in considerable detail, was the design of a *Panopticon* – a prison in which the conduct of the inmates was to be controlled by total surveillance throughout the day. Bentham stated that its object was 'to grind rogues honest'. This process was to be achieved by an uninterrupted survey of behaviour, which would result in the remodelling of the offenders' attitudes. Bentham had in mind reform of the prisoners – mere punishment with no objective other than retributive detention seemed to him a wasted opportunity. Bentham's radical approach to law and punishment was vigorously opposed in his time, although a number of penal reforms are now attributed to him. Controversy surrounds his approach to punishment even today. It is argued that the utilitarians disregarded the claims of justice in determining whether or not a punishment was 'right'. For them, the utility of the punishment was the sole consideration, but for many jurists other matters would have to be taken into account before accepting the 'correctness' of a particular type of punishment. Objection is taken, too, to the 'pleasure-pain calculus' which is considered unreal and absurd, particularly in relation to the criminal law. Principles of punishment derived from a construct of this nature are considered flawed and, therefore, unreliable.

Opposition to Bentham's views stems also from jurists who cannot accept his reasoning concerning the general happiness of society as constituting the *summum bonum*. It is thought that Bentham's view of mankind was naive in the extreme. People are much more complex than the principle of utility suggests, and the causes of crime are much more complicated than the utilitarian model indicates. Modern investigations of criminal psychology put forward a psychological picture of anti-social motivation which is at odds with Bentham's views.

Plamenatz, the historian of the utilitarian movement, suggests that, although much of Bentham's work was often superficial and crude, it was far ahead of its time in proposing new methods of analysing social and legal problems. These methods and the resulting proposals for reform of the criminal law can be accepted, Plamenatz argues, on their own terms. It is not necessary, therefore, to accept Bentham's 'felicific calculus' or his belief in 'the greatest happiness of the greatest number' in order to agree with his powerful pleas for a rethinking of the fundamental purposes and modes of punishment. There is much in his analysis which is ingenious, original and thought-provoking. It remains worthy, according to Plamenatz and others, of consideration by jurists of all persuasions. The contemporary school of penology which accepts the utilitarian (or 'reductive') justification of penalising offences, holds that penalties imposed by the law act to reduce the frequency of offences by deterring the offender and potential imitators, reforming the offender, and educating the public by incarcerating some offenders. Bentham's influence remains much in evidence here.

NOTES

Bentham's *Introduction to the Principles of Morals and Legislation* is published in an edition by Burns and Hart. Ogden has edited his *Theory of Legislation*. Summaries of Bentham's views are given in Dias, Chapter 20; Harris, Chapter 4; Lloyd, Chapter 4; and Bodenheimer, Chapter 6. Extracts from Bentham's work are presented in Davies and Holdcroft, Chapter 7. Interesting background material is provided by *Utilitarianism: For and Against*, by Smart and Williams, and *Bentham: An Odyssey of Ideas*, by Mack. *The English Utilitarians*, by Plamenatz, contains a history of the movement. For the extraordinary story of the trial and execution of Bentham's servant, Franks, on a charge of 'burglarously breaking and entering the dwelling house' of his master, see Chapter 10 of *The London Hanged: Crime and Civil Society in the Eighteenth Century*, by Linebaugh. Note, also, *Bentham's Prison*, by Semple. *A Reader on Punishment*, edited by Duff and Garland, explores the concepts underpinning contemporary penology. Hart's *Punishment and Responsibility* examines Bentham's views in detail.

Legal Positivism

INTRODUCTION

Legal positivism is the name given to a great school of juristic thought, which includes such luminaries of philosophy as Hobbes (1588–1679), Bentham (1748–1832), Austin (1790–1859) and Professor HLA Hart (1907–1992). The main feature of legal positivism is its insistence that the law of a society be identified purely by 'social facts' and that one does not need a moral argument to work out the content of the law – what the modern legal positivist, Professor Raz, calls 'the sources thesis'. The legal positivist does not deny that law is very often influenced by morality, or even that there may be necessary connections between law and morality; therefore, the traditional division and conflict in the presentation of jurisprudence between 'natural lawyers' and 'legal positivists' can be seen to be a false and misleading distinction. The questions in the chapter include definitions of legal positivism, discussion of the 'command theory' of law, Professor Hart's restatement of legal positivism and the attack on the doctrine of legal positivism from Professor Ronald Dworkin.

Checklist ✔

Ensure that you are acquainted with the following topics:

- the definition of legal positivism;
- the virtues and drawbacks of the 'command theory' of law;
- Professor Hart's definition of law as 'a union of primary and secondary rules';
- the methodology of Professor Hart;
- the contribution of Professor Raz to legal positivistic thought;
- the attack on legal positivism by Professor Dworkin.

QUESTION 16

What do you understand by 'legal positivism'?

Answer Plan

The question calls for a discussion of the great school of juristic thought called 'legal positivism'. The origins of legal positivism are usually taken to be with Bentham (1748–1832) and Austin (1790–1859), but the tradition can be dated as far back as Thomas Hobbes (1588–1679). The essence of legal positivism is not a denial of the 'natural law' claim that law and morality are heavily interlinked; it is rather that the identification of the law is not dependent on moral argument but that it depends on social facts alone – what Professor Raz (the leading living legal positivist) calls the 'sources thesis'. The legal positivist will point to the function of law in providing authoritative co-ordination of human activity as justifying the necessity of law being clearly and crisply identified from social facts such as Parliamentary enactment and judicial precedent. The *locus classicus* of legal positivistic texts is *The Concept of Law* (1961, 2nd edition 1994) by Professor Hart, which sought to reinvigorate the legal positivist tradition from the defects of earlier 'command theories' propagated by Bentham and Austin. The main attack on legal positivism has not come from traditional natural law; indeed, Professor Finnis (author of *Natural Law and Natural Rights* (1980)) accepts the legal positivist 'sources thesis', but from the courtroom-driven vision of the American Professor, Ronald Dworkin. Dworkin argues that legal positivism cannot account for the fact that legal argument in the higher appeal courts in the USA and UK often has recourse to moral arguments to support propositions of law. Dworkin's attack on legal positivism remains controversial, as does his denial of the central methodological claim of legal positivism that there can be descriptive legal theory only with no justificatory ambitions towards law. A skeleton argument is included.

❖ Introduction, the history of legal positivism from Hobbes to Bentham and Austin;

❖ description of the central tenet of legal positivism: 'the sources thesis';

❖ Hart's reformulation of legal positivism in *The Concept of Law*;

❖ the attack on legal positivism by Professor Dworkin;

❖ conclusion, Dworkin's attack remains the most potent threat to legal positivism.

ANSWER

In his important essay 'Authority, law and morality' (reprinted in *Ethics in the Public Domain* (1994)), Professor Raz comments that Professor Hart was the torch-bearer of a 'great tradition'. That 'great tradition' is legal positivism. The great figures of the tradition of legal positivism are usually considered to include Bentham (1748–1832), Austin (1790–1859), Herbert Hart (1907–1992) and Joseph Raz. However, the true philosophical origins of legal positivism probably reside in the great seventeenth century philosopher, Thomas Hobbes (1588–1679). For Hobbes, the law was an exercise in the expression of the sovereign will. As Hobbes commented: 'The civil laws are the commands of him who hath the chief authority for direction of the future actions of his citizens.' On this view of the law, the laws are essentially rules laid down and upheld by the sovereign and the sovereign is the person or persons with effective authority in a society. The law represented for Hobbes the sovereign's will and judgment as to what the law's subjects, the citizens, must do. The Hobbesian conception of law, 'the command theory', was later developed by the two great positivist thinkers of the nineteenth century, Jeremy Bentham and John Austin. Austin developed and popularised Bentham's approach and Austin's account became the more influential, given the fact that Bentham's writings on this subject were not published until after the halfway point of the twentieth century.

However, Bentham's views are of note because they reveal a legal positivistic distaste for judge-made law in contrast to the certainties and forward looking nature of legislation. Indeed, it was Bentham who first used the term 'judge-made law', using it as a term of abuse and contempt for English common law. As Gerald Postema comments in 'Philosophy of the Common Law' (in *Oxford Handbook of Jurisprudence and Philosophy* (2002), edited by Coleman and Shapiro), Bentham spent a large part of his life trying to undermine the grip of the common law on lawyers in England. Bentham compared judge-made common law to the way people train dogs; as he commented: 'When your dog does anything you want to break him of, you wait till he does it, and then beat him for it. This is the way you make laws for your dog, and this is the way the judges make law for you and me.' The retroactive and reactive nature of the common law compared unfavourably with statutory codification. Bentham favoured statutory codification, which looked to the future and not the past. Bentham's aim (which he hoped to extend beyond England to other countries, such as the United States) was to create a complete code of laws which he eventually called the 'pannomion' (meaning 'all the laws'). Legislation (or codification) fits better the 'commands of the sovereign' model of law than the vagueness and uncertainties of the common law, which Bentham derided in the following terms: 'A law is to be extracted (from common law) by every man who can fancy that he is able; by each man perhaps a different law.' Arguably, English law has moved in a general direction that Bentham would have approved of. One of the long-term processes witnessed by the twentieth century in the legal system of England and Wales was the transition from the common law dominated system of the nineteenth century to the statute dominated system of the twenty-first century. Statute, not common law, is generally how new legal rights and duties are now created in England and Wales.

A landmark in the legal positivist tradition was the publication of Austin's *The Province of Jurisprudence Determined* in 1832. Austin's conception of law was that the law was essentially the result of the 'commands of the sovereign'. The law of any society with a 'sovereign' was to be identified by asking two fundamental questions: (a) who is the 'sovereign'? (Austin believed every organised society had a 'sovereign' who obeyed no other authority and was itself obeyed by the bulk of the population), and (b) what has the sovereign commanded? In this simple way the law of any society could be distinguished from the norms of morality, religion and custom of that society. Therefore, legal positivism recognises that the virtue of law is that it forms a public and dependable set of standards for the guidance of officials and citizens whatever the disagreements in that society over the dictates of morality, religion or custom. The method by which legal positivism distinguishes law from other systems of norms (such as morality) is by the stipulation that the law is to be identified by 'social sources' – that is, the law can be identified by asking certain questions about human behaviour (such as 'what has the sovereign commanded?').

This doctrine – that the law can be identified by reference to social facts alone, and that law is not identified by engaging in a moral argument – is called 'the sources thesis' by Professor Raz. The 'sources thesis' has been identified by Raz as the key doctrine of legal positivism. Raz states in *The Authority of Law* (1979) that the legal positivist thesis is that what is law, and what is not, is a matter of social fact; he states further that a jurisprudential theory is acceptable only if its test for identifying the content of the law and determining its existence depends exclusively on facts of human behaviour, capable of being described in value-neutral terms, and applied without resort to moral argument. Other legal positivists have differed somewhat in the exact test to be used to identify the law, and the history of legal positivism as a doctrine can be seen partially as a more and more sophisticated attempt to capture the essence of a proper test for law.

'The command theory' of Bentham and Austin was effectively replaced by the 'rule of recognition' of Hart's analysis (in essence, that the identification of law was to be made upon the observance of the behaviour of legal officials and how they identified legal rules in their society) as the test for the identification of law. Both the 'command theory' and the Hartian 'rule of recognition' are examples of Raz's 'sources thesis' – that is, that the law of a society is to be identified by social facts alone.

Legal positivists do not deny that law is influenced by morality at many points and, indeed, Professor Raz has denied that the heart of legal positivism is about denying necessary connections between law and morality. When Austin commented 'the existence of law is one thing; its merit and demerit another', this should not be taken to mean that legal positivism denies the connections between law and morality, but merely that the identification of law is a separate question from its moral merit. As Raz comments (in a recent article 'About Morality and the Nature of Law' (2006)) there can be no doubt that there are necessary connections between law and morality and that legal positivism does not deny this. However, the most potent criticisms of legal positivism all emanate from the view that legal positivism fails to accept fully the intimate connections between law and morality. The attack on legal positivism comes in two main forms. First, there is the 'natural law' view that law and legal systems can be properly understood only if it is understood that the point or ultimate value of legal systems is a moral function – that law is the primary means by which civil society is co-ordinated and ordered for the benefit of the 'common good'. This 'natural law' critique suggests that legal positivism gives a very 'thin' and underdeveloped view of the concept of law. The legal positivist could suggest that he does not deny law's 'higher functions' but that his main thesis that law is identified by social facts alone is unaffected by the whole 'natural law' apparatus. Indeed, plausibly a legal theorist could assent to the truth of legal positivism whilst developing a fully fledged 'natural law' theory, as Professor Finnis has done in *Natural Law and Natural Rights* (1980).

The second attack on 'legal positivism' is not possible to reconcile with the legal positivist tradition as it asserts that the central idea of positivism, that law is identified by 'social sources' alone, is fundamentally flawed. The leading proponent of the attack on the legal positivist 'sources thesis' is Professor RM Dworkin, as exemplified in his *magnum opus* on legal theory, *Law's Empire* (1986). Dworkin has argued that legal positivism cannot properly account for legal argumentation by lawyers and legal decision by appellate judges in so-called 'hard cases' where the source based law does not provide a clear answer. Dworkin argues that the law consists not merely of the settled legal rules but also legal principles, which are identified not from the 'social sources' but from the moral interpretation of settled law. Dworkin, in his theory of law, makes the identification of law at least partly dependent on moral interpretation carried out by the law's interpreter – the appellate judge. This argument, if true, undermines the central positivist tenet of the 'sources thesis'. As Raz comments in an essay 'Two views of the nature of the theory of law' (2001) (see Hart's 'Postscript: essays on the concept of law' (2001)), if Dworkin's theory of law is correct then Hart's theory is flawed at its foundations. The focus of Dworkin has been very much on appeal cases where legal positivism has had difficulty in explaining the moral driven nature of legal argumentation in 'hard cases'. However,

Dworkin has probably overestimated the amount of controversy in legal cases where, most frequently, the argument of counsel concerns not the law but the facts of the case. Yet Dworkin does seem to capture the judicial atmosphere in hard cases; indeed, the natural lawyer, Professor John Finnis (who accepts legal positivism's 'sources thesis' in *Natural Law and Natural Rights*) comments that we should broadly accept some main elements of Ronald Dworkin's account of adjudication in appeal cases (see Finnis, 'Natural law: the classical tradition' in *The Oxford Handbook of Jurisprudence and Philosophy of Law* (2002)).

The legal positivist tradition explains well the role of legislation in society. Raz comments that the law is a structure of authority and that the normal exercise of political authority is by the making of laws and legally binding orders (see *The Morality of Freedom* (1986)), and legal positivism can explain the rule-governed and appellate-controlled operations of the lower courts, such as the magistrates court, county court and Crown Court. Indeed, Hart commented in *The Concept of Law* (1961) that, in great measure, the prestige gathered by the courts is from their unquestionably rule-governed operations over the vast, central areas of the law. However, legal positivism has an underdeveloped account of legal argumentation and legal judgment in appeal cases where the law runs out compared to Dworkin's rich and nuanced account, which seems to capture the judicial scene where legal argument and moral standards often are interwoven. Legal positivists could argue that the nature of legal argumentation in 'hard cases' in the Anglo-American legal systems was never the focus of legal positivism, which aimed to give a general account of the concept of law as it appears to people in all cultures where law appears. Although it can be accepted that legal positivism is, in the words of Hart, not tied to any particular legal system, but seeks to give an explanatory and clarifying account of law as a complex social and political institution with a rule-governed aspect (see Hart, *The Concept of Law* (1994, 2nd edition)), legal positivism does have an implicit theory of judicial adjudication in 'hard cases'. For example, both Raz and Hart think that the existence and content of law depend on social facts and not on moral considerations but, given the unforeseeability of the facts of future cases and the lack of clarity of language, then the law is riddled with gaps, leaving judges with significant discretion to make law. As Hart commented in *The Concept of Law*, in every legal system a large and important field is open for the discretion of courts. Where legal questions turn on moral argumentation the judges are not controlled by law and they have discretion to make 'new law'. Of course, in making new law judges must proceed carefully by analogy with decided cases and consider what the will of Parliament may be on the matter, as pointed out by Hart in *The Concept of Law* (1994, 2nd edition). However, this characterisation by legal positivists of judicial decision in 'hard cases' has been criticised by Dworkin as 'wholly inadequate' (see 'Hard cases' (1975), reprinted in *Taking Rights Seriously* (1977)). Dworkin has argued that judges in hard cases should not be nor are 'deputy legislators' but should 'find' the law to any 'hard case' by re-interpreting the existing law in the best moral light possible with an acceptable level of consistency with decided law. Even if Professor Dworkin overstates somewhat the amount of interpretation needed in the law, where in most cases the law can be understood and applied without the need for Dworkinian interpretation the fact remains that Dworkin's legal theory represents the greatest challenge to the tradition of legal positivism currently debated.

Common Pitfalls

Students can avoid the pitfall that legal positivism argues that there is no necessary connection between law and morality – the so-called 'separability thesis'. Students can gain extra marks by arguing that legal positivists such as Raz and Gardner argue that there are necessary connections between law and morality, such as (a) the law by its nature always claims moral authority (b) the language of law and morality are virtually identical with terms such as 'rights' 'duties' and 'normative' in both discourses of law and morality. Students can also gain extra marks by arguing that the central claim of legal positivism is 'the sources thesis' – that the content and existence of the law is made without resort to a moral argument.

NOTES

The reader should first approach 'legal positivism' through the pages of the greatest legal philosopher of the twentieth century, Professor Hart, in *The Concept of Law* (1961), especially Chapters 2–5 of that book. The most readable account by Raz of legal positivism is the essay 'Authority, law and morality', (1985) The Monist, reprinted in *Ethics in the Public Domain* (1994).

Dworkin's frontal attack on legal positivism can be gathered from the article 'Hard cases' (1975), republished in *Taking Rights Seriously* (1977). Hart's reply to Dworkin's criticisms can be found in the 'Postscript' to *The Concept of Law*, published in the second edition in 1994 and edited by Raz and Bulloch. A very useful essay 'Legal positivism' by Leslie Green is to be found in the online and free *Stanford Encyclopedia of Philosophy* (http://plato.stanford.edu/).

QUESTION 17

Has the 'command theory' any virtue as a theory of law?

Answer Plan

The 'command theory of law' is widely considered to have been effectively demolished by Professor Hart in *The Concept of Law* (1961). However, it is possible to see valuable insights in this theory, as Hart himself recognised. The 'command theory' of Austin (1780–1859) and Bentham (1748–1832) saw a clear conceptual separation between the identification of law and the claims of morality, which remains the basis of legal positivism today (see Raz's 'sources thesis'). The 'command theory' also captures valuable insights into the relationship between law, power and coercion which may reflect the reality of power even in so-called 'democracies'. A skeleton plan is suggested.

- ❖ Introduction;
- ❖ the 'command theory' explained;
- ❖ the virtues of the 'command theory';
- ❖ the conceptual separation of law and morality;
- ❖ the coercive aspect of law stressed;
- ❖ the relationship between law, coercion and power exposed;
- ❖ the 'reality' of the 'command theory';
- ❖ conclusion, despite all the attacks the 'command theories' have some valuable insights.

ANSWER

The 'command theory' of law dominated jurisprudence in the nineteenth century through the writings of John Austin (1790–1859) and owes its philosophical origins to two giants of philosophy, Thomas Hobbes (1588–1679) and Jeremy Bentham (1748–1832).

Jeremy Bentham was a product of the eighteenth century Enlightenment or 'age of reason'. The Enlightenment was an attack on old habits of thought which were alleged to rest on the dark forces of superstition, irrationality and religion. One doctrine which came under attack during the Enlightenment was the doctrine of natural law which had been the dominant jurisprudential doctrine before the Enlightenment. Bentham and other Enlightenment thinkers such as Montesquieu attacked the idea that there was a universal natural law applicable to and binding on all mankind, created by God and discoverable through reason and which formed a basis for the promulgation and authority of man-made law. Bentham argued that the natural law was 'a mere work of the fancy' having no basis in reality and that it was not a God-given natural law which gave man-made law its authority but rather human authority alone which established the authority of man made law. In other words human law was merely the result of the 'commands of the sovereign' and did not derive its authority from any link to a mystical and fictitious 'natural law'.

It is important to take note of the historical context in which Bentham formulated his 'command theory of law'. Bentham was keen to refute the idea of natural law thinkers such as Grotius that there could be property rights in the 'natural law sphere' even before man-made law had spoken. For Grotius the ultimate origin of the right of property was that God at creation had given the earth to mankind and so there could be 'natural' rights of property before the say-so of man-made law. For Bentham this natural law doctrine was to be completely rejected. For Bentham, following Hobbes and Hume, only such goods and property that had been assigned to a man by positive law (man-made law) could be said to belong to him. For Bentham property and man-made law were born together and there could be no property rights before man-made law had spoken and therefore for Bentham natural law theory was to be rejected. Indeed natural law theory went into a steep decline in the nineteenth century following the Enlightenment attack of Bentham and others and natural law theory only revived in importance in the twentieth century. For Bentham the man-made law derived its authority not from God or the natural law but from the fact of promulgation by a sovereign – the law was the 'commands of the sovereign' – no more, no less.

It is now seen as a theory whose account of law is too simplistic and too 'thin' to account for the important legal phenomena that we find in complex legal systems. However, on reconsideration, the 'command theory' does have some valuable insights into the relationship between law, coercion and power.

Early in his career, Austin came under the influence of his mentor, Bentham, although Austin's work on legal theory was more influential, especially *The Province of Jurisprudence Determined* (1832). In the great tradition of legal positivism, Austin sought to give a general descriptive account of all legal systems. As to what is the heart of the concept of law, Austin's answer is to say that positive law (that is, man-made or 'posited' law) is the 'commands of a sovereign'. Positive law consists of those commands laid down by a sovereign to be contrasted with those dictates of religion or morality. The 'sovereign' is defined as a person or collection of persons who receives habitual obedience from the bulk of the population but who does not habitually obey any other person or institution. When, in a law case, the 'commands' (the laws) do not determine the issues, Austin had no objection to judicial law making which Austin called 'highly beneficial and even absolutely necessary'. Judge-made law could be accommodated within the 'command theory' by regarding such law as the 'tacit' commands of the sovereign, who then affirms those fresh judicial law making acts by not repealing them; those judicial acts of law making then become 'the commands of the sovereign'. Austin is therefore in the tradition of legal positivism (see Hart and Raz) in according a limited law-making discretion to the judiciary. Bentham objected to judicial law making and would have such disputed legal questions referred back to the legislature for decision.

The 'command theory' makes the identification of the law of a community depend on social facts: one does not need to make a moral argument to identify the law; it is enough merely to identify the 'sovereign' (the sovereign is identified by looking at patterns of obedience in the bulk of the population) and then ask 'what has the sovereign commanded?' Even though Professor Hart ultimately rejected the 'command theory' as a satisfactory description of law (Hart said in *The Concept of Law* that the simple model of law as the sovereign's coercive orders fails to reproduce some of the important features of a legal system) he does maintain, in the legal positivistic tradition, that the law is identified by social facts alone and that this insight was provided by Austin following Hobbes and Bentham. As Hart comments, in *Essays on Bentham* (1982), the 'command' theory's conceptual separation of law and morality is a permanently valuable insight which should be retained when the 'command' (or 'imperative') theory is discarded. That the law is identified independent of morality not only reproduces the way the law in modern societies appears to many citizens but also permits the construction of a general theory of law applicable to every society where law is found. Therefore, the 'command theory' is the source not only of the 'sources thesis' but also the view that the ambitions of legal theory are universal, in that it aims to describe law as a specific type of social organisation wherever it is found. For both Raz and Hart, the 'sources thesis' and the universality of legal theory are important themes.

The 'command theory' builds the idea of a sanction into the very idea of law. A 'command' involves an expressed wish from a 'superior' that something be done or not done by an 'inferior' and a sanction to be imposed if that wish is not complied with. In the understanding of citizens, the image of the law conjures up pictures of police, judges and prisons. As Professor Galligan writes, in *Law in Modern Society* (2007), the coercive aspect of law colours the common perception of law and how people talk about it. People rely upon the law because of the assumption that the law will ultimately use coercion to protect them or enforce their rights. Coercion is then a significant feature of modern legal systems, which Austin in the 'command theory' captured well. Indeed, Professor Hart, the foremost critic of the Austinian 'command theory', can be criticised for underplaying the importance of coercion to modern legal orders in *The Concept of Law*. The 'command theory' captures the inherent coerciveness of many systems of law and the importance of power to the maintenance of the state. Austin's conception of law and legal systems perhaps captures in a cynical way the relationship between law, coercion and power in modern states. Austin's 'command theory' is a theory of the 'rule of men' of government using law not as an instrument for the realisation of the 'common good' but as a way of controlling populations for the ultimate benefit of those few in real power. As John Locke realised, in his *Treatise on Civil Government* (1690), there is a tendency in some human beings to strongly aim for power; as Locke wrote: 'human frailty, apt to grasp at power'. The 'command theory' conceives law not as a specific method for the co-ordination of the common good as natural lawyers, such as John Finnis would have us believe in *Natural Law and Natural Rights* (1980), but rather the Austinian conception sees law as an instrument of power in which a 'superior' authority addresses the 'inferior' mass of humanity not necessarily for the true benefit of the 'inferior' mass of the people.

NOTES

The Stanford Encyclopedia of Philosophy (http://plato.stanford.edu/) has a free online and very useful essay on John Austin written by Brian Bix in 2005. The critical analysis of Austin's 'command theory' given by Professor Hart in Chapters 2–4 of *The Concept of Law* (1961) should be examined carefully. Professor Hart's more positive remarks on 'the command theory' can be found in his *Essays on Bentham* (1982).

QUESTION 18

Explain how later legal positivists, such as Hart and Raz, criticised Austin's 'command theory'.

Answer Plan

The 'command theory', despite its virtues, has fundamental and near fatal flaws as an explanation of the concept of law. Professor Hart (1907–1992), in *The Concept of Law*, exposed the weaknesses of the 'command theory' in that Austin's theory failed to account for the reality and complexity of legal phenomena, such as the variety of legal rules which cannot all be reduced to the 'commands' of the sovereign and the 'internal' point of view of legal officials in a legal system. Professor Raz added to the weight of criticisms of the 'command theory' in that the old Austinian theory cannot account for the law's claim to legitimate authority, such a claim of authority being a central feature of the law's method of social organisation. A skeleton plan is given.

- ❖ Introduction;
- ❖ the attack on Austin's 'command theory' by Hart in *The Concept of Law*;
- ❖ the variety of legal rules;
- ❖ the facilitating role of law;

❖   the 'internal point of view';
❖   law as a system of rules not 'commands';
❖   Raz's notion of the law as an 'exclusionary reason' for action;
❖   the law's claim to authority;
❖   conclusion, the 'command theory' misses salient features of law and makes all legal systems seem like a 'gangster writ large'.

ANSWER

It is now widely accepted that Austin's 'command theory' account of law is inadequate as an explanation of key legal phenomena. Although not without critics in the nineteenth century, the mortal blow to the 'command theory' was delivered by Professor Hart in *The Concept of Law* (1961) where, in Chapters 2–4, Hart effectively demolishes the edifice of the Austinian account of law. Hart argues persuasively that Austin's model of law as 'the sovereign's coercive orders' failed to reproduce some of the key features of a legal system. There are two main angles of attack on Austin: (1) the different kinds of rules in a modern legal system which cannot be reduced to 'commands' and (2) the 'internal aspect of rules'.

Hart points out that there are important categories of legal rules (other than the criminal law) where the model of laws as commands – orders backed by threats – fails completely, since these rules perform a different social function from commanding behaviour. Legal rules defining the ways in which valid contracts, wills or marriages are made do not require persons to act in certain ways whether they wish to or not. Such laws do not impose duties or obligations. Instead, they provide individuals with facilities for realising their wishes to create new rights, duties and relationships within the coercive framework of law. Hart comments that the power conferred on individuals to mould their legal relations with others – by, for example, contracts, wills and marriages – is one of the great contributions of law to social life and it is a feature of laws obscured by representing all law as a matter of orders backed by threats. Perhaps an important criticism of Austin's 'command theory of law' is that it does not capture the totality of the relationship expressed through the law between the modern liberal state and its citizens. The law certainly has important coercive aspects, but the law is also an enabler and facilitator for the autonomous citizen to shape his life through meaningful choice offered by the law through the legal institutions of contract, marriage and probate. Austin gives the reader the model of the 'submissive, inferior citizen' through law. Hart gives the reader the more benign and realistic portrait of the 'autonomous citizen' through law. As Professor Raz comments (in an article in 2003, 'Between authority and morality') even fairly straightforward legal institutions like contract law enable the creation of business relationships which would not exist outside institutional contexts – for example, neither corporations nor intellectual property could exist outside the law. The law makes a significant and decisive contribution to the realisation of the moral goal of the autonomous citizen under law.

Austin's view of the law as 'coercive commands from a sovereign' neglects another important social fact of modern legal systems – namely, that many of the legal officials and some citizens actually accept the law without being coerced into compliance. This is the 'internal point of view' which Hart sought to understand and which is completely missed by the 'command' account of law. The central message of Hart is that law must be understood from the 'internal' point of view. This 'internal point of view' is the way of thinking of someone who treats a legal rule as a reason for action. Austin's account of law, with its emphasis on coercion, cannot account for the view of many officials of a legal system who regard the existence of a legal rule as a 'reason for action' independent of any threatened sanction for non-compliance.

More generally, Hart commented in *The Concept of Law* that the model of laws as commands should be replaced by an idea of law as a system of rules for the guidance of officials and citizens alike, both in and out of court. The notion of law as a series of 'commands' cannot account for the conduct guidance feature of law whereby persons use law as standards for conduct as well as using the law to plan their lives. Hart's central conception of law as 'the union of primary and secondary rules' has been very influential and must be taken to have effectively replaced the view of laws as being 'commands of the sovereign'.

Although Professor Raz is a legal positivist and accepts the 'sources thesis', he believes that the Austinian model of law is fundamentally flawed because it cannot account for the 'authority of law'. Professor Raz points out that a central feature of law is that it claims authority. The existence of a sanction is not supposed to be the primary reason why the law insists it should be obeyed. The law claims itself to be 'an exclusionary reason for action' in that the law claims binding force for itself to the exclusion of any reasons for non-compliance the citizen may have. The existence of a sanction is merely an auxiliary (supporting) reason for obeying the law. As Raz explains, in his 1975 book *Practical Reason and Norms*, the fact that so far as sanctions go the law is merely an auxiliary reason is not intended to belittle the importance of legal sanctions. Sanctions are an important way of securing social co-ordination and of providing persons with reasons for conforming to the law. However, the sanction-based attempt to explain the authority of law leads to a dead end, says Raz. So it is the fact that the law has been promulgated by the legitimate authority (such as Parliament) which is intended by the lawmakers to be the exclusionary reason for the obedience of citizens, and the sanction attached to the law is only a supporting reason for the recalcitrant. Raz claims that the law's claim to supreme authority within a territory is a significant and distinctive feature of the law's method of social organisation; this is missed by the Austinian model of law, which sees the law ultimately as the tool of a 'gangster writ large'.

NOTES

The critique of Austin in Hart's *The Concept of Law* (1961) is justly famous (see Chapters 2, 3 and 4) but Raz's account of 'exclusionary reasons' should be examined in *Practical Reason and Norms* (1975). Raz's important essay 'Authority, law and morality', (1985) The Monist, reprinted in *Ethics in the Public Domain* (1994), should also be consulted.

QUESTION 19

Was Professor Hart engaged in mere description of the concept of law when he wrote *The Concept of Law* in 1961?

Answer Plan

An issue currently forming one of the main controversies in jurisprudence is whether it is possible to have a descriptive account of the concept of law, or rather whether all legal theorists are committed to some ultimate view as to the point, value or purpose of law. Professor Hart (1907–1992) has always maintained that his analysis of law has been from a detached 'external' point of view, even if he acknowledges that legal theory must take into account the 'internal committed' point of view of participants in the legal system. The recognition of the 'internal point of view' has a major role to play in Hart's *The Concept of Law* (1961). However, acceptance of the reality of the 'internal point of view' does not entail personal acceptance of the legitimacy of law from the legal theorist himself. Hart must be correct because an anarchist (Hart is not an anarchist) who denies the legitimacy of all coercive law could still give an account of a modern legal system, including the 'internal' point of view. However, Professor Dworkin has argued that all meaningful theories of law are driven by a view of law's point or function and that this entails a 'justification' of law in liberal democracies. Professor Raz has sought to defend Hart by arguing that general descriptive legal theory is possible despite Dworkin's assertions. A skeleton plan is given.

- ❖ Introduction;
- ❖ description of Hart's methodology in *The Concept of Law* mirroring Thomas Hobbes;
- ❖ Hart's views on the advantages of a legal system over the 'pre-legal' order;
- ❖ Dworkin's attack on Hart's claim to a 'descriptive' 'neutral' legal theory;
- ❖ Raz's defence of Hart and general descriptive jurisprudence;
- ❖ conclusion, the issue of the proper methodology of legal theory, one of the most contested issues in jurisprudence today.

ANSWER

Professor Hart (1907–1992), in the preface to *The Concept of Law* (1961), comments that his aim has been to further the understanding of law, coercion and morality as different but related social phenomena and that the book can be viewed as an essay in descriptive sociology. Certainly, Hart's jurisprudence is not tied to a particular legal system but aims to give a general account of the concept of law as it has appeared in different human societies. The key question is whether a general descriptive theory of law is possible, as Hart asserts, or whether even Hart's legal positivism was driven by some contestable view of law's function or value and is therefore a view of law that can be contested by rival theories of law, such as that propounded by Professor Dworkin.

As well as attacking Austin's concept of law, Hart also builds his own theory out of the ashes of the 'command theory'. As Hart comments, Austin's account of law is the record of a failure and there is plainly need for a fresh start. That fresh start is introduced on pages 89–96 of *The Concept of Law* in which Hart invents a story designed to show the value to any 'pre-legal' society of having a legal system. The story is not intended by Hart to describe any historical reality but rather is meant to illustrate how a pre-legal system might benefit from a legal system. The story begins in what Hart calls a pre-legal society, which is governed purely by rules of obligation – a set of commands and prohibitions. Hart points out the social defects of such a regime and how the addition of secondary rules to the primary rules of obligation cures the defects of the pre-legal order. The methodology of Hart here is interesting as it recalls the work of Thomas Hobbes (1588–1679) in his work *Leviathan* in 1651, in which Hobbes, as a conceptual device, imagines a society without any central authority, such a situation being termed by Hobbes 'the state of nature'. The defects of 'the state of nature' – which include a perpetual state of war as man fights man and an ever present risk of violent death – are cured by the establishment of an absolute authority through a social covenant when each person acquiesces to absolute authority which, in turn, guarantees the safety of person and property.

In the spirit of Thomas Hobbes, who asked us to imagine the horrors of life without state authority, Professor Hart asks us to consider life without law and how the introduction of secondary rules helps to cure the defects of the pre-legal order. There is no claim by Hart that pre-legal societies ever did exist; rather, as for the Hobbesian 'state of nature', the Hartian 'pre-legal society' serves as an analytical or conceptual device in order to better illustrate an important point. Hart points out the defects of a pre-legal regime. Those defects in the pre-legal order are threefold: (1) uncertainty, (2) static quality – an inability to change the rules, and (3) inefficiency.

As Hart explains in *The Concept of Law*, the rules by which the pre-legal society lives will not form a system but will simply be a separate set of standards without any identifying mark. Therefore, as Hart rightly points out, if doubts arise as to what the rules are or as to the precise scope of some given rule, there will be no procedure for settling the doubts by reference to an authority set up by secondary rules to determine the issue. This is the defect of uncertainty cured by the addition to the primary rules of secondary rules concerning the establishment, authority and jurisdiction of courts. A second defect is the static character of the primary rules. There will be no means in the pre-legal order of deliberately adapting or eliminating old rules in the light of changing circumstances. The remedy for this defect is the addition of secondary rules concerning the introduction, variation and repeal of primary rules. The third defect of the pre-legal order is inefficiency of that society as disputes arise as to whether a rule has or has not been breached. Again, the introduction of secondary rules to set up courts to deal quickly and authoritatively with the question of breach of the primary rules is the remedy for the pre-legal problems.

Hart argues that the introduction of secondary rules to deal with the three main defects sees the emergence of a recognisable legal order and, in a key phrase of Hart, the concept of law may be most illuminatingly characterised as 'a union of primary and secondary rules'.

For Hart, the most important secondary rule is the 'rule of recognition'. This rule specifies some feature or features, possession of which by a purported rule is a conclusive indication that the rule is a legal rule and not only a mere rule of morality, custom or religion. As Hart says, where a secondary rule of recognition is accepted and used for the identification of primary rules of obligation, then that situation is the foundation of a legal system. This all seems as if Hart was, in value-neutral terms, merely describing the benefits to a society of adopting a legal system over a pre-legal order of simple primary rules. However, Hart has a firm view of the value of law, which is related to the co-ordinating virtues of clarity and certainty that law provides to a society. For Hart, a legal system provides a settled, public and dependable set of standards for private and official conduct which cannot be called into question by any person's sense of morality or policy. If Hart had identified other defects in the pre-legal order – such as that the regime of primary rules does not provide any forum for discussion as to whether the primary rules form a set of coherent principles – then Hart might have been led to a different account of legal order, one in which adjudication in 'hard cases' was a prominent feature of his theory of law.

Indeed, Professor Dworkin believes that Hart and other legal positivists are driven by a contestable vision of the value of law and that Hart is not merely presenting a description of the concept of law for use by sociologists or historians of legal systems. Dworkin, in an important article for students of jurisprudence entitled 'Hart's Postscript and the character of political philosophy' (in the 2004 Oxford Journal of Legal Studies), has argued that proper legal theory is concerned with the interpretation of law so as to justify its use as the mechanism by which the state's monopoly on the use of legitimate force is expressed. Dworkin rejects Hart's view that whilst Dworkin is engaged in the important but narrow issue of how judges should decide hard cases, Hart simply describes these activities in a general and philosophical way and describes them as a detached observer from the outside. Dworkin insists that legal positivism – in particular, Hart's legal positivism – is driven by ethical claims about the value of law. As Dworkin states, legal positivists all stress the role of law in substituting crisp direction for the uncertainties of morality and custom. For Bentham, the law's efficiency would be undermined if the identification of law was made to turn even in part on moral argument, since persons disagree about the requirements of morality; the consequent disorganisation in the identification of the law would produce chaos, thought Bentham. Hart wrote that law cures the inefficiencies of a mythical pre-legal state of custom. Raz argues that the essence of law is authority and that authority through law is undermined if the identification of law, even partly, depends on moral argument. For legal positivists, from Hobbes to Bentham to Hart and Raz, the idea of law makes social co-ordination possible, so positivism insists that morality should and does play no role in identifying true claims of law. Dworkin concludes that legal positivism has appeal only when its underlying views of the function of law are brought out because mere description of the concept of law is not possible.

Dworkin's views of the purposes of legal theory are hotly contested in Hart's 'Postscript' to The Concept of Law (1994, 2nd edition) and in the jurisprudential writings of Raz. Hart, in his 'Postscript', claims that his account of law is descriptive in that it has no justificatory aims – it does not seek to commend law to anyone. Hart comments that his legal theory is descriptive and general in a way Dworkin's theory of law is not, as Dworkin's theory is addressed to the particular culture of Anglo-American law. As contributors in a recent book celebrating Hart's contribution to legal thought maintain (*The Legacy of HLA Hart* (2008), edited by Kramer and Grant), Hart always said that legal philosophers themselves need not adopt the internal perspective of a committed participant in a legal system but that the best vantage point for a legal philosopher was to analyse law from a detached 'external' point of view, even though the astute legal philosopher will attend to the 'internal' point of view – the 'outlook' of the persons who are being subject to philosophical enquiry without the legal philosopher sharing that 'internal' point of view himself. Hart comments that he finds it hard to follow why Dworkin appears to rule out general and descriptive legal theory as at best 'useless', in Dworkin's word, to describe legal theory. Indeed, Hart has a strong ally in Professor Raz who believes that the true purpose of legal theory is to be general and value-neutral in approach. In an article published in 2004, 'Can there be a theory of law?', Raz comments that legal theory is an attempt to explain the nature of a certain kind of social institution and that law as a concept occupies a central role in our understanding of our own and other societies. Raz comments that the inquiry of true legal theory is universal in that it explores the nature of law wherever it is to be found, not merely a justification of the Anglo-American legal system as found in Dworkin's 'localised' legal theory.

The question as to whether legal theory can be usefully descriptive or must inevitably have some justificatory purpose is one of the most contested issues in legal theory today. In this issue not only the content of jurisprudence but its whole methodology and its purpose are in contest. It is perhaps the 'holy grail' of jurisprudential questions.

NOTES

The preface to the original *The Concept of Law* (1961) by Professor Hart should be consulted, as should the 'Postscript' by Hart to the second edition of *The Concept of Law* (1994), for Hart's own views as to his aims in legal theory. The most important source for Professor Dworkin's views on the proper methodology for legal theory is the essay 'Hart's Postscript and the character of political philosophy' (2004) *Oxford Journal of Legal Studies*, vol 24, no 1, pp 1–37. Raz's views can be found in his essay 'Can there be a theory of law' (2004) available on Raz's website (http://josephnraz. googlepages.com/home). A useful discussion of the 'methodological' debate in legal theory between Dworkin on the one side and Hart and Raz on the other can be found in Andrei Marmor's essay 'The nature of law' (2007), to be found on the online and free *Stanford Encyclopedia of Philosophy* (http://plato.stanford.edu/)

QUESTION 20

How have later legal theorists sought to improve upon Hart's analysis in *The Concept of Law* (1961)?

Answer Plan

Professor Hart only intended *The Concept of Law* published in 1961 to be a student text in the Clarendon Law Series of which he was the editor. It is ironic that *The Concept* as it is known in jurisprudential circles has come to be treated as Hart's *magnum opus* or masterwork on legal philosophy, when it was only meant to function as an introductory student text. Hart moved away from cutting edge work in legal philosophy after 1961 in favour of topics such as 'Causation in the Law' and 'Punishment and Responsibility' so *The Concept of Law* came to be viewed as Hart's defining work in pure jurisprudence. As Nicola Lacey points out, in her very readable biography of Hart: *The Nightmare and the Noble Dream* (2004), Hart's aim was to present his own theory of law as an accessible student text. Lacey quotes Hart's notebook written at the time (1961) on his aims with the publication of *The Concept of Law*:

> My ambition . . . is to dispel forever the definitional will o' the wisps- the search for 'definitions' of law- by showing that all that can be done and is important to do is to characterise the *Concept* of law by identifying the main elements and organization of elements which constitute a *standard* legal *system*.

Therefore *The Concept of Law* (1961) should be read as an effort to provide a general and descriptive account of the main elements of a standard legal system. It is not correct then for Professor Finnis in his various writings to suggest that his own 'ideal theory of law' – a rational system of norms for the co-ordination of the common good – is an improvement on Hart's theory. Hart's descriptive value-neutral account of law, not commending the institution of law to anyone was a radically different jurisprudential enterprise to Finnis's description of law from the standpoint of an approved ideal form of law – see *Natural Law and Natural Rights* (1980). Of course Hart's theory of law in *The Concept of Law*(1961) is by no means perfect. Hart in his description of a standard legal system says too little about the subtleties of common law adjudication which Professor Dworkin so ruthlessly exploited in subsequent years and led to Hart becoming somewhat preoccupied with his American critic so that nearly all Hart's 'Postscript' to the second edition of *The Concept of Law* (1994) is taken up with replying to Dworkin's criticisms of Hart's own legal theory. Indeed in the 'Postscript' Hart says a lot more about common law reasoning in 'hard cases' that was omitted in the original *The Concept of Law*. Other writers have used Hart as a starting point. including Dennis Galligan in *Law in Modern Society* (2007) who refers to Hart's 1961 work as 'a classic'. Whatever subsequent critics have said about Hart's work in *The Concept of Law* (1961) it will always have the status of reviving serious philosophical interest in the philosophy of law. Hart is the modern heir of the legal methodology adopted by Bentham, which is what Hart terms in 'Essays on Bentham' as the 'sane and healthy centre of legal positivism' – the calculatedly neutral approach to the definition of legal and social phenomena.

A skeleton plan is suggested.

- ❖ Introduction;
- ❖ Hart's main purposes in writing *The Concept of Law* (1961);
- ❖ Dworkin's attack on Hart's underdeveloped theory in *The Concept of Law* of judicial adjudication in a 'hard case';
- ❖ Raz's reference to the 'Authority of Law' as an improvement on Hart's account;
- ❖ Finnis's critique of Hart's methodology from the standpoint of an 'ideal' legal theory;
- ❖ Galligan's narrowing of the focus of Hart to 'modern legal orders' but Galligan's approval of Hart's text as a 'classic' which has stood up to critics.

ANSWER

Hart's *The Concept of Law* (1961) is widely considered to be the canonical text of modern jurisprudence. The book in many ways represented 'year zero' for jurisprudence, a new start after the failures of Austinian jurisprudence which had dominated English jurisprudence for over a century. As John Finnis comments in 'Natural Law: The Classical Tradition' (in *The Oxford Handbook of Jurisprudence and Philosophy* edited by Coleman and Shapiro 2002) :

> Late twentieth century legal theory's paradigm text is called 'The Concept of Law ... Hart might more accurately, if less elegantly, have called his book "A New and Improved Concept of Law".

It is somewhat ironic that Hart's book should have this 'central text' status since the book was originally conceived by Hart as a book for undergraduate students, a product of his lecture notes at Oxford University. The aim was to produce his own theory of law as an accessible student text. In his biographical note for Hart in the *Oxford Dictionary of National Biography*, Tony Honore comments of Hart's book:

> his aim was to give beginners in jurisprudence a book that that was more than a catalogue of great names spiced with superficial comments on their theories.

Instead they would be introduced to the main issues in the subject of which two stood out: the relation of law to brute force on the one hand and morality on the other.... For writers on jurisprudence criticism of Hart at once replaced criticism of Austin as the starting point of their thinking. It seeks to lay bare the structure of modern legal systems and to show what it is that separates them from other forms of social control such as brute force or morality.

So a 'student text' became treated as Hart's major work in legal theory and this trend was confirmed by the fact that Hart, quite early on, abandoned major work in legal theory in favour of other pursuits such as academic administration (Hart was President of Brasenose College, Oxford), editing Bentham's copious works and writing on other aspects of law such as *Punishment and Responsibility* (1968).

Hart is sometimes criticised for not analysing in *The Concept of Law* the role of the common law with its conflicting principles in the 'rule' dominated analysis of law found in *The Concept of Law*. Brian Simpson, drawing on his deep knowledge of the common law, argued that Hart's analysis of a legal system does not fit the 'muddle' of the common law (see 'The Common Law and Legal Theory' in *Oxford Essays in Jurisprudence* (1973)). Brian Simpson further criticises Hart in his comments (Michigan Law Review 2005) that:

> the book (*The Concept of Law*) devotes virtually no attention whatever to the working of the common law tradition: indeed the common law does not appear in the index and is hardly mentioned in the entire book.

It may be said that Hart was overly influenced by the 'legislation model' of law so beloved of the 'command theorists', Austin and Bentham, and also by Kelsen's legislation slanted legal theory and that as a consequence Hart adopted the view that law is fundamentally a matter of varied but still legislated 'rules'. However, to defend Hart against this charge of neglecting the common law's place in the legal system, we may return to the point that Hart was interested in describing a 'standard' or 'archetypal' legal system and in such an archetype, the common law may not necessarily be a feature. It is wise to remember that Hart, in his legal theory, was concerned with generality of scope, aiming to describe a 'standard' legal system and was not in the business of giving an accurate definition of the Anglo-American legal systems with its common law element.

Hart's text in *The Concept of Law* was used as the basis for the launch of Professor Dworkin's own anti-positivistic theory of law, such as the article 'The Model of Rules' (1967) which heavily criticised Hart's notion that law could be understood as a system of different kind of rules. Dworkin argued through a number of articles and finally in his book *Law's Empire* (1986) that, contrary to Hart's analysis, law could not be identified in the form of a master rule or recognition, but rather that the law of the Anglo-American legal system was identified through the moral interpretation of existing law. However a way has been suggested to defend Hart from Dworkin's attack, whilst acknowledging that judges in the Anglo-American legal system sometimes use moral arguments to identify the law. Jules Coleman in a 1982 article 'Negative and Positive Positivism' argues that in the Anglo-American legal system there is an 'accepted social practice' among judges that where the law is unclear then the case will be decided by the moral interpretation of existing law. This 'accepted social practice' amongst judges to decide cases in that way is itself part of the rule of recognition. Moreover, because that 'accepted judicial practice' of using morality to identify law is true only of certain legal systems then the legal positivist argument of Hart, that law everywhere is identified by reference to sources, is unaffected. Hart can therefore agree with Dworkin that certain legal systems recognise a judicial social practice where difficult cases are resolved by reference to moral arguments but that it is the 'social practice' that gives such moral arguments their legitimacy and not the moral principles themselves as Dworkin argues. This 'inclusive legal positivism' suggested by Coleman was given approval by Hart in the second edition of *The Concept of Law* (1994).

However, some legal positivists, such as Professor Raz, reject 'inclusive legal positivism' in favour of a hardline 'exclusive positivism'. For Raz the identification of law can never turn on a moral argument for the very essence of law is that it is an exercise in authority to replace the moral reasons underlying the legal directive with the finality of law's authority. If citizens had to employ moral arguments to work out the content of the law then this would undermine the very point of the law, which is to replace the uncertainties of morality with the crisp authority of law. Raz has stood fast to the 'sources thesis' namely that the existence and content of the law can be determined without resorting to any moral argument.

Raz has generally been sympathetic to Hart's *The Concept of Law* but a few points of distinction need to be made. First of all Raz maintains a harder version of legal positivism than Hart. Raz believes morality plays no part in the identification of law (although Raz agrees that law is often heavily influenced by morality), whereas Hart is prepared to accept a softer version of legal positivism where in some jurisdictions accepted judicial practice allows morality some place in the identification of law in hard cases. Secondly, Hart in *The Concept of Law* correctly pointed out that there was a crucial difference between the demands of the taxman and the gangster and that this distinction was captured in the difference between 'being obliged' and 'being under an obligation'. However although Hart noted descriptively the legitimacy of law's demands over the demands of a gangster, apparent also in Hart's idea of the 'internal point of view' of someone who endorses a legal order as valid irrespective of sanctions for non-compliance, Hart did not fully bring out the point that the law by its nature claims legitimate authority. It was Raz, in works such as *The Authority of Law* (1979) who firmly made the point concerning law's authority that law is differentiated from the brute force of the gangster by law's claim to authority. In a development of the legal positivist tradition, of which Hart himself represented a significant improvement over Austin's 'command theory', Raz comments in *The Authority of Law*:

> Put in a nutshell, the law is a system of guidance and adjudication claiming supreme authority within a certain society.

This is a definition which Hart was feeling towards in *The Concept of Law* but perhaps because of his dislike of 'definitions' of law he was not as crisp on the point of the law's authority as he should have been in *The Concept of Law*.

Perhaps because Hart was writing *The Concept of Law* primarily for a student audience then his analysis of law and legal systems can seem simplistic. A good example of Hart's simplistic reduction of legal systems to a basic level of description is Hart's claim that :

> **law may most illuminatingly be characterized as a union of primary rules . . . with . . . secondary rules.**

This alleged 'key' to understanding law and legal systems offered by Hart is similar in its distorting simplicity to Austin's claim that the 'key' to jurisprudence was understanding law as 'the commands of the sovereign' a view of law which Hart was at such pains to reject in *The Concept of Law*.

The simplistic reduction by Hart, in *The Concept of Law*, of the institution of law to a system of primary and secondary rules **'will not do'**, as MacCormick comments in *Institutions of Law* (2007). As a final analysis of legal systems the reducing of legal systems to a union of primary rules and secondary rules about those primary rules is inadequate even as an explanation for Hart's undergraduate students in 1961. On this account of legal systems provided by Hart, the law is not distinguished from sporting organizations or social clubs that also have basic primary rules of permitted and prohibited conduct but also have secondary rules specifying the procedure for the variation or elimination or replacement of the basic primary rules. Hart had, therefore, failed to distinguish between law and sporting or social clubs in his account of legal systems as consisting of a union of 'primary and secondary rules'. Indeed Hart commented in *The Concept of Law*:

"a legal system is a complex union of primary and secondary rules . . ." and that such a union of rules is: "the heart of a legal system".

Hart could have added that such a union of rules is also the heart of a sporting association or social club. Hart therefore failed in one of his tasks in *The Concept of Law* (1961) which was to distinguish law from other social institutions. Hart's 'key' to understanding law does not provide in its structure a way of distinguishing legal systems from organised sports. For the source of this biting criticism of Hart's theory of law, which holds that Hart does not distinguish legal systems from sporting clubs, see Professor Dworkin in the Harvard Law Review Forum (2006): 'Hart and the Concepts of Law'.

Professor Finnis in *Natural Law and Natural Rights* (1980) took Hart's analysis in *The Concept of Law* as the starting point for his breathing of new life into the old tradition of natural law theorizing. As Finnis has commented in 'On Hart's Ways: Law as Reason and as Fact' (in *The Legacy of HLA Hart* (2008), edited by Kramer et al), Hart's work:

is a standing invitation to develop legal theory's critical account and promotion of those considerations of justice, of concern for the common good and make law salient as a means of governance . . .

For Finnis, Hart's account of a modern legal system found in *The Concept of Law* (1961) is incomplete because Hart did not, in his descriptive account of law, tie that description to the 'central case' of a legal system, which is an ordering of reason for the common good. Finnis believes that an adequate description of those legal systems which work for the common good (such as modern Western democracies) cannot be given without attending to the moral purposes of those legal systems, which is to further the common good. For Finnis the human institution we call 'law' has a specific moral purpose, namely the common good of a community. For Finnis the 'central case' or 'central example' legal system is an arrangement rationally prescribed by those responsible for the community for the common good of its members. Hart in *The Concept of Law* famously introduced the 'internal point of view', the point of view of participants in a legal system who accepted the law as a valid set of standards for conduct. Hart famously said 'acceptance' of law by legal officials could be based on habit, a wish to conform, calculations of long term interest etc. Finnis argued in *Natural Law and Natural Rights* that the 'central case' of the internal point of view was the legal official who accepted the law because he saw a moral duty to uphold the legal order for the common good of the community. Therefore Finnis seeks to improve Hart's analysis by seeking to widen and deepen the description of a legal system by reference to an 'ideal' type of legal system, namely a legal system that is working for the common good. Of course Hart himself was seeking to describe law and legal systems in descriptive social-scientific terms, as he famously said in the Preface to the original *The Concept of Law* the book could read as an essay in 'descriptive sociology'. Indeed in the 'Postscript' to the second edition of *The Concept of Law* Hart commented:

> **like other forms of positivism my theory makes no claim to identify the point or purpose of law and legal practices as such. . . . In fact I think it quite vain to seek any more specific purpose which law as such serves beyond providing guides to human conduct and standards of criticism of such conduct.**

Ultimately then it is not possible to see the work of Finnis as an 'improvement' upon Hart for Hart was aiming at general, even universal, coverage of legal systems morally good, morally bad or indifferent whereas Finnis was aiming at an account of those few legal systems working genuinely for the common good. In other words Finnis's work is 'engaged' with law as a social institution, Hart's work is 'disengaged' from law as a social institution and it is absurd to see Finnis's work as an improvement upon Hart's *The Concept of Law*.

Another legal philosopher who sought to 'improve' upon Hart's account in *The Concept of Law* is Dennis Galligan who, in 2007, published *Law in Modern Society*. Galligan aims to give a rich descriptive account of what he calls 'modern legal orders' – the few legal orders, mainly of Europe, North America and the former British Empire such as Australia, where the rule of law is virtually fully realised. Galligan pays his respects to Hart's *The Concept of Law* by commenting:

> his account is illuminating, has acquired the status of a classic, and on the whole has stood up to critics.

However, by narrowing his focus to the few 'modern legal orders', Galligan hoped to bring out certain crucial features missed by Hart in his general account of all modern legal systems. As Galligan notes:

> In modern legal orders, officials have special relations with citizens . . . A noticeable aspect of Hart's account is that, while officials are placed at the centre, citizens are relegated to the margins. For Hart a legal system in its essentials consists of general obedience to law by the people and acceptance by officials of the rules of the system. The idea of citizens needing only to obey, while officials accept, may be justified in a very general way in relation to legal systems generally, but hardly matches the character of modern legal orders and needs to be reconsidered.

For Galligan in *Law in Modern Society* the special relations between citizens and officials is one of the defining features of a modern legal order and explains legal doctrines such as the separation of powers, judicial review of executive action and the possibility of bringing civil actions, such as false imprisonment against the police for example. Galligan argues that in Hart's concern in *The Concept of Law* to settle on a description of law wide enough to cover all legal orders from the good to the bad to the intolerable, Hart had to take account of legal systems sustained by legal officials with the barest support of the people – hence the criticism that Hart's account is 'legal official centred'.

However, Galligan argues in practice that in order for legal systems to be stable over the long term they need the support, not just the obedience, of the people. As Galligan comments:

> the support (not just the obedience) of the people is essential to preserve any form of rule, no matter how strong. In its absence or loss, inherent instability or fragility will be manifest.

Galligan is clearly in the business of justifying and supporting the great social benefits that modern Western legal orders bring in terms of social peace and prosperity. Although valuable this is very different legal theory from Hart's in *The Concept of Law* who aimed to describe legal systems in terms which would cover the very wide range of human situations and societies where law appears.

However, it may be that Hart was right in his analysis to focus on legal officials in his account of a legal system and that Galligan is unduly romantic and optimistic in his description of the 'bond of trust' between legal officials and citizens in a modern legal order. In an article in 2010 (*Oxford Journal of Legal Studies*) Michael Wilkinson argues:

> Is it in the nature of modern society for subjects to become alienated from their laws? Do the features of modern society tend to distance subjects from genuine engagement with the law and can this be seen in the way modern law becomes official, specialised and institutionalised.? There may well be something about modern society that promotes a retreat by the subject to the private sphere, and the adoption of a limited and deficient sense of acceptance of law that is purely self-interested or sheep-like.

This vision of modern Western society and its legal system is far removed from the 'bond of trust' between legal officials and citizens that Galligan said characterised modern legal orders. Perhaps Hart, in his unromantic and realistic way, was correct to give an account of law in terms of the acceptance by legal officials of legal norms. Citizens in anonymous, massive consumerist Western societies can view the legal order as remote, technical and arcane. Law is then on this pessimistic view a 'distinctively official practice' – an account which Hart caught well in *The Concept of Law*.

Hart was well aware of the risks involved in the institution of law and refused to be romantic (as Finnis and Galligan are romantic about law in their different ways) about law.

Law has of course been used for hideous oppression in the past but law also brings with it other forms of dangers as Leslie Green argues in 'The Inseparability of Law and Morality':

> **the necessary moral hazards of law include not just better organized and more efficient instruments of oppression; but also new forms of oppression: the alienation of community and value, the rise of hierarchy, domination by experts, and the docility of those who are bought off by the goods that legal order brings.**

Given the moral hazards of instituting a system of law then it was wise of Hart to seek to frame his explanation of law in terms of an institutionalised normative system resting on a consensus of thought and action amongst legal elites. Hart was right to distance himself from any 'romantic' view of law that seeks to give an account of law from the standpoint of some alleged ideal, whether that ideal be 'Law as Integrity' (Dworkin), 'law as an ordering of rationality for the common good' (Finnis) or 'a bond of trust' between legal officials and citizens in a 'modern legal order' (Galligan).

HLA Hart in *The Concept of Law* (1961) aimed to give his students a 'road map' of the main features of a legal system without offering himself any endorsement of such a system. Hart's 'general and descriptive' purposes can be seen in the following features he highlighted:

(1) The different types of legal rules performing differing functions, some rules prohibitory such as the criminal law but some enabling and facilitating the lives of citizens such as laws on contract, wills and marriage.
(2) The 'internal' point of view of legal officials and some citizens who accept the legal rules as valid for a variety of reasons- self-interest, habit, a desire to conform but at least an acceptance of the law going beyond a fear of sanctions
(3) The 'rule of recognition' as the criteria for validity in a legal system differentiating the law from morality, social custom and other social rules. Hart provided an account of how the rule of recognition is identified- through observing the actions and attitudes of legal officials and an account of its importance- Hart said that the rule of recognition was the knot of the legal system.

(4) The minimum necessary conditions for a legal system to exist which Hart defined as (a) acceptance by legal officials of the rule of recognition and hence the legal system, (b) obedience to the law by the bulk of the population.

(5) The general benefits that a legal system can bring to a society which Hart explains in his famous 'fable' of the pre-legal society which by adding the institution of law to the pre-legal social rules gains the benefits of certainty, efficiency and adaptability in the handling of the basic rules of the pre-legal society.

(6) Hart stressed how law is used in society to plan and organise life out of court.

However, in all this description of law and legal systems generally Hart was not committing himself (unlike other theorists such as Dworkin or Finnis) to a view that law was 'a good thing' or 'intrinsically valuable'. Although he was not an anarchist Hart could have been an anarchist sociologist writing *The Concept of Law* as a rough guide for his students as to what a legal system was and its possible benefits, but in the end reserving judgment as to the inherent value of law to society knowing that law is 'morally risky'. Hart was, above all, keen not to romanticise legal phenomena. As Hart said in *Essays in Jurisprudence and Philosophy* (1983):

> **The identification of the central meaning of law with what is morally legitimate, because oriented towards the common good, seems to me in view of the hideous record of the evil use of law to be an unbalanced perspective, and as great a distortion of the opposite Marxist identification of the central case of law with the pursuit of the interests of a dominant economic class.**

Given man's inherent moral imperfection and a consequent tendency in human affairs for things to go badly then Hart may have been correct to have said that the institution of law itself could be used for evil purposes as equally as good purposes.

However, a conservative thinker might argue that it is precisely because of mankind's inherent moral imperfection that law and government are a necessity and that therefore **law cannot be separated from the realization of the common good** through law's restraining of the evil impulses within mankind. As Anthony Quinton comments on the traditions of conservative thought in England:

> **The consequence of men's moral imperfection is that men, acting on their own uncontrolled impulses, will on the whole act badly, however elevated their professed intentions may be. They need, therefore, the restraint of customary and established laws and institutions, of an objective and impersonal barrier to the dangerous extravagance of subjective, personal impulse.**

Therefore on the conservative reading of human nature, which is not purely inspired by the Christian religion's doctrine of 'original sin' but was also shared by the atheistic Thomas Hobbes and David Hume from observation of human nature, **law and Government are accepted as necessities** given the moral imperfection of mankind. Perhaps then there is **a closer connection** between the institution of law and the realization of the common good than Professor Hart allowed for in his legal philosophy: the institution of law is a necessity given the inherent human tendency to do the morally bad rather than the morally good. Anthony Quinton expressed the point well about the necessity of government and law in *The Politics of Imperfection* (1978):

> **the conservative . . . locates the need for government in the propensity for anti-social conduct that is to be found in every-one . . . His ideal government has to be strong, since it has to control a universal impulse . . .**

The institution of law, given the unpleasant realities of human nature, is then tied to the realisation of the common good in a way which is much more in tune with the views of natural lawyers such as Finnis in *Natural Law and Natural Rights* (1980) than Professor Hart's detached social-scientific approach to law found in *The Concept of Law* (1961).

Aim Higher ★

Students can gain extra marks by noting how, even to the very end of his writings (see the 'Postscript' to the second edition of *The Concept of Law* (1994)). Hart maintained that his purpose in legal theory was general and descriptive with no agenda to justify or recommend law to anyone. Students can avoid the pitfall of thinking that Hart was, in *The Concept of Law*, arguing for the moral superiority of law over a pre-legal order. Hart merely pointed out some very general benefits of the institution of law, whilst at the same time recognising the risks law can bring in terms of the organised coercion of the population.

NOTES

Professor Hart's reply to Dworkin's criticisms of Hart's theory of law is best seen in 'The Postscript' to *The Concept of Law* (1994, 2nd edition) edited by Bulloch and Raz. Galligan's praise of Hart can be found in *Law in Modern Society* (2007) pp 6–18. Nicola Lacey's insightful biography of Hart: *A Life of H.L.A. Hart: The Nightmare and the Noble Dream* (2005) has good material on *The Concept of Law* at pp 221–233.

ESTION 21

vorkin, in his theory of law, successfully overcome the appeal of legal positivism?

Answer Plan

Professor Dworkin has for 40 years ('The model of rules', his first attack on legal positivism, appeared in 1967 and has been reprinted in *Taking Rights Seriously* (1977)) been the most erudite and eloquent critic of the tradition of legal thought we call 'legal positivism'. Dworkin initially attacked the account of judicial adjudication in appeal cases offered by legal positivism – namely, that the judge has an inescapable law making function. This characterisation of the judicial role in a 'hard case' (where settled law does not dictate an answer) was severely criticised by Dworkin, who developed his own 'gapless' theory of adjudication and law in response. By the time of *Law's Empire* in 1986, Dworkin had broadened his attack on 'legal positivism' to suggest that it offered a poor vision of the value and potential of law in a modern liberal democracy compared to Dworkin's own vision of 'law's empire', namely, 'law as integrity'. The debate between Dworkin and modern legal positivists, such as Professor Raz, continues today but Dworkin's vision of law represents the most complete and serious attack in legal thought on the legal positivistic tradition. A skeleton plan is suggested.

* Introduction;
* the legal positivistic account of judicial law making 'discretion';
* Dworkin's counter-attack suggesting such a view of judicial adjudication is wrong in practice and principle;
* Dworkin's 'gapless' theory of law;
* the updated attack on 'legal positivism' in *Law's Empire* (1986);
* Raz's criticisms of Dworkin's theory;
* conclusion, Dworkin has not killed off legal positivism but Dworkin has forced, through trenchant criticism, Hart and Raz to defend the theory of legal positivism.

ANSWER

Ronald Dworkin's attack on legal positivism as the reigning theory of law, from Austin and Bentham in the nineteenth century to Professor Hart in the mid-twentieth century, has been complex, shifting and sometimes persuasive. The original attack by Dworkin was on Hart's conception of legal positivism and what Dworkin took to be the inadequacies of the legal positivist account of judicial adjudication in 'hard cases', as exemplified in Dworkin's influential articles, 'The model of rules' (1967) and 'Hard cases' (1975), both collected in *Taking Rights Seriously* in 1977. The fact that Hart was never focally interested in describing the judicial role in a 'hard case' (a case where the settled legal rules do not dictate an answer) in *The Concept of Law* (1961) was never acknowledged by Dworkin, and the true scope and methodology of legal theory remains a contested issue between Dworkin and the legal positivists today (see, for example, Dworkin's article on the methodology of legal theory in *Oxford Journal of Legal Studies* 2004).

Dworkin's core idea in his attack on the legal positivistic conception of law is that the idea that the law is solely identified by social sources is wrong and fails to capture the reality of legal argumentation and judicial judgment in 'hard cases' at appeal court level. Dworkin holds that what he calls the 'true grounds of law' include the best moral interpretation of existing law. If Dworkin is right then he has indeed overcome Hart's legal positivism where the 'grounds of law' are to be determined without recourse to moral argument but depend on a master factual test – 'the rule of recognition'. As a later positivist, Professor Raz comments (in his essay 'Two views of the nature of the theory of law' (2001) – see *Hart's Postscript: Essays on the Postscript to the Concept of Law*, edited by Professor Jules Coleman) that if Dworkin is right to maintain that his theory of law is correct, then Hart's theory of legal positivism is flawed at its foundations. The main issue then is whether Dworkin is correct? We can accept that Hart's and Dworkin's understanding of the character of legal philosophy differ and that Hart views his own theory as a general description of law as a type of social institution (and this 'internal point of view' of Hart's conception of his own theory deserves some weight) whereas Dworkin's focus is on Anglo-American adjudication in 'hard cases', but this difference in approach does not mean that Dworkin's theory and Hart's legal positivism can be reconciled.

Dworkin argues, in an article called 'Hard cases' (1975), that legal positivism provides a theory of hard cases. When a particular lawsuit cannot be brought under a clear rule of law, laid down by some institution in advance, then the judge has, according to legal positivism a 'discretion' to decide the case either way. The judge, for the legal positivist, must create new law – legislate when the law runs out. For the legal positivist, the law begins and ends with the sources – the statutes, cases and conventions. Beyond the sources lies judicial discretion and judicial legislation in 'hard cases'. Dworkin argued that this theory of adjudication inherent within legal positivism is wholly inadequate. Dworkin built his immense reputation as a legal theorist by constructing an alternative theory of judicial adjudication to that offered by legal positivism, a theory of adjudication which found its most mature expression in *Law's Empire* (1986). Legal positivism is sometimes defended from Dworkin's attack by pointing out that Hart's legal positivism was concerned with a general and descriptive account of law and was not concerned with the judicial role in 'hard cases' – indeed, judicial adjudication in hard cases receives only passing reference in the whole of *The Concept of Law*. Professor Finnis writes, in *Natural Law and Natural Rights* (1980), that Dworkin's theory of law offers guidance to the judge as to his judicial duty in a 'hard case'. Hart's theory of law is a descriptive account offered to historians to enable a history of legal systems to be written. Finnis believes that Dworkin's debate with positivists such as Hart and Raz miscarries because Dworkin fails to acknowledge that Hart and Raz have no intention in their legal positivist theories of law to offer solutions to 'hard cases' disputed amongst competent lawyers.

However, against this view of Finnis we can argue that legal positivism does have a theory of 'hard cases' implicitly, even if 'hard case' adjudication is not the main or even subsidiary focus of legal positivist legal theory. We have seen that legal positivism limits the law by stipulation to the 'social sources' so that the law can perform its various functions of social co-ordination through authoritative directives. Inevitably, as the law is a bounded institution, there will be gaps in the law and here the judge has a limited law making function, say legal positivists. Indeed, Professor Hart, in his 'Postscript' to *The Concept of Law* (1994, 2nd edition), went to some length to defend a theory of judicial law creation in 'hard cases' from Dworkinian attack. 'Hard cases' might not be central to legal positivism but legal positivism has a theory of 'hard cases' anyway. For Dworkin, an acceptable legal theory must provide a plausible account of certain features; Dworkin finds in adjudication that, even in 'hard cases' where the 'sources' run out, the lawyers and judges argue as though there are legally binding standards to be applied. Dworkin's theory of law therefore emerges from his theory of adjudication. It may be questioned whether a theory of adjudication should not follow a theory of law. Whilst, for the legal positivist, the central legal figure is the law-maker or legislator, the central legal figure for Dworkin's theory of law is the law's interpreter: the appellate judge. Although the focus of the two theories is different, there is a small but crucial overlap between the theories concerning 'hard cases'. Dworkin has found his ground to attack legal positivism and has consistently attacked legal positivism because it fails to capture the reality of judicial adjudication in 'hard cases'.

Dworkin starts from the idea that legal positivism is both wrong as a description of 'hard case' adjudication and also politically objectionable. Judges, in the Anglo-American legal system, when they give judgment in 'hard cases' talk as if they were 'finding' the law, not 'inventing' new rights and duties. However, we can counter this argument of Dworkin by commenting that, for reasons of political acceptability, unelected judges should talk as though they are 'constrained' by law rather than owning up to their exercise of discretion in actually making law. Indeed, judges sometimes do admit that they make law, as Professor Hart points out in his 'Postscript' to *The Concept of Law* (1994). Hart comments that judges of the stature of Oliver Wendell Holmes and Cardozo in the United States, or Lord MacMillan, Lord Radcliffe or Lord Reid in England, have insisted that there are legal cases left incompletely regulated by the law where the judge has an inescapable law making task.

Professor Dworkin has several political arguments for the view that judges should not legislate in even the hardest 'hard case'. In a democracy the power to make new law is not vested in judges but in Parliament. The law making power should not be exercised by unelected judges. Hart responds by commenting in the 'Postscript' that the fact that judges should be entrusted with law making powers to deal with disputes which the law fails to regulate may be regarded as a necessary price to pay for avoiding the inconveniences of alternative methods of regulating them, such as reference to the legislature; the price may seem small if judges are constrained in the exercise of these powers and cannot introduce wide reforms of the law, but only rules to deal with the specific issues thrown up by particular cases. In any case the legislature has final control over judicial legislation and may repeal or amend any judge-made law that Parliament finds unacceptable. These responses by Hart, in the second edition of *The Concept of Law* (1994), considerably take the 'sting' out of Dworkin's attack on legal positivism that judges should not make law. Hart is also determined to point out that, on his theory of judicial legislation in 'hard cases', when judges make new law it should be in accordance with principles or underpinning reasons recognised as already having a footing in the existing law. Judges in 'hard cases' do not and should not push away their law books and start to legislate without further guidance from the law. However, there is still the need to legislate new law since, in any hard case, different principles may present themselves and a judge will often have to choose between them, relying like a conscientious legislator on the judge's sense of what is best in terms of new law.

Dworkin, however, has been insistent that in complex legal systems, like the Anglo-American systems, the law never runs out and that a judge, if clever enough, can always find the 'right answer' already within the existing law to any 'hard case'; this can be understood as the 'gapless' theory of law, to be contrasted with legal positivism as exemplified by Hart and Raz who regard the law as riddled with gaps. Hart, in *Essays in Jurisprudence and Philosophy* (1983), comments that Dworkin's theory of law as a gapless system of entitlements is a 'noble dream'.

Dworkin's attack on legal positivism is not just on its theory of judicial legislation but on its whole theory of law, especially the legal positivist idea that there is a single master test for law in the form of a 'rule of recognition'. Dworkin argues that there is no master test which can be devised which could capture all the legal principles in a complex legal system and, even if such a new 'rule of recognition' could be devised, it would not perform the function that the legal positivists require of it – to sharply distinguish law from other social standards. Dworkin comments, in *Taking Rights Seriously*, that if we treat principles as law we must reject the legal positivist view that the law of a community is distinguished from other social standards by some test in the form of a master rule. Dworkin argues for a much more expansive conception of the scope of legal considerations than do the positivists. For Dworkin, the law at least in the USA and UK, encompasses not only court decisions and legislation but the totality of the law seen by the interpreting judge as an internally coherent and consistent set of individual rights and duties. This view of law obliterates the legal positivist view of judicial legislation in 'hard cases'. It must be said that Dworkin's theory of law represents the most influential and subtle attack on legal positivism in current legal theory. It is therefore wrong for Brian Leiter (in an article in Rutgers Law Journal 2005, called 'The end of empire') to comment that Dworkin's theory of law and adjudication is implausible, badly argued and largely without philosophical merit. As the respected legal theorist, Professor Finnis argues (in *The Oxford Handbook of Jurisprudence and Philosophy of Law* (2002)) we should broadly accept at least some of the main elements of Ronald Dworkin's account of adjudication. Indeed, Gerald Postema (in an article entitled 'Philosophy of the common law', in *The Oxford Handbook of Jurisprudence and Philosophy* (2002)) comments that Dworkin's 'interpretive' account of legal reasoning may be the best available characterisation of the intellectual process in common law reasoning.

Dworkin's core concept is that the distinction between the law and moral standards is much more blurred than legal positivism says that division is. For Dworkin, the identification of law in 'hard cases' depends in part on a best moral interpretation of existing law. Professor Raz comments, in *The Authority of Law* (1979) that Professor Dworkin has opted for the most conservative interpretation of the judicial role. Judges on Dworkin's view, according to Raz, are not entitled to assume a reforming role. The judges on Dworkin's view, according to Raz, must rely in 'hard cases' only on analogical arguments which perpetuate and extend the existing legal ideology. However, to defend Dworkin from Raz, the Dworkinian judge may come up with the best moral interpretation of the law that has never occurred to previous judges and the 'reforming' judge through Dworkinian interpretation could take the law into new territory.

A legal principle exists, according to Dworkin, if that principle follows from the best moral and political interpretation of past judicial and legislative decisions in the relevant legal areas. What is interpretation of law? The judge must apply two central criteria in assessing the acceptability of legal principles discovered in the law. Those judicial criteria are 'fit' and 'justification'. The judge must choose as the 'right legal answer' that legal principle which 'fits' the law to a 'satisfactory' level (that is, the legal principle is consistent with past legal decisions to a certain degree) and which also illustrates the law in the best moral light. There are several consequences which follow from Dworkin's theory of adjudication:

(a) Judges do not and should not legislate in a 'hard case' because in the existing law the 'one right answer' is potentially to be found in every case, at least in complex legal systems such as the UK and the USA.

(b) The law is not applied retroactively to the litigants by the judge but the law is already in existence, for Dworkin, waiting to be found by the judge in a 'hard case'.

(c) There is always, according to Dworkin, one legally right answer to cover the 'hard case' that 'fits' the previous law well enough and justifies the law in the best moral light possible. A real life judge might identify the 'wrong' legal principle but this does not alter the fact for Dworkin that 'the one right answer' already exists in the existing legal materials. An ideal judge called 'Hercules' by Dworkin in his legal writings (such as *Law's Empire* (1986)) always finds the 'one right answer' in every 'hard case' however real life judges make mistakes.

The Dworkinian characterisation of adjudication in 'hard cases' has come under criticism. Professor Finnis (in an article in 1987 'On reason and authority in law's empire') has the following trenchant criticisms of Dworkin's notions of 'fit' and 'justification' as the governing criteria in adjudication in a 'hard case'. Finnis comments that Dworkin provides no guidance as to how much 'fit' a legal principle has to have with previous legal decisions before it is acceptable as a legal principle for application in a 'hard case' – what is the threshold level of 'fit' in a 'hard case?' Finnis also comments that Dworkin provides no means of balancing the two criteria of 'fit' and 'justification' against each other so that the judge in a 'hard case' is provided with little concrete guidance on how to apply the Dworkinian method of adjudication in a 'hard case'. Finnis also comments that in a 'hard case' there will often be more than one answer which is a 'correct' legal answer, even if many answers will be clearly wrong on the criteria of 'fit' and 'justification', and that it is wrong to say that there will always be 'one right answer', as Dworkin does.

Whatever the indeterminacy and vagueness of Dworkin's theory of adjudication, Dworkin's aspiration is a 'noble dream'. Dworkin, in *Law's Empire*, comments that he asks judges to assume, so far as this is possible, that the law is structured by a coherent set of principles about justice, fairness and procedural due process, and that judges should enforce these standards in the fresh cases that come before them so that each citizen's situation is fair and just according to the same standards. Such a legal system turns that society into a community of principle. In *Law's Empire*, Dworkin's own Empire is extended from the small but important colony of 'hard case' adjudication to the large country of the justification of the authority of the state and the moral obligation by the citizen to obey the law. Dworkin has expanded his theory of law, known as 'Law as Integrity', to answer some of the major questions of political philosophy. Dworkin writes in *Law's Empire* (1986) that a political society that accepts integrity as a virtue in the courts and legislation becomes a special form of community, special in a way that promotes that society's moral authority to assume and deploy a monopoly of coercive force. Dworkin now takes this as the central task of legal theory that a theory of law must explain how the law provides a general justification for the exercise of coercive power by the state. Therefore, from a theory of adjudication in 'hard cases', Dworkin has not only developed a theory of law, but also a theory for the moral legitimacy of the state itself. Professor Hart never claimed to have such justificatory aims in *The Concept of Law*; he was merely trying to describe the essential features of a familiar social institution – the law.

There is one more major criticism of Dworkin's legal theory and that is from Hart's heir in the legal positivist tradition, Professor Raz. Raz has criticised Dworkin's theory of law as being inconsistent with a central feature of law – namely, its claim to authority (see Raz's essay, 'Authority, law and morality', reproduced in *Ethics in the Public Domain*). Dworkin's theory of law undermines the guidance function of law by making the content of the law depend somewhat on controversial moral interpretation of settled law. As Raz comments, much of the law of a country may, according to Dworkin, be unknown. Yet it is already legally binding, waiting there to be discovered by the judge in a 'hard case'. Hence, the 'hidden' law is neither, nor is presented as being, anyone's judgment on what the law's subjects ought to do. Raz holds that Dworkin's theory is inconsistent with the authoritative nature of law. The law is a structure of authority; it is in the business of telling people what they must do. This conduct guidance function of law, the key to its method of social organisation, is undermined by Dworkin's theory of law. Raz thinks that the key problem for Dworkin is that Dworkin's theory is a theory of law developed out of a theory of adjudication. Raz argues that legal philosophy must stand back from the lawyers perspective, not in order to ignore it, but in order to examine lawyers and courts in the wider perspective of social organisation and political institutions generally, which is what Hart tried to do in *The Concept of Law*.

Professor Dworkin's subtle, influential and wide ranging attack on the legal positivism of Hart has not killed off the theory as Hart killed off the 'command theory' of Austin, but legal positivism remains alive and kicking as the continued influence of both Professors Hart and Raz illustrates.

Common Pitfalls ✖

Students can avoid the pitfall of thinking that legal positivists such as Raz and Hart have no answer to Dworkin's claim that judicial law-making is anti-democratic since judges are unelected. Students can gain extra marks by pointing out that Raz and Hart argue that judicial law-making is very different from Parliamentary legislation because: (a) judges engage in small scale improvements to the law not whole-scale reforms (b) judges on the whole avoid law-making in areas of political or social controversy (c) judges have to make their law reforms fit in with existing legal principle: judges in making new law have to have regard to 'legal reasoning': making sure the new judge created law fits with the existing law as far as possible (d) Parliament has final control, overturning any judge-made law it finds objectionable. All these factors take the 'sting' out of Dworkin's criticisms that judicial legislation is objectionable because anti-democratic Judicial law-making is a very different process compared to Parliamentary legislation, and the 'anti-democratic' criticism loses much of its force when the differences are fully appreciated.

NOTES

The best starting point for Professor Dworkin's initial attack on 'legal positivism' is to read two essays collected in *Taking Rights Seriously* (1977), namely 'The model of rules' and 'Hard cases'. The response of Professor Hart to many of Dworkin's criticisms can be read in 'The Postscript' to the second edition of *The Concept of Law* (1994) edited by Raz and Bulloch.

In *The Oxford Handbook of Jurisprudence and Philosophy of Law* (2002), edited by Coleman and Shapiro, Gerald Postema, in an essay entitled 'Philosophy of the common law' pays tribute to Dworkin's work on the judge's task in common law adjudication, commenting: 'There is much to be said for Dworkin's characterisation of this process as an account of an important part of common law reasoning.'

Professor Raz's criticisms of Dworkin's legal theory, from a modern legal positivistic background, can be found in the essay 'Authority, law and morality' (1985) The Monist, reprinted in the collection of Raz's essays, *Ethics in the Public Domain* (1994).

A useful summary of the changing nature of the debate between Dworkin and legal positivism can be found in the online and free essay 'The nature of law' (2007) by Andrei Marmor in the *Stanford Encyclopedia of Philosophy* (http://plato. stanford.edu/)

QUESTION 22

Discuss Professor Raz's contribution to legal theory.

Answer Plan

The contribution of Professor Raz to legal philosophy has been immense. Raz has restated and recast the traditional central legal positivistic position, that law is identified by 'social sources' only, by tying that thesis to the function of law as a type of social organisation which claims legitimate supreme authority within a territory. Raz has also defended legal positivism from the trenchant attacks of Professor Dworkin by emphasising the 'authoritative' nature of law. Raz has also stressed the importance of law to the realisation of the goal of personal autonomy for citizens through the creation of legally protected rights and interests. A skeleton plan is suggested.

- ❖ Introduction;
- ❖ the general influence of Raz on modern legal theory;
- ❖ the 'sources thesis' of Raz;
- ❖ the law's claim to authority;
- ❖ the law's role in supporting modern urban civilisation;
- ❖ the role of law in furthering and upholding the value of personal autonomy;
- ❖ conclusion, the law is not just a structure of authority but a vital support for personal freedom.

ANSWER

Professor Joseph Raz is perhaps the best known legal philosopher who generally supports the main ideas of the legal positivistic tradition. His best known work in legal philosophy is his collection of essays in *The Authority of Law* (1979) but Raz's legal philosophy includes *The Concept of a Legal System* (1970), *Practical Reason and Norms* (1975) and essays in *Ethics in the Public Domain* (1994). Raz has also written widely on moral, political and ethical philosophy, including *The Morality of Freedom* (1986) and *Practice of Value* (2003).

In an article in *The Oxford Journal of Legal Studies* (2005) Leslie Green writes, in 'Three themes from Raz', that the widespread interest in jurisprudence is testament to the great influence of Raz and that, to find another legal philosopher who has not only produced an indispensable body of work but who has influenced so many legal scholars, one has to go back to Professor Hart.

It is not possible in the space provided to do full justice to the richness of Raz's legal theory, but a few important 'Razian' themes will be highlighted.

Raz defends the central tenet of legal positivism that the law of a community is identified by reference to social sources alone – the 'sources thesis', as Raz terms it. The basic argument of Raz is that law, by its nature, claims to be a legitimate practical authority for its citizens. However, to be an authority, Raz claims, legal rules must be able to guide citizens without any evaluation needing to be taken concerning the moral reasons that the law claims to replace. Therefore, Raz concludes, the content of law must be ascertainable without resort to moral argument. The 'service conception' of authority, in which the law aims to make citizens better comply with right reason, is used to justify a hard line legal positivism in that Raz argues that it is not in the nature of law to contain moral tests for the content and validity of legal rules. A theory of law such as Professor Dworkin's (see *Law's Empire* (1986)), which makes moral judgments part of the grounds of law, undercuts and undermines the inherent claim to authority that law makes for itself.

Raz claims in *The Authority of Law* (1979) that a normative system is a 'legal system' only if it claims to be authoritative and to occupy a position of supremacy within society – in that the law claims the right to legitimise or outlaw all other social institutions. For Raz, the law is a system of guidance and adjudication claiming supreme authority within a certain society. This 'definition of law' represents an evolution in the legal positivistic tradition from the 'law as commands' view of Austin and Bentham, and the later Hartian view of 'law as a union of primary and secondary rules' (see *The Concept of Law* (1961)).

Indeed, 'the authority' of law is a key feature for Raz for whom the law's claim to authority is a significant and distinctive feature of the law's method of social organisation. Therefore, following Raz's analysis, the legal positivist thesis that the law is identified solely by reference to social sources is a necessary and inevitable consequence derived from the very nature of law itself, especially the law's institutionalised, conduct-guiding, authoritative character.

The basic underlying function of the law, for Raz, is to provide publicly ascertainable standards by which members of the society are held to be bound and by which legal standards cannot be made non-binding by moral argument either by citizens or officials. The 'sources thesis' identifies the law as a kind of human institution which is of crucial importance to the regulation of social life.

When the 'source based' law runs out in a 'hard case', Raz, like earlier legal positivists such as Austin and Hart, believes that the judge has an inescapable law making function. For Raz, the law begins and ends with the 'sources' – beyond the 'sources' lies judicial discretion to make new law.

Raz not only believes that the law is the primary means by which political authority is expressed, but that without the intervention of the law personal autonomy as a moral ideal would be very difficult to realise for the majority of citizens. As Raz has written (in a 2003 article 'Between authority and morality: first Storrs lecture') law and legal institutions have made possible the whole urban civilisation as we know it over the last century or two. Personal autonomy is the capacity to make significant 'life choices' for oneself. As Raz writes (in an article 'Autonomy, toleration, and the harm principle' (1987)) the ruling idea of personal autonomy is that persons should make their own lives. The autonomous person is a part author of his own life. The ideal of personal autonomy is the vision of persons controlling, in some degree, their own destiny, fashioning it through successive decisions throughout their lives. To be autonomous, a person must not only be given a choice but he must be given an adequate range of options. The autonomous person is the one who makes his own life. The law's role in fostering and protecting personal autonomy is vital for Raz. Part of the function of legal rights not to be enslaved, falsely imprisoned or assaulted is that the law forms a protective bastion enabling an individual to achieve his own ends in a life he shapes himself. However, not only does the law bestow protective 'negative' rights on persons, it also bestows 'positive' legal rights which allow the autonomous life to be lived by offering legally protected choices to marry, travel or make contracts, for example. For Raz, the goal of personal autonomy is partly dependent on an adequate range of choice and the law protects that range of choice by offering protected 'rights' to X as well as rights to be protected from various harms.

Raz wrote, in an important article in *Ratio Juris* (1992) 'Rights and individual well-being', that the law protects freedom of religion, freedom of speech, freedom of association, of occupation, of movement, of marriage not because it is important that persons should practice religion, get married or travel, but because it is important that persons should decide for themselves whether to do so or not. Through the legally protected rights, such as a right to marry or a right to travel or worship religion, the individual can fashion his own life, be the part author of his own life.

In summary, although Raz has a distinctive conception of the law as a structure of authority and as Raz notes authority involves essentially the power to require action, the law has a more benign face than merely telling people what to do. The law has, for Raz, a crucial role in securing, through protected and protective legal rights, the moral ideal of personal autonomy.

NOTES

A good starting point for an overview of the juristic thought of Raz is Leslie Green's article 'Three themes from Raz' in *The Oxford Journal of Legal Studies* (2005). The essay by Raz, 'The claims of law' in *The Authority of Law* (1979), should be consulted for the idea of the law's claim to authority. Many of Raz's recent essays can be found on his own personal website by going to http://josephnraz. googlepages.com/home. His 2003 article 'Between authority and morality: first Storrs lecture' is particularly useful on the role of law in supporting urban civilisation. The link between law and personal freedom is explored in Raz's book *The Morality of Freedom* (1986).

QUESTION 23 --

Has the law any intrinsic value beyond its great instrumental benefit to society?

Answer Plan

This question concerns the issue as to whether the institution of law has any value in itself, independent of any instrumental benefit law may have to society. Traditional legal theory has usually tended to view law in purely instrumental terms, seeing law as the instrument of the state to achieve civil peace (Hobbes in *Leviathan* (1651)) or as co-ordinating society for the common good (Finnis in *Natural Law and Natural Rights* (1980)) to give two prominent examples of law's instrumentality. The famous Austrian jurist Hans Kelsen, in *Introduction to the Problems of Legal Theory* (1934) positively asserted that law had no value in itself beyond the goals that law could achieve for society. Kelsen said:

> The law is a coercive apparatus having in and of itself no political or ethical value, a coercive apparatus whose value depends, rather, on ends that transcend the law qua means.

However a number of legal theorists, most notably Professor Raz, have asserted that law can be a focus for the identification of a person with his society. Since the law is the political voice of a community then the law can be a means by which a person self-identifies with his own society through an attitude of 'respect for the law'. Kelsen's extreme view is therefore in need of modification. Law has a dual aspect: instrumentally important to achieve societal goals but also potentially intrinsically important as a focus for the self-identification of citizens with their society.

A skeleton plan is suggested.

* Introduction;
* Kelsen's view that law is of purely instrumental value only and has no intrinsic worth;
* the major trend in legal philosophy to view law in instrumental terms to the neglect of law's intrinsic worth: see Hobbes's *Leviathan* (1651) Hart's *The Concept of Law* (1961) and Finnis's *Natural Law and Natural Rights* (1980);
* Professor Raz's view that law can have intrinsic value in itself as a focus for the self-identification of citizens with their society: law as the authoritative voice of a political community;
* conclusion, Kelsen's extreme view is in need of modification.

ANSWER

The great Austrian jurist, Hans Kelsen (d 1973) was firmly of the view that law was only of purely instrumental value to a society. Kelsen wrote on this matter in *Introduction to the Problems of Legal Theory*:

> the law is a coercive apparatus having in and of itself no political or ethical value, a coercive apparatus whose value depends rather on ends that transcend the law qua means.

Kelsen, to bring the point home, commented further:

> Law is a means, a specific social means, not an end' and also that the law is 'a specific social means, not an end.

This instrumentalist approach to law's authority in society, propagated by Kelsen, has dominated jurisprudence – the idea that law is there to achieve mighty social goals, but has no intrinsic worth itself – like a piece of cheap cutlery such as a fork which can be put to the great end of eating food but has no real value in itself. Bentham elevated legislation above the common law because of legislation's superior ability to co-ordinate society, so as to maximise utility. Professor Hart in *The Concept of Law* (1961) regarded the emergence of law to a pre-legal society as bringing instrumental benefits of certainty, efficiency and adaptability in terms of legal rules of that society. Thomas Hobbes in *Leviathan* (1651) regarded the law of the sovereign power as a mighty instrument for achieving the supreme goal of civil peace over the anarchic 'state of nature' without law. Professor Raz has written extensively on how the authority of law brings instrumental benefits to society and individuals through the guidance of reason and expertise as expressed by policy-makers through law.

However it is clear that the instrumentalist conception of authority is not the whole picture. It is possible to view the law as a public order of rules loyalty to which by citizens can be seen as a valuable way of showing commitment to a particular political community whose law the citizen loyally obeys. As Raz comments in *Between Authority and Interpretation* (2009): the law 'is the authoritative voice of a particular community'. As Raz further explains:

> the law and its institutions are among the central constituents of a community: a political community . . . in being partly constitutive of a community which is normally a focus of identification, the law can be intrinsically valuable.

It is important to be clear what Raz is saying here. Raz is not denying that many persons in Western societies actually feel a sense of profound alienation from their own society and legal system and who therefore feel unable to identify with the law of their society. Raz also insists that the sense of identification or respect for their own legal system or law that is valuable for some citizens is not a morally obligatory position to take, even in a liberal democracy. The issue is one of choice:

> I can choose to identify with my own society by identifying with the legal system of that society. This is entirely optional but such a choice has value for me if I choose to identify with the law. However the anarchist who despises all State law is entitled to his stance in the sense of not being required to identify with the law of his own society even if he must obey the law.

Raz comments in *Between Authority and Interpretation* (2009):

> identification with a community depends on our ability and willingness to accept the standards which these communities endorse as our own. . . . Given the importance of political communities in the life of their members, an ability to identify with one's political community is intrinsically valuable. Any account of the law which disregards that aspect of it is incomplete. To understand the nature of the law we have to understand its role as partly constitutive of a

political community and therefore as an object for identification, as playing an important role in people's sense of who they are.

The extent to which the law has intrinsic value depends crucially on the particular cultural and political mix in a particular society. In the United States the Supreme Court is venerated by many Americans, but ignored by many as well. The common law of England may in the past have held intrinsic value for some English persons. Raz writes in *Ethics in the Public Domain* (1994) that Professor Hart disliked **'the excessive veneration in which the law is held in common law countries'**.

The discussion has shown that the original view expressed by Kelsen – that the law has instrumental value – only has to be modified in the light of the observation that law can have a value inherent in itself beyond any instrumental value the law undoubtedly possesses. This inherent value of law is found in those societies where some citizens voluntarily adopt an attitude of 'respect for law' out of a sense of self-identification with their society, of which the law is the authoritative product of the political institutions of that society. To that extent the law can have an 'inherent' value.

NOTES

Hans Kelsen's view that law was purely of instrumental value – 'a coercive apparatus', can be found in his *Introduction to the Problems of Legal Theory* (1934) at p 31. Professor Raz's view that law can have intrinsic as well as instrumental value can be found in his *Between Authority and Interpretation* (2009) at pp 102–106.

Authority

8

INTRODUCTION

The related but distinct questions concerning the justification of state authority and the moral obligation to obey the law are crucial and enduring questions of political philosophy and legal theory. The question as to how the authority of the state is to be justified has drawn the attention of philosophers of the stature of Hobbes (1588–1679) and Locke (1632–1704), and the question continues to be debated between 'philosophical anarchists' and defenders of the possibility of legitimate state authority such as Professor Raz. The question of the moral obligation to obey the law first taxed Socrates (470–399 BC) (as reported in Plato's *Crito*), as he debated whether to flee the judgment of death that the state had passed on him. The question of the moral obligation to obey the law has occupied virtually every leading legal philosopher from Finnis and Raz to Dworkin and Greenawalt. The questions in the chapter consider how state authority is to be justified, if at all, and whether there is any general moral obligation to obey the law.

Checklist ✔

Ensure that you are acquainted with the following topics:

- the 'social contract' theories of state authority propounded by Hobbes and Locke;
- the challenge to state authority presented by 'philosophical anarchism';
- the 'normal justification thesis' for legitimate state authority given by Professor Raz;
- the attempt to ground a moral obligation to obey the law variously on 'consent', 'gratitude', 'fair play' and 'associative obligations';
- the special moral obligation to obey the law of public office holders;
- the denial of a general moral obligation to obey the law by Raz.

QUESTION 24

Critically examine how the authority of the state is to be justified.

Answer Plan

Professor Raz (in the essay 'Legitimate authority', collected in *The Authority of Law* (1979)) commented that there is little surprise that the notion of authority is one of the most controversial concepts in legal and political philosophy, since the concept of authority has a central role in any discussion of legitimate forms of social organisation. The attempt to justify political authority starts with the end of Bible based arguments for political authority in the mid-seventeenth century. Both Hobbes (1588–1679) and Locke (1632–1704) attempted to justify political authority through the emergence of authority from an anarchic 'state of nature'. In modern times, the whole notion of political authority has come under severest attack from the school of thought known as 'philosophical anarchism'. The 'normal justification thesis' for justifying political authority given by Professor Raz can be viewed as the most persuasive rebuttal of the challenge posed by philosophical anarchism to the possibility of legitimate political authority. A skeleton argument is given.

- ❖ Introduction;
- ❖ the 'Divine right' of Kings;
- ❖ 'social contract' theories of Hobbes and Locke;
- ❖ the challenge of philosophical anarchism to the legitimacy of the authority of the state;
- ❖ the definition of a state given by Nozick;
- ❖ the 'service conception of authority' given by Raz;
- ❖ conclusion, the 'normal justification thesis' of Raz is the most persuasive defence of legitimate authority.

ANSWER

In *The Authority of the State* (1988) Leslie Green comments that all modern states claim authority over their citizens and that the state's authority claims to be supreme. Indeed, as a form of social order, the state is distinctive in claiming supreme and wide authority over the lives of citizens. Widespread belief in the legitimacy of state authority can itself strengthen the stability of the state in question. For these interrelated reasons it is a crucial question in jurisprudence and in political philosophy to determine when a belief in the authority of a state is justified, and if such justification is possible at all.

The connection of this question with the subject of jurisprudence is not difficult to understand. The authority of the modern state is typically expressed through the laws and legal directives of those in authority. The study of the authority of the state is crucially linked to how that authority is usually expressed, namely, through law. As Raz comments in *The Morality of Freedom* (1986), the normal exercise of political authority is by the making of laws and legally binding orders. As Raz notes in his essay, 'The claims of law' (in *The Authority of Law* (1979)): 'The notion of authority is inextricably tied up with that of law ... for it is an essential feature of law that it claims legitimate authority.' Therefore, the concept of authority plays a crucial part in our understanding of the concept of law.

The attempt to justify political authority is an ancient one and can be traced back to Plato's (428–347 BC) philosophical work, *Crito*, when Socrates debates whether to flee Athens or face execution. However, the usual starting point for discussion of the legitimacy of the authority of the state is the once powerful doctrine that political authority had been ordained by God and was, for that reason, legitimate. Christian doctrine held that rulers existed as a result of Divine will, the key text being St Paul's Epistle to the Romans (Chapter 13, verses 1–2): 'For there is no authority except from God, and those that exist have been instituted by God. Therefore he who resists the authorities resists what God has appointed.' This Christian doctrine justified the 'Divine right' of Kings in an era when the Bible was paramount. Therefore, James I (1566–1625) of England and Scotland, in his 1598–1599 work *Basilikon Doron*, wrote for his son that 'God made you a little God to sitte on his throne, and rule over other men'. This doctrine of the 'Divine right' of Kings also justified another observation of James I that he could not be subject to the law since it was his law. However, the English Civil War (1642–1651), culminating in the execution of Charles I in 1649, effectively ended the power of the 'Divine right' of Kings as a justification of political authority. Indeed, the Bible itself was used to justify the execution of Charles I since he was 'a man of blood', a Biblical concept; this was used to undermine his Divinity and justify his execution.

Thomas Hobbes, who had lived through the English civil war and revolution, wrote his secular justification for political authority, called *Leviathan*, in 1651. As the leading historian of the seventeenth century, Christopher Hill, commented in *The World Turned Upside Down* (1972), anyone in 1651 who was convinced by the arguments in Hobbes's *Leviathan* would no longer find it possible to look to the Bible alone for answers to political problems. The work of Hobbes in *Leviathan* can be seen as a decisive break with the past as it sought to justify political authority in secular terms. Hobbes, having lived through the political disintegration of the English civil war period, asked the reader in *Leviathan* to imagine society in a 'state of nature', a condition of society without government; as Hobbes comments, the state of nature is 'the time men live without a common Power to keep them all in awe'. In this 'state of nature' there is a continual fear and danger of violent death as man fights against man and human life is 'solitary, poor, nasty, brutish and short'. As Hobbes comments: 'All men in the state of nature have a desire and will to hurt, they are in that condition which is called War.'

Hobbes characterises the natural condition of humankind as a mutually unprofitable state of war of every person against every other person and, since Hobbesian persons value self-preservation above all else, there will emerge the beginnings of political power as each person submits to some mutually recognised public authority who will protect person and property. However, this central authority must have absolute power, according to Hobbes, in order to prevent society from falling back into the anarchic 'state of nature'. So the way out of the desperate 'state of nature' is for men to make a 'social contract' and establish a very strong state to keep peace and order. Hobbes can be criticised for exaggerating the horrors of the 'state of nature', for having an 'obsession' with the risks of violent death in the 'state of nature' and for proposing absolute authority as the only alternative to the horrors of the 'state of nature'. Indeed, Hobbes can be criticised for replacing the horrors of the 'state of nature' with the horrors of absolute authority in the hands of one ruler. However, despite these criticisms, the writings of Hobbes mark a decisive shift away from justifying political authority on the basis of the Bible to some sort of secular 'social contract'. Hobbes, often in his own era described as an atheist, did, however, share the prevailing 'Calvinistic' religious view that the depravity of man in his 'natural state' necessitated an authoritarian state. (The Calvinistic view was that 'original sin' had depraved and distorted human nature and that only the few 'elect' of God would be saved – from the teachings of John Calvin (1509–1564).) The evil majority must be controlled, kept in subordination, or anarchy would result, said both the secular Hobbes and religious men like Oliver Cromwell (1599–1658).

John Locke (1632–1704) followed Hobbes in postulating a 'state of nature' followed by a 'social contract' to establish political authority but, unlike Hobbes, Locke accepted legal limits on government and accepted that those in authority could be removed if their actions threatened the property of men. Locke argued, in contrast with Hobbes, that the executive may forfeit its rights if it endangers the stability of property. Hobbes thought that any revolution against the authority of the sovereign must dissolve society into anarchy. Locke held that society could continue to exist even if the men of property found it necessary to change the sovereign, as they did in 1688. In the *Second Treatise of Civil Government* (1690), Locke comments that legitimate civil government is instituted by the explicit consent of those governed. What counts as legitimate consent is a matter of dispute amongst political philosophers but the important point is that, despite Locke's own religious Christian faith, his theory of political authority is a further development of the 'social contract' theory of authority away from explicit reliance on the Bible as the source of political authority. As

Christopher Hill comments, in *The English Bible and the Seventeenth Century Revolution* (1993), the political revolution starting with the execution of Charles I shattered the universal acceptance of the Bible as an infallible text the pronouncements of which were to be followed implicitly. As Karl Marx commented, 'when the bourgeois transformation had been accomplished, Locke supplanted Habbukuk (of the Old Testament)' (from *Selected Works of Marx and Engels* (1935)).

The question of the justification of political authority has continued to be fiercely debated in the modern era. Indeed, the great attempt to justify a 'minimal State' by Robert Nozick in *Anarchy, State and Utopia* (1974) uses the old device used by Hobbes and Locke of the 'state of nature' to show how a legitimate state might evolve without infringing individual rights. Although Nozick's explanation of the kind of state that emerges from 'the state of nature' differs radically from the view of the state propounded by both Hobbes and Locke, the basic methodology is the same – namely, to see what defects in the 'state of nature' the emergence of a state might cure. As Nozick observes, 'state of nature' explanations of the emergence of states have punch and illumination in political philosophy. Nozick also gives us a useful definition of what a state is when he comments, in *Anarchy, State and Utopia*, that a state claims a monopoly on deciding who may use force when it says that only the state may decide who may use force and under what conditions: the state reserves to itself the sole right to pass on the legitimacy and permissibility of any use of force within its boundaries; furthermore the state claims the right to punish all those who violate its claimed monopoly of force. It should be noted that the law's claim to a monopoly on the use of force, which has been recognised as the defining mark of a state by political philosophers from Max Weber (1864–1920) to Robert Nozick (1938–2002), is part of the definition of a state but does not justify the authority of the state. Force secures authority and enables it to be effective but force does not justify authority. The mere fact of possession of effective force in a territory may have justified authority for Thomas Hobbes in *Leviathan* (1651) but few philosophers have followed Hobbes in so holding. The horrors of the English civil war so conditioned Hobbes that he equated the fact of authority with the justification of authority. However there is something of a proper justification for State authority in the 'Leviathan' of Hobbes beyond the mere assertion that effective authority exists so therefore it is legitimate. For Hobbes authority, 'The Leviathan', was only legitimate if the state authority honoured the 'pact of protection' guaranteed to all citizens by the all mighty State in return or exchange for citizens giving complete obedience to the State. Hobbes accepted the old Latin proverb 'homo homini lupus' – 'man is a wolf to man' (a summation of man's inhumanity to man) and the State by offering protection of all against all justified its awesome possession of absolute power. The question is: does the mere fact that the State guarantees security of citizen's property and persons in itself justify the depositing of complete power in the hands of that monster-State?

The greatest challenge to the attempt to justify political authority has come from the tradition of political thought known as 'philosophical anarchism'. As Robert Nozick observes, the fundamental question of political philosophy, one that precedes questions about how the state should be organised, is whether there should be any state at all and that, if valid, anarchist theory undercuts the whole subject of political philosophy. The *locus classicus* of the philosophical anarchist tradition is to be found in the work of Robert Paul Woolf in his *In Defense of Anarchism* (1970). Following Kant (1724–1804), Woolf argues that persons are endowed with reason and free will and, as such, persons have a duty to themselves to be autonomous. It is therefore the primary moral duty of each person to form his own judgment on matters concerning himself. However, as Woolf observes, to recognise the authority of another is to surrender one's own judgment to his and, as a result, if the person submits to the state and accepts its claim to authority then he loses his autonomy. The rational and autonomous person does not ignore the state's commands, says the philosophical anarchist; he will treat them as requests or advice, but not as binding orders. As Robert Woolf comments, for the truly autonomous man there is no such thing, strictly speaking, as a command and as long as we recognise our responsibility for our actions, and acknowledge the power of reason within us, we must acknowledge the continuing obligation to be the authors of the commands we choose to obey. For Woolf, the philosophical anarchist, the defining mark of the state is authority, the right to rule. The primary obligation of man is autonomy, the refusal to be ruled. There is, for Woolf, no resolution of the conflict between the autonomy of the individual and the authority of the state and that, in so far as a person fulfils his obligation to make himself the author of his decisions, he will resist the state's claim to have authority over him. Woolf concludes that the concept of a legitimate state is empty and that philosophical anarchism is the only reasonable practical position for an enlightened man.

This challenge of philosophical anarchism to the legitimacy of the state is a serious challenge for it denies the possibility of any justification of state authority, whether that justification is 'social contract' or otherwise. Recognition of authority does involve in some way a 'surrender of judgment' by the citizen and the whole concept of authority is a social relation of domination and subordination between a superior and a subject. Perhaps the philosophical anarchists, such as Robert Paul Woolf, have a point that there is something inherently troubling about the notion of authority. The question is, does this troubling intuition make all political authority illegitimate? Professor Raz, in *Ethics in the Public Domain* (1994), makes the following claim about legitimate governments: that they claim the right to rule us by right reason, that is to take over from us the task of deciding what we should do on certain matters. Does it follow that the philosophical anarchist is right and that there cannot be legitimate government over autonomous people? Raz, in defending the notion of legitimate authority, denies against Woolf that autonomy means never handing over to anyone the right to decide for a person on any matter. Raz comments that a person does not abandon his autonomy when he authorises an agent to represent him in a sale or in some complex commercial negotiations. A person, says Raz, does not abandon his autonomy when joining a trade union which has power to reach binding agreements concerning one's wages and conditions of employment. A person, argues Raz, does not surrender his autonomy by appointing an attorney to conduct a lawsuit on his behalf. Raz, drawing an analogy with the legitimate state, says that these are just a few of the innumerable occasions on which people find it reasonable to give up their right to decide for themselves on certain matters. Raz concludes that the philosophical anarchist attack on the notion of authority is a misconception. As Raz comments, one way of wisely exercising one's autonomy is to realise that, in certain matters, one would do best to abide by the authority of another.

As long as government leaves significant areas of personal choice to the decision of the individual citizen, then over matters such as taxation and health and safety policy the state can exercise legitimate authority based on its superior expertise and ability to co-ordinate human action. Indeed, the argument for legitimate authority is bolstered by the observation that a functioning liberal state is needed for the realisation of personal autonomy, as Raz notes in *The Morality of Freedom* (1986). The law protects and promotes personal autonomy by protecting and promoting certain fundamental rights, such as the right to marry, the right to travel and the right make contracts, as well as protecting personal autonomy through laws against violence and false imprisonment.

It is true that it is possible to have an over-reliance on authority and when this happens a person does, to some extent, forfeit his own humanity. This 'dehumanising' effect of authority concerned the 'father' of philosophical anarchism, William Godwin (1756–1836), who argued 'where I make the voluntary surrender of my judgment . . . I annihilate my individuality as a man' (*An Enquiry Concerning Political Justice* (1793)). However, as Scott Shapiro comments, while the dangers of reliance on authority are real it is important not to exaggerate them. The world is simply too complex for anyone to live a life in Western society completely unaided by experts who typically advise governmental authority (see 'Authority' in *The Oxford Handbook of Jurisprudence and Philosophy of Law*, edited by Coleman and Shapiro (2002)).

The most persuasive justifications of modern political authority point to the ability of authorities to co-ordinate human activity for the common good and on the superior expertise of those authorities in such areas as economic policy, health and safety policy, defence policy, foreign relations with other states, etc. There are many problems of great importance to the orderly conduct of any society of complexity. There will be a range of possible solutions to those problems. There is a need for authority to designate the chosen options – there is a need for decision. Professor Finnis has argued, in *Natural Law and Natural Rights* (1980), that the ultimate basis of a ruler's authority is that he has the responsibility of furthering the common good by stipulating solutions to the community's co-ordination problems. Raz, the legal positivist, agrees with Finnis, the natural lawyer, that the ability of government to co-ordinate action for the common good is a core justification for modern political authority (see Raz, *Practical Reason and Norms* (1975)).

Raz has developed perhaps the most persuasive justification for modern political authority, namely, the 'service conception'. The 'service conception' of authority reminds us that the function of authorities is to serve the governed. Raz argues that authority can be legitimate if by complying with the authority the subjects are better able to follow the moral reasons that otherwise apply to them. Raz calls the 'service conception' of authority the 'normal justification thesis' for authority in that it is not the only way to justify political authority but is the 'normal justification' of authority.

Raz gives two main ways in which a political authority can meet 'the service conception', the 'normal justification thesis'. In a collection of essays entitled *Authority*, edited by Raz (1990), Raz mentions two primary arguments in support of political authority: (1) the expertise of government and its policy-making advisers in such matters as consumer protection legislation, and (2) the ability of government to secure social co-ordination.

Both of these are aspects of the 'service conception' of authority in that the authority, by relying on its expertise in certain areas and its ability to co-ordinate human activity, can enable citizens to better conform to the requirements of morality, such as the duty to help those in need, than if the citizens were to decide for themselves.

Raz comments that the expertise of government is most clearly seen in consumer protection legislation, the regulation of the pharmaceutical industry, laws to secure safety at work or on the roads. The ability of government to co-ordinate is most evident in the provision of public goods (clean air and water, for example). Both factors, superior expertise and an ability for co-ordination, are present, says Raz, in most cases of justified governmental action. This is fundamentally an instrumental approach to justifying authority. There is no appeal here to any 'social contract', real or imagined, that appealed to Hobbes and Locke in the seventeenth century; the basis of legitimate authority is in getting citizens to better conform to right reason. The 'service conception' of authority propounded by Raz has intuitive appeal because it justifies authority only to the extent that it serves the governed. A lot of the feelings of misgiving and unease, which philosophical anarchists trade on, about authority disappear when legitimate authority is understood from the viewpoint of Raz – that legitimate authority is there to help citizens do the right thing in reason. Raz's 'service conception' of authority helps to meet the challenge of philosophical anarchism to the legitimacy of any state. The philosophical anarchist uses the powerful intuition that submission to political authority constitutes a breach of a person's personal autonomy. After all, authority involves essentially the power by the authority to require action on the part of the subject. However, if submission to authority is not global but leaves significant choice in the hands of the citizen, and if submission to authority is only justified by the idea that authority exists to serve the governed, then the philosophical anarchist challenge to authority is largely met.

Professor Raz, in a 2005 lecture, 'The Problem of authority: revisiting the service conception', returned to the topic of the justification of authority and its relation to autonomy. Raz gives the example of decisions about the safety of pharmaceutical products, which are not the sort of decisions which people should make for themselves rather than follow authority which has superior expertise on the matter. However, Raz admits there are many decisions in life – such as who to marry, where to live, whether to do this job or that job – where it is better to decide for oneself unaided by authority. Raz concludes by saying that the primary point of authority is to improve conformity with reason. The normal understanding of authority is that it does involve a hierarchical relationship involving an imposition on the subject. The unease which these facts of authority can induce in us are somewhat dissipated by the Razian 'service conception' of authority which explains how authority can be legitimate if it serves the public good.

Aim Higher ★

Students can gain extra marks by pointing out that Hobbes is the true father of modern political philosophy with his *Leviathan* in 1651. Hobbes was rational and secularist in his approach not using any argument from the Bible to justify his political conclusions but basing his arguments on rationally observed principles. Students can avoid the pitfall of thinking that 'anarchism' is merely a violent political movement without realising the existence of 'philosophical anarchism' which is non-violent but teaches that a rejection of the state is the only position for a reasonable enlightened person. Students to gain extra marks will note the truth of Weber's statement that authority strives for acceptance not submission.

NOTES

The political thought of both Hobbes and Locke is captured in essays in the online and free *Stanford Encyclopedia of Philosophy* (http://plato.stanford.edu/): 'John Locke' is covered by William Uzgalis; 'Locke's political philosophy' is examined by Alex Tuckness; 'Hobbes's moral and political philosophy' is examined by Sharon A Lloyd and Susanne Sreedhar.

The general concept of 'Authority' in the *Stanford Encyclopedia* is examined by Tom Christiano.

The general philosophy of Hobbes can be further explored in a collection of essays: 'Perspectives on Thomas Hobbes' (1988, reprinted 2002) edited by Rogers and Ryan. The general topic of 'Authority' is examined by Leslie Green in his book, *The Authority of the State* (1988), as well as in the collection of essays edited by Professor Raz called *Authority: Readings in social and political authority* (1990); the introduction in that volume by Professor Raz is particularly valuable. An account and explanation of 'the normal justification thesis' for legitimate authority is given by Raz in the early chapters of *The Morality of Freedom* (1986).

QUESTION 25

Examine how the question of the moral obligation to obey the law has been treated by philosophers.

Answer Plan

The issue of the obligation to obey the law has attracted much philosophical thought from the time of Socrates (470–399 BC) (see *Crito* by Plato) to the present day. There have been many candidates put forward to justify such a general moral obligation based on the 'consent' of the governed, the 'gratitude' of the governed to the state, duties based on 'fair play' and the need to 'support just institutions', to give the major examples. However, all of the attempts to justify a general moral obligation have been found to be defective and the better view probably resides with Professor Raz who denies any general moral obligation to obey the law but argues that the moral obligation to obey the law varies from person to person. A skeleton answer is sketched.

- ❖ Introduction;
- ❖ a denial of a general moral obligation to obey the law;
- ❖ reasons for that position (Raz);
- ❖ the special moral obligations of holders of public office such as police officers;
- ❖ moral obligation to obey the law based on 'respect for law';
- ❖ 'consent' theories such as Locke's;
- ❖ arguments from 'gratitude' and 'fair play;
- ❖ arguments for moral obligation based on communitarian or 'associative' obligations (Dworkin);
- ❖ conclusion, the failure of all theories for a general moral obligation suggests there is no such general moral obligation to obey the law.

ANSWER

It may at first sight appear obvious that there is an obligation to obey the law in a liberal democratic state. As Klosko comments, the feeling that we have a moral obligation to obey the law is one of our deepest intuitions (quoted in 'Law and obligations' by Leslie Green in *The Oxford Handbook of Jurisprudence and Philosophy of Law*, edited by Coleman and Shapiro (2002)).

However, the surprising consensus of opinion among legal philosophers today is that citizens do not have a general moral obligation to obey the law and such obligation as exists varies from person to person.

Professor Raz, the leading proponent of the view denying a general moral obligation to obey the law, comments that there are risks, moral and other, in uncritical acceptance of authority (*The Authority of Law* (1979)). Raz argues that often persons do have a moral obligation to obey individual laws based on concern for others, trying to avoid setting a bad example and the need for social co-ordination, but Raz denies any unthinking general moral obedience to any legal system, no matter how virtuous. Whilst defending the idea of legitimate authority from the philosophical anarchists, Raz comments that the question of moral obedience to a legal system is a different question and he seems to take on board the insight of philosophical anarchism (see Robert Paul Woolf's *In Defense of Anarchism* (1970)) concerning a person's moral independence from the legal system under which he exists. Raz argues that the extent of the moral duty to obey the law in a relatively just state varies from person to person. There is, says Raz, a common core of cases regarding which the moral obligation exists and applies equally to all. Some duties based on the co-ordinative argument (for example, the moral duty to pay lawful taxation), and on the avoiding of setting a 'bad example' (for example, avoiding political terrorism) are likely to apply equally to all citizens. Beyond this core, says Raz the extent of the moral obligation to obey the law will vary greatly among persons. The Prime Minister's moral obligation to obey the law will be much stronger, due to his high office, than the average citizen. For example, as Kent Greenawalt comments, persons who have taken an oath to obey the law are under a much stronger moral obligation to obey the law than the average citizen. Persons such as police officers, judges, magistrates and government ministers of the state who voluntarily assume positions of official responsibility have promised to uphold the law and perform their duties in a lawful manner. As Greenawalt concludes, although most citizens make no promise – like undertaking to obey the law – some persons do engage to obey in a general way and such promises have moral force and constitute a substantial moral reason for obedience ('Promissory obligation', in *Authority*, edited by Raz (1990)).

It is necessary to understand Raz's argument denying a general moral obligation to obey all the laws of even a relatively just state on the following concern based on historical experience, in that too often in the past, the fallibility of human judgment has led to submission to authority from a misguided sense of duty where this was a morally reprehensible attitude (Raz, *The Authority of Law* (1979)).

Raz is a defender of the idea of legitimate authority against philosophical anarchists, but believes the question of moral obedience to law is a separate though related issue. Generally, persons should take the existence of a law from legitimate authority very seriously because those in authority usually have superior knowledge and expertise on matters requiring law than ourselves. However, the superior wisdom and expertise of those in legitimate authority cannot, according to Raz, justify a general moral obligation to obey the law. Raz goes on to identify one possible source of a general moral obligation to obey the law for some persons: this is the situation where an individual voluntarily accepts such an obligation as a way of identifying with his society. Raz comments that the government and the law are official organs of the community. If the government and law represent the community and express its will justly, then a natural indication of a member's sense of belonging is one's attitude toward the community's laws. Such an attitude Raz terms 'respect for law'. This is the belief that one is under a moral obligation to obey because the law is one's law, and the law of one's country. However, such a belief binds only those who choose to adopt such a 'respect for law', says Raz. There are many who do not feel this way about their country and the law of their country. Alienation from country and law is a sad and widespread fact of modern states. As Raz comments, in *The Morality of Freedom* (1986), those who consent to respect the laws of a state have a moral obligation to obey the laws of that state. But not everyone does have this attitude. Obligations undertaken through consent or respect are voluntary obligations; they bind only those who undertake them. It cannot ground a general moral obligation to obey the law. Those who do not voluntarily place themselves under the authority of relatively just governments are under only a partial and qualified obligation to obey the law. In particular, they have a moral obligation to obey the law where that is necessary for social co-ordination. However, as Raz concludes, a general moral obligation to obey the law is the result of a special relationship between an individual and his state; however, by no means everyone has this attitude towards their own state.

The modern view of most legal theorists is that there is no general moral obligation to obey the law but, for many years, the 'traditionalist' view was that there is a prima facie moral obligation to obey the law of a reasonably just state. A modern legal theorist who does argue for a general moral obligation to obey the law of a reasonably just state is Professor Finnis, the natural law author of *Natural Law and Natural Rights* (1980). Finnis argues from 'fairness' to a general moral obligation to obey the law. In a

1989 article, 'Law as co-ordination', Finnis argues that the law presents itself as a seamless web of rights and duties by forbidding its subjects to pick and choose; all the subjects of the law are put in like case and linked to each other by that network of protections and other benefits which the law secures for each by imposing restraints on all. Finnis argues that the point of law is not merely to ensure the survival of government; part of the point of law is to maintain real fairness between the members of a community. This is why there might be a general moral obligation to obey the law because of the fairness we owe to others in the community governed by law. We benefit as individuals from others obeying the law; therefore, we owe our fellow citizens in the community a general moral obligation to obey the law. Insightfully, Professor Finnis locates the moral obligation to obey the law not to the rulers of society but to our fellow citizens – the law is a web of fairness. However, Finnis also believes that not endorsing a general moral obligation to obey the law will undermine the effectiveness of law as well. In his 1998 book, *Aquinas*, Finnis writes that picking and choosing among the law's requirements will inevitably undermine the law's protection of rights and interests. However, this argument for a general moral obligation to obey the law from the consequences to the effectiveness of the legal system of disobedience must face the fact that most legal systems function in the light of many acts of disobedience. Many unlawful acts such as trespass, breach of contract and breach of copyright do not threaten the effectiveness of a robust legal system.

The traditional argument for a general moral obligation to obey the law has been based on 'consent' or 'social contract'. For most of the history of liberal democracies the dominant theory about why citizens are morally obligated to obey the law has been social contract. The citizen has an obligation to obey the law because he has in some way 'consented' to the authority of government. The history of 'social contract' theories of obligation to obey really start with John Locke's account of social contract which makes a citizen's relationship to the state like that of a promisor: the citizen has made something like a promise to obey the law. Locke (1632–1704) based the citizen's obligation to obey the law on an implied consent to authority. This 'implied consent' for Locke is stated (in *The Second Treatise on Civil Government* (1690)) to arise when any citizen remains within the country: the 'very being of anyone within the territories' of a government amounts to tacit or implied consent. This is obviously a very weak argument in favour of a moral obligation to obey the law – that the citizen fails to emigrate to build a new life from scratch under a foreign flag. Indeed, the philosopher David Hume (1711–1776) commented on Locke's theory of obligation to the state that a poor peasant or artisan has no free choice at all to leave his country. Remaining in a country cannot be taken to render tacit agreement to obey the laws. Citizens remain in a country because of family, career, friends and culture, among other reasons. No one can maintain with a straight face that a refusal to emigrate constitutes tacit consent to the laws of that country. Indeed, the citizen under Locke's theory has no real choice at all since if he leaves one country he merely puts himself under the sovereignty of another country and so the problem arises again; 'consent to law or emigrate': perpetual emigration is the only solution to the dilemma posed by Locke's theory. There are more promising avenues of exploration for 'tacit consent' than Locke's 'remaining in the territory' argument. Tacit consent to the laws of the realm could arise from (a) voting in elections, or (b) receipt of benefits from the state, such as housing, transport systems, pension, education, etc.

With regard to voting, an argument based on 'tacit consent' could be that the very act of voting implies a recognition of the legitimacy of the state and its laws and that, therefore, an implied promise to abide by the laws of that state could be developed from the act of voting – a participation in government. Such a theory for a general moral obligation to obey the law faces formidable objections. As a preliminary point, voting could not amount to any form of 'consent' in Australia, where voting is mandatory and required by law. A more universal objection is the reality that many millions of citizens do not vote whether due to inertia, objection to the political system, or whatever. Therefore, 'voting' cannot ground a general obligation to obey the law that would reach all citizens. Perhaps the killing objection to voting as a ground of moral obligation to obey the law is that the act of voting is not understood as involving any undertaking as to obedience to the law. Voting in an election is not like an oath of office; it is merely an act of political preference.

An argument for a general moral obligation to obey the law based on benefits received from the state is a more fertile line of argument than either 'residence' or 'voting' as a basis for 'tacit consent'.

The argument based on 'gratitude' for benefits received from government is not a recent one. It has an ancient lineage. Socrates (470–399 BC) mentions the gratitude he feels for the benefits he has received from the Athenian state when he explains why he will not disobey, by escaping, the ruling of the jury that sentenced him to death (Socrates' dilemma is recounted in Plato's *Crito*).

In a modern setting, the argument from gratitude for benefits received from government to a general moral obligation to obey the law can be stated as follows: although citizens differ greatly in the amount of benefits they receive from government, all liberal democratic governments do confer substantial benefits on all citizens, such as a transport system, police force, education, social services, clean water and other utilities. As a general principle of morality, when a person accepts benefits from another, that person therefore incurs a debt of gratitude towards his benefactor. If, for example, someone saves my life then only a moral idiot would say that I was under no debt of gratitude to that life saver. Therefore, the argument goes, showing obedience to the law is the best way of showing gratitude to the state for benefits received. But there are a number of objections to the argument from 'gratitude' for benefits received from government. In the ordinary course of life, if someone confers benefits on me without any consideration of whether I want them I have no obligation to be grateful towards my unsolicited benefactor. Robert Nozick, in his 1974 book *Anarchy, State and Utopia*, gives some striking examples to show that there is no obligation of gratitude for benefits received which are not solicited by the recipient. Nozick says if each day a different person on your street sweeps the entire street, must you do so when your time comes? Even if you don't care that much about a clean street? Nozick, in addition, imagines a brilliant lecture from a philosopher from the back of a sound truck in a suburban street. Nozick asks do all those who hear it – even all those who enjoy and profit by the brilliant lecture – owe the philosopher a lecture fee? Of course, they do not owe him a lecture fee, says Nozick. In the same way, the most important benefits of government – such as a transport system – are provided for citizens without the citizens ever asking for them.

A more fruitful argument to a moral obligation to obey the law is based on 'fairness'. Professor Finnis, we saw earlier, had a variation on this theme when he argued that the moral obligation to obey the law is owed to our fellow citizens in 'fairness'. This is the so-called argument from 'fair play' first explained by Professor Hart in an article entitled 'Are there any natural rights?' (*Philosophical Review* (1955)). Hart basically argues that a person who has accepted the benefits of a scheme of mutual co-operation is then bound by a duty of fair play to do his part and not to take advantage of the free benefits by not co-operating. This obligation of fair play seems to arise most clearly within small, tightly knit voluntary co-operative enterprises such as working men's clubs, sporting and religious organisations. Can the duty of fair play really be adequately extended to modern societies of millions of persons where they hardly know their neighbours?

The next argument for the general obligation to obey the law is the argument that there is a moral duty to support just institutions. The American philosopher, John Rawls, argued such a duty in his 1971 book, *A Theory of Justice*. Rawls argued that reasonable people recognise a natural moral duty to support reasonably fair and just institutions. Most liberal democratic states have reasonably fair and just legal orders; therefore, there is a general moral obligation to support those institutions by general moral obedience to the law in those societies. Raz accepts that the most common theme to liberal political theorising on authority is that the legitimacy of authority rests on the duty to support and uphold just institutions as, following Rawls, the duty is now usually called ('Authority and justification', in *Authority*, edited by Raz (1990)). Raz rejects the attempt to found a general moral obligation to obey the law on the moral duty to uphold reasonably just institutions. Raz comments (in *The Morality of Freedom* (1986)) that the duty to uphold reasonably just institutions may entail an obligation to obey certain of the more politically sensitive laws such as laws against the use of political violence. However, Raz says it is an exaggeration to suppose that every breach of the law threatens, by however small a degree, the survival of government or of law and order. Moreover, Raz argues, if we take seriously the duty to support reasonably just institutions, this will entail duties far above those of obedience to the law. Lawful strikes may threaten the fabric of a society much more than many unlawful acts. So a person wanting to support the institutions of government would abstain from lawful strikes, etc. Indeed, the duty to support reasonably just institutions would entail a duty to play a part in political participation in government.

The criticisms of Raz of the argument from a duty to support reasonably just institutions to the moral obligation to obey the law can be summarised in two propositions: (1) many breaches of the law – such as acts of trespass, breach of copyright – have no implications for the stability of government, and (2) the full implications of the moral duty to support reasonably just institutions could entail such onerous and oppressive duties as actual political participation to support the state.

The failure of many of the traditional arguments for the general moral obligation to obey the law has led some legal scholars in the last 20 years to try to base a moral obligation to obey the law upon the idea that 'membership' of an 'associative' ideal, such as 'society', grounds such an obligation. At the heart of the 'associative' approach is the idea that political obligation is a form of non-voluntary obligation similar to obligations owed to family members. Professor Dworkin, in *Law's Empire* (1986), has the most well known explanation of this theory. Dworkin argues that political association, like family and friendship, is in itself pregnant of obligation. Dworkin argues that a state which accepts 'integrity' (treating all citizens as equals under the rule of principle in law and legislation) thereby becomes a 'special' kind of community which justifies a moral obligation to obey the law of that 'society under the rule of law as integrity'. This view of Dworkin does fit with a common intuition of many persons who do think of themselves as members of political societies who have an obligation to obey their polities' laws. The true essence of 'associative obligation does not rest on any fictitious social contract or gratitude but on a feeling of "belonging"'.

Just as many persons feel a sense of belonging and obligation to family members they never chose to belong to, therefore, the argument goes, there is a moral obligation to obey the law of a fair society that a person never chose to be born into. There are problems, though, with trying to base a moral obligation to obey the law on the model of family obligations:

(a) Members of modern political societies lack the close relationships with each other that family members typically share. The family is a very small close-knit unit. A political society is massive in number, anonymous and alienating to many persons.

(b) Many families have a developed sense of paternalism and surveillance of its members which would be unacceptable in a modern liberal democratic state.

(c) A philosophical anarchist would argue that a person's sense of 'belonging' to his state is as a result of false consciousness and that no state is ever legitimate.

(d) Many persons feel a sense of 'belonging' to groups which challenge the authority of the state (for example, religions or radical political ideologies).

'Associative obligations' are often competing with each other and this is why, ultimately, any appeal to 'communitarianism' as a ground of moral obligation to obey the law must fail.

The history of attempts to justify a general moral obligation to obey the law is a history of ultimate failure and perhaps the cumulative failure of all the theories from Locke in the seventeenth century to modern day theories, such as Dworkin's 'associative' theory, suggests that there is no general moral obligation to obey the law and that any moral obligation varies from person to person in society.

George Klosko in *Political Obligations* (2005) has argued for a general moral obligation to obey the law based on citizens receipt of essential public goods from the state. Klosko writes:

> One of my governing assumptions is that the overwhelming majority of inhabitants of modern societies do not prefer to live in the woods or some remote outpost. (Persons want acceptable lives) and by "acceptable" lives I mean lives in modern industrial societies, as we know them. These societies are relatively safe, have functioning economies, and allow a wide range of occupations, activities and modes of life. "Acceptable" lives are led by persons who are integrated into such societies and take advantage of the amenities they provide.

Klosko goes on to write:

> the organised force of society, in the form of the State, able to be channeled in different directions is itself arguably indispensable to acceptable life. A number of public goods are required for acceptable lives and private or non-State provision of these goods will not work adequately therefore traditional States possessing both authority and a monopoly of force are necessary for acceptable

lives. To have a safe and secure environment, an economy that functions healthily, efficient transportation and communication and other "essential services" require a high degree of efficient coordination which Klosko argues only an organised modern democratic State can provide.

Klosko's conclusion is as follows:

Because we need public goods supplied by the State in order to lead acceptable lives, we all have obligations to support their production. Political obligations are based on the principle of fairness. Political obligations are rooted in receipt of essential public goods from the State.

Klosko's argument is essentially a variant on the argument from gratitude for benefits received from the state but with the emphasis that such benefits from the state are 'essential' to the living of 'acceptable lives' by citizens. A critique of such an argument might focus on the consumerist and materialistic driven vision of many of those 'acceptable' lives in modern Western societies. An even stronger critique would argue that modern Western democratic states far from producing 'acceptable' lives for their citizens actually produce morally corrupting and spiritually stultifying effects on their citizens: materially rich but spiritually empty wastelands. It is by no means as obvious as Klosko seems to imply that the 'essential' nature of modern Western states to the living of 'acceptable lives' by citizens actually produces a general moral obligation to support those Western industrial democracies.

NOTES

In the online free *Stanford Encyclopedia of Philosophy* (http://plato.stanford.edu/) there are a couple of useful essays on the issue of moral obligation to obey the law. 'Political obligation' is by Richard Dagger; 'Legal obligation and authority' is by Leslie Green. In *The Oxford Handbook of Philosophy and Law* (2002), edited by Coleman and Shapiro, there is an essay by Leslie Green called 'Law and obligations', which is a survey of the issues in this area. In the collection of essays, *Authority* (1990), edited by Professor Raz, there is an essay by Kent Greenawalt called 'Promissory obligation: the theme of social contract', which is particularly valuable. The best collection of various essays on this topic from writers as diverse as Robert Paul Woolf to Joseph Raz is to be found in: *The Duty to Obey the Law: Selected Philosophical Readings* (1999), edited by William A Edmunson.

American Realism

INTRODUCTION

The American Realist movement developed during the 1930s from the philosophical views associated with James and Dewey. Both rejected 'closed systems, pretended absolutes and origins' and turned towards 'facts, action and powers'. James insisted upon the study of 'factual reality'; Dewey called for an investigation of probabilities in law and reminded jurists that 'knowledge is successful practice'. The realists studied law on the basis of a rejection of 'myths and preconceived notions' and on the acceptance of recording accurately things as they are as contrasted with things as they ought to be. A true science of law demands a study of law in action. 'Law is as law does.' The two jurists noted in this chapter, who contributed to the foundations and growth of American Realism, are Holmes (1841–1935) and Cardozo (1870–1938).

Checklist ✔

Ensure that you are acquainted with the following topics:

- legal certainty;
- law as what the courts do;
- judicial hunches;
- law as rules laid down by the judge.

QUESTION 26

'You see how the vague circumference of the notion of duty shrinks and at the same time grows more precise when we wash it with cynical acid and expel everything except the object of our study, the operations of the law': Holmes.

In what ways does this observation characterise Holmes's view of the 'path of the law'?

Answer Plan

Holmes exerted very great influence as a jurist and a long-serving member of the Supreme Court. He inspired the American Realist movement with a jurisprudential theory based on the need to 'think things, not words'. The examination of facts must dominate legal investigation. The object of a study of the law is 'prediction' – that is, 'the prediction of the incidence of the public force through the instrumentality of the courts'. The study of the law's operations demands that the positive law be kept in focus and that it be investigated in a methodical, realistic fashion. The following skeleton plan is used:

- ❖ Introduction;
- ❖ Holmes's emphasis on objective investigation;
- ❖ importance of removing extraneous factors from an investigation;
- ❖ law as more than mere logic;
- ❖ operations of the courts;
- ❖ criticisms of Holmes's approach;
- ❖ conclusion, significance for Holmes of pragmatism.

ANSWER

More than a century has passed since Holmes (1841–1935) published *The Path of the Law* (1897), which assisted in the provision of a theoretical basis for American Realism. Holmes, whose long career included 30 years as a member of the Supreme Court (an experience which contributed to his declared views on the significance of the judiciary in the American legal process), stressed that the essence of the 'realist' contribution to jurisprudence was to be found in the careful *examination and verification of factual data*. Concepts incapable of verification (such as 'the vague notion of duty') had to be scrapped. The jurist should be guided by what a contemporary of Holmes referred to as 'the humility of the experimental scientist', who wastes no time in worrying about the absence of 'ultimates'. In Holmes's early writings, such as *The Path of the Law*, there is emphasis on the need to identify problems and to investigate them by keeping one's observations uncontaminated by irrelevancies. The application of 'cynical acid' should remove extraneous factors, allowing the true form and proportions of problems to emerge. By studying the real operations of law, one would discover the facts which constituted 'the law'.

This quasi-scientific approach involved a deliberate exclusion from the pattern of study of 'every word of moral significance'. (It is not surprising to note that Holmes rejected 'the muddled metaphysic of the concept of natural law'.) This was not to suggest that society's moral standards were of no consequence. They were, however, rarely significant for an analysis of *operational* matters. Indeed, Holmes suggested, it might be advantageous for the jurist if he were to use only words which could carry legal ideas uncoloured by matters outside the law.

Holmes illustrated the importance of 'dissolving' extraneous irrelevance, by reference to the notion of 'legal duty'. We have filled the word 'duty' with a content drawn from morality. But when we wash away from the phrase 'legal duty' its moral overtones, we are left with 'duty' viewed in terms of the *consequences* for those who break the law. It is what the law *does* (as seen in sanctions, for example) that gives 'duty' its real meaning and significance. The law of contract provides further examples of confusion engendered by the use of 'moral phraseology'. The concept of 'irrefragable undertakings', with its high-sounding overtones of moral purpose, should be washed away from any study of the principles of contract as known to the business community. Remove the irrelevancies and discover the realities of the contractual relationship: this is the guidance to be given to those who seek to discover the meaning of the law.

Holmes considers it necessary to expose as a fallacy, which has seriously affected investigation of the law, the notion that 'the only force at work in the development of the law is logic'. On the contrary, *the life of the law has been, not logic, but experience*. In a very broad sense, he argues, it may be true that the law is partly the result of some kind of logical development, but the danger is in confusion among jurists relating to the *logical format* of a judicial decision and the inarticulate, unconscious attitudes of judges as to the relative worth and significance of competing claims. The language of logic, which may be used to provide the 'wrappings' of a judicial decision, may mask 'the very root and nerve' of unconscious determinants of legal judgments. To understand the precise reasons behind a judgment requires, in Holmes's colourful language, the use of an 'acid' of an investigation which will 'eat away' expressive formalities and the confusion of logic with legal principle, exposing at the heart of the problem a shifting array of preferences and values – often unacknowledged.

In *The Common Law* (1923), Holmes repeats and elaborates his injunction to jurists to discount the part supposedly played by logical reasoning in the courts' processes of adjudication. The rules by which people should be governed may owe something to formal modes of logical expression (such as the syllogism), but this must not be exaggerated. The role played by the perceived 'necessities of the time', prevalent political ideologies, intuitions concerning public policy and shared prejudice cannot be overemphasised in considering the basis of the law. Indeed, law may be seen as the embodiment of a nation's long development; it cannot be interpreted merely in terms of logic. Hence, it is important that lawyers and judges be well acquainted with the historical and social contexts of the law they administer. To be a master of the law, one must master the branches of knowledge that lie *next to it*. Anthropology and history should not be neglected by the jurist, since 'In order to know what is, we must know what it has been, and what it tends to become'.

Holmes stated clearly what he understood by 'the law'. In his celebrated epigrammatic definition, which became one of the starting points of American 'functional' jurisprudence, he notes: '*The prophecies of what the courts will do in fact, and nothing more pretentious, are what I mean by the law.*' This is an application of the doctrine of 'washing away with cynical acid' the so-called 'logical certainties' and the 'moral essence' of the law. Concentrate upon the law in action; the data produced will lend themselves to an interpretation of law *as reality*.

It has been objected repeatedly that Holmes's observation is, simply, incorrect. Cohen, in his analysis of 'definition in law', suggests that the real test of a definition is whether it is useful or useless. The words of a definition carry their own problems of ambiguity. 'What courts do' is a phrase heavy with a variety of meanings. Does it have equal application to *all* types of court – the magistrates' courts as well as the House of Lords? Is there a significant distinction between what courts *do* and what they *say*, given the fact that many jurists and lawyers tend to perceive most 'judicial behaviour' as verbal? It may be that the real value of Holmes's definition is in its power to draw attention to operations, to the functioning, of the courts. It is arguable, however, whether or not the definition advances our understanding of the *basis* of law. Goodhart criticised Holmes's formulation by suggesting that 'Law is what the courts do' can be no more satisfactory to the jurist than the statement 'Medicine is what the doctor gives you'.

In an interesting extension of his argument concerning the perception of the essential features of law, Holmes suggested that if one wants to know the 'real law', and nothing else, one ought to consider it from the point of view of 'the bad man' who cares only for the material consequences which such knowledge enables him to predict. Do not, he urged, take into account the point of view of 'the good man', who may find reasons for his conduct in 'the vaguer sanctions of conscience'. The 'bad man' cares nothing for axioms or deductions; he wants to know what 'the Massachusetts or the English courts' are likely to do *in fact*. 'I am much of his mind', declares Holmes. It is the *consequence* of the mode of operations of the courts that is of importance; this constitutes, in reality, 'the law'. The events which follow on, say, failure to register a registrable land charge under the **Land Charges Act 1972**, or the pickpocket placing his hand into an empty pocket, intending to steal, as interpreted under the **Criminal Attempts Act 1981** constitute parts of 'the law'.

Although Holmes draws attention to the importance of the consequences of the courts' decisions, he is emphatic in his belief that the making of laws is the business not of the courts but of the legislative bodies within communities. He proclaims the urgency of recognising the principle that the people have the right to make, through their elected representatives, whatever legislation they feel to be necessary, given the needs of the community. Further, he reminds judges of their important duty of 'weighing considerations of social advantage'. The training of lawyers ought to lead them, and judges, 'habitually to consider more definitely and explicitly' the advantages to society of the rules they lay down. The workings of the legislature and the courts should not be seen in isolation from the societies from which they spring and from which alone they derive their significance.

To view the law in its true relationships, clearly and free from linguistic and moral overtones which distort the picture, forms the basis of the advice which Holmes offers to jurists who seek to understand the reality of the legal process. 'The common law is not a brooding omnipresence in the sky . . . the United States is not subject to some mystic overlaw that it is bound to obey.' A *rational study* of law in action is possible and necessary. In investigating the work of the courts, one must keep in mind William James's insistence that adherence to the philosophy of Pragmatism involved 'looking towards last things, fruits, consequences'. Factual analysis of data from which 'cynical acid' has taken away layers of prejudice and invisible preconceptions is the key to the methodology required by jurists in their attempts to understand the path of the law.

It would be a mistake, however, to imagine that Holmes rejected the need for legal theory. The philosophy of Pragmatism, to which he adhered, is itself the product of a complicated process of applying principles to an interpretation of data. Holmes believed that 'we have too little theory in the law, rather than too much . . . Read the works of the great German jurists and see how much more the world is governed today by Kant than by Bonaparte'. The 'path of the law' demands from those who seek to explore it a knowledge of legal theory, an awareness of historical development, and the continuous observation and analysis of the practical activities of the courts.

Aim Higher ★

Students can gain extra marks by pointing out that Holmes tells the young lawyer in his audience that if he wants to avoid confusion, he should imagine the bad man seated across the desk in his offices and think the matter through from his point of view. Holmes explains that this perspective will avoid three confusions: (1) the belief that if something is one of the rights of man in a moral sense, it must therefore be a legal right as well (2) the belief that law is a system of reason. . .a deduction from principles of ethics (3) the belief that legal duty is filled with all the content which we draw from morals.

NOTES

Holmes's *The Path of the Law* appears in several anthologies of jurisprudential texts; see, for example, *Philosophy of Law*, edited by Feinberg and Gross. *The Collected Legal Papers of Holmes*, edited by Laski, is a valuable anthology of Holmes's views on the essence of Realism. Lerner's *The Mind and Faith of Justice Holmes* provides an interesting picture of 'the Great Dissenter', as Holmes was called (particularly in view of his celebrated dissenting opinions in the Supreme Court). The most recent biography of Holmes, *Justice Oliver Wendell Holmes: Law and the Inner Self*, by White, contains a bibliographic essay. White suggests that understanding Holmes's life is crucial to understanding his work.

QUESTION 27

What does Cardozo tell us about the nature of the judicial process?

Answer Plan

Cardozo (1870–1938) was a very successful New York lawyer who became Chief Judge of the Court of Appeals for the State of New York in 1917. He was appointed to the Supreme Court in 1932, following the resignation of Justice Holmes, and served until 1938. He wrote widely on aspects of jurisprudence, basing his views on the realist approach of the 'integrative jurisprudence' school, whose members stressed the importance of viewing the aims and procedures of the law in relation to specific social conditions. A humanitarian and liberal, Cardozo's thinking concentrated in large measure on the tasks and responsibilities of the judge. The following answer plan is suggested:

- ❖ Introduction;
- ❖ Cardozo and integrative jurisprudence;
- ❖ the task of the judge;
- ❖ the significance of the will of the judge;
- ❖ precedent and its importance for the legal process;
- ❖ the essence of rational coherence in the law;
- ❖ criticisms of Cardozo;
- ❖ conclusion, Cardozo's contribution to our comprehension of the judicial process.

ANSWER

Cardozo (1870–1938) was a New York lawyer who was appointed to high judicial office in the Court of Appeals, prior to his elevation in 1932 to the Supreme Court. He produced a large number of essays on aspects of realist jurisprudence and became widely known as an analyst and interpreter of the American judicial process and, in particular, the role of the judge. He was one of a number of jurists who participated in the work of the 'integrative jurisprudence' school, founded by Hall, which had as its general outlook the utilisation of a 'realist' approach, based upon some findings of legal sociology. The basis of the 'integrated approach' was the search for 'adequacy' in legal philosophy. 'Adequacy' requires of jurisprudence 'ultimacy', 'comprehensiveness' and 'consistency'. An adequate legal philosophy will be constructed on simple ideas that are intellectually defensible; it will take account of all significant aspects of legal problems and will produce a coherent and consistent general theory. This approach characterised Cardozo's analysis of the processes of the courts and culminated in *The Nature of the Judicial Process* (1921), which was a record of a series of lectures delivered at Yale University.

Cardozo wrote of the judicial process as revealing to him the necessity for that process to show three approaches if it is to reflect not only 'the fugitive exigencies of the hour', but the necessity for the ordering of social life and its changing needs. The method of *philosophy* would allow the judge to utilise aspects of reasoning, such as those presented by the analogy. The method of *evolution* would allow the judge to recognise the importance of processes of development in the work in which he takes part and in the rules that he is expected to apply. The method of *tradition* would draw upon ideas of justice, morality and social welfare in the procedures resulting in a judicial decision. These methods are often to be discerned in the workings of the courts, and their integration into a unified approach to the problems arising from the functioning of the courts is to be encouraged. Such an approach becomes of unusual importance when the needs of society require from the judge 'the bending of symmetry, the ignoring of some aspects of history and the sacrifice of some customs' in the pursuit of justice.

The thinking of the judge affects the nature of the judicial process, often in a decisive manner. The need for his tasks to be guided by patterns of utility and morals which he may perceive in the life of the community is important. It is the judge's task to declare the law on the basis of reason and judgment and, where appropriate, in accordance with custom. A judgment is rarely made *in vacuo* and the judge's thinking should take into account the basic morality of 'right-minded men and women'; where this is ignored, the judge has contributed to a degeneration of the law into 'a jurisprudence of mere sentiment of feeling'. It is the nature of the judicial process that the communal support which feeds and sustains it demands recognition from the judges of the power of commonly held attitudes towards justice, punishment and rehabilitation. Where a judge perceives that the customs of society are of unusual importance in a particular series of events, he must balance demands of custom against the specific problems of the case he is hearing. How the question of balance is to be determined necessitates the judge weighing up 'problems of experience and of life itself'.

The nature of the judicial process, Cardozo maintained, reflects the nature of the judge: his sympathies, conscious and unconscious, must not be forgotten in any analysis of his work. Cardozo's contemporary, Marshall CJ, insisted that judicial power is never exercised for the purpose of 'giving effect to the will of the judge'. In rejecting this point of view, Cardozo stressed that the nature of the judicial process could never be understood completely if the significance of 'the judicial will' were to be ignored. The Chief Justice's opinion, said Cardozo, 'has a lofty sound; it is well and finely said; but it can never be more than partly true'. A judge's consciously held opinions and attitudes are affected by a subconscious element in his thought. In accepting this, Cardozo is aware of the problems this may create in the administration of justice. He advocates programmes of training for judges, designed to improve 'the judicial temperament' and urges that judges be made aware of the disproportionate effect of their likes and dislikes, so that the desirable neutrality of the judicial process be maintained and enhanced. He feels, in particular, that the judicial process demands, for its efficacy, judges who have been trained not only in the letter of the law, but in philosophy and social science, allowing them to see in the round the true nature of their work and the well-springs from which order and justice emerge.

Any investigation of the judicial process that ignores the significance of precedent in the growth of the law is vitiated from the outset. Cardozo acknowledges that stability in the law is one of the key determinants in the work of judges and lawyers. 'Existing rules and principles can give us our present location, our bearings, our latitude and longitude'; anything in legal procedures which suggests the presence of arbitrary whim in the rulings of the court is to be avoided. In general, there must be adherence to precedent if the law is to achieve stability and if it is to be seen by the community as based upon a principled approach. *Stare decisis* cannot be ignored as an everyday working rule. The importance of precedent in maintaining the sense of continuity which must be perceived as entering into the judicial process cannot be overstated. At the back of precedents are 'the basic juridical conceptions which are the postulates of judicial reasoning, and farther back are the habits of life, the institutions of society, in which those conceptions had their origin and which, by a process of interaction, they have modified in turn'.

A slavish adherence to precedent is to be deplored. Cardozo gives his approval to a statement by Wheeler J that it is essential to recognise that 'the rules of law which grew up in a remote generation may, in the fullness of experience, be found to serve another generation badly'. Where precedent provides no answer to a problem, or where it suggests an answer which is demonstrably out of keeping with the changed aspirations of the community and the declared intentions of the legislature, a judge must not hesitate to consider moving along new pathways, and this may demand, in turn, an extension, or even rejection, of an existing set of rules. Where the experiences of life indicate that precedent is out of step with widely accepted perceptions of social life, then the law must move ahead in arguing for the acceptance of new perspectives.

The creative function of the judge in the processes of the courts is seen by Cardozo as of profound significance in any attempt to analyse the true nature of justice in the common law jurisdictions. Although stability remains a key element in the workings of the law, it must not be seen to be equated with a refusal to change with the times. *Balance is all.* Acceptance of and adherence to the principles of 'rational coherence' will assist in ensuring that the judicial process is seen as respecting the need for stability *and* the need to modify, change and reject in the interests of growth of the law. It is for the judge to recognise that, at any given time, there will be within the community a group of jural principles, customs, rules, canons of behaviour and attitudes towards moral questions which may cohere so as to restrain his freedom to act as he wishes. He will consider the significance of prevailing attitudes and exercise a 'rational discretion' in matters affecting communal standards. The judge is never completely free in the performance of his judicial role and must accept the many pressures of convention, morality, habit and the inscrutable force of professional opinion when contemplating decisions which may be perceived as introducing fundamental change.

'Where doubt enters in, there enters the judicial function.' Cardozo notes that study of the judicial process indicates that important moves in judicial attitudes often seem to be preceded by periods of 'sustained and intense doubt' as to the relevance of parts of the law. It is then, in this period of doubt, that the exercise of the judicial function assumes much importance. The judge is faced, on the one hand, with the need to preserve the workings of society and to do nothing to affect its stability and, on the other hand, with the need to shift the frontiers of the law so as to recognise the inevitability of necessary change. How is the judicial process to operate? 'We go forward with our *logic*, with our *analogies*, our *philosophies*, until we reach a certain point.' At that point, the judge may have no trouble with the paths he is pursuing – they will seem to follow the same lines. But they then begin to diverge and it is for the judge to make his choices, conscious of the pressures upon him. His actions will be determined in large measure, says Cardozo, by history or custom or social utility or some other vital and compelling sentiment of justice '*or perhaps by a semi-intuitive apprehension of the pervading spirit of the law*'. The principles of 'rational coherence' will prevail where the desire for change is balanced by awareness of the dictates of reason. The judicial process is, in these circumstances, highly effective where the judge balances his philosophy, logic, sense of right, and all the rest, 'adding a little here and taking out a little there [so as to determine], as wisely as he can, which weight shall tip the scales'. Where exercise of the judicial process produces a result which is widely perceived as straining credulity or moving beyond the bounds of social acceptability, the various courts of appeal and, ultimately, the legislature will act, on the basis of principle, to overturn and nullify the judgment. In general, says Cardozo, the nature of the judicial process will be taken as 'the expression of a principle of order to which men must conform in their conduct and relations as members of society . . . and the judge, so far as freedom of choice is given to him, tends to a result that attaches legal obligation to the folkways, the norms, or standards of behaviour exemplified in the life about him'. In no sense is he 'a knight-errant, roaming at will in pursuit of his own ideal of beauty and goodness'. Service to the ideals of justice and the demands of social living must play a determining role in his judicial activities.

Cardozo refers repeatedly in his writings to the significance of *Riggs v Palmer* (1889). He discerns in the decision of the New York Court of Appeals an illustration of the 'directive force of a principle' in affecting the nature of the judicial process. In that case, a grandson who was named in his grandfather's will as his heir murdered the grandfather so that he might inherit swiftly. Could the murderer inherit under the will? Cardozo drew attention to two principles favouring the murderer. First, the principle of the binding force of a will disposing of the testator's estate in accordance with the law. Secondly, the principle that civil courts may not add to the pains and penalties of a crime. To follow these principles would, according to Cardozo, offend against the universal sentiment that no person should be allowed to derive an advantage from his own wrong. If we were to hold otherwise, that would be to support a dissolution of the bonds which link members of a family. It was held that the grandson could not take the legacy under the will. Cardozo suggested that attention be paid to the judgment of Earl J, who stated: 'No man may be permitted to profit from his own fraud . . . no man may acquire property by his own crime. These maxims are dictated by public policy, they have their foundation in universal law administered in all civilised countries, and have nowhere been superseded by statute.' This ruling exemplifies for Cardozo the essential nature of the judicial process: principles direct a decision, law is seen as a means to a social end and the links between morality and law are deliberately recognised and strengthened. 'Justice reacted upon logic, sentiment upon reason, by guiding the choice to be made between one logic and another. Reason in its turn reacted upon sentiment by purging it of what is arbitrary, by checking it when it might otherwise have been extravagant, by relating it to method and order and coherence and tradition.'

Cardozo sums up his analysis of the nature of the judicial process thus: an analysis comes to this and little more – that logic, history, custom and utility, and the generally acceptable standards of right conduct are the forces which, singly or in combination, mould the law's progress. Which force shall be dominant in a given case will depend largely upon the comparative significance of the social interests that stand to be promoted or impaired. A vital matter is that law shall be uniform and impartial; nothing savouring of prejudice is to be allowed. Adherence to precedent becomes essential. 'There shall be symmetrical development, consistently with history or custom when history or custom has been the motive force, or the chief one, in giving shape to existing rules and with logic or philosophy when the motive power has been theirs.' But symmetrical development may be too expensive: uniformity is no longer good when it has become uniformity of oppression. It then becomes necessary to balance the social interest served by symmetry against the social interest served by equity. The judge's duty is then to consider a departure from existing practice where he feels that this has become necessary. Stability and necessary change are the keys to interpreting the nature of the judicial process. Criticisms of Cardozo have centred on the suggestion that he seems to have built his theories around observation and analysis of the work of the appeal courts. Frank, in his *Cardozo and the Upper Court Myth*, states that Cardozo rarely mentions the problem of the measure of discretion resting in trial judges and juries. The 'certainty' which Cardozo appears to find in the judicial process is often absent from the deliberations of jury members involved in matters relating to the significance of facts. It is suggested, further, that Cardozo has seen the workings of principles where none can be discerned, even on close analysis, and that the 'balancing' of stability and social desires for improvement is difficult to find in practice.

Cardozo's contribution to our knowledge of the judicial process may be said to rest on his having emphasised the social nature of the law and his belief that the judicial process cannot be interpreted as though it were an isolate, a 'thing-in-itself'. Law is nothing if not a means to an end, and the judicial process must respond continuously to that end if it is to flourish.

NOTES

Cardozo's writings include *The Nature of the Judicial Process, The Paradoxes of Legal Science* and *The Growth of the Law*. Posner's *Cardozo, A Study in Reputation*, analyses aspects of Cardozo's fundamental thought. Criticisms of Cardozo appear in Pollock's *Jurisprudence*.

The Nature of Law

INTRODUCTION

The purpose of legal theory as conceived by Professor Raz is to seek to uncover and explain the nature of law, so that the explanation of law covers law wherever law is found. As Raz comments in *The Authority of Law* (1979) at p 105:

> Legal philosophy has to be content with those few features which all legal systems necessarily possess.

Two essential features of law are (1) the 'sources' thesis – that the identification of law does not depend upon a moral argument and (2) the law's claim to legitimate moral authority. This second essential and inescapable feature of law is part of the explanation of one of the key concerns in jurisprudence – the 'normativity of law'. Of course Professor Dworkin has denied that legal theory is essentially about the 'essential' properties of law but rather Dworkin conceives that the proper function of legal theory is to justify the use of state coercion through law: see Dworkin, *Justice in Robes* (2006) p 13. For Dworkin the 'nature of law' is not as central to legal theory as he conceives it to be.

However, it is possible to talk about the 'nature of law' in terms of law's essential properties and also the role law plays in modern Western societies. The institution of law may have, in modern Western societies, a much more expansive role than law's relation to societies in the past. Law in the past may have been mainly limited to the maintenance of law and order and the regulation of a few central aspects of social life such as marriage, contracts, wills etc. However, modern law in Western societies pervades deeply into social life in a way that would have astounded our ancestors. Symbolic of that penetration of law into the social space is the ban on smoking in public places which came into effect in 2007 as a result of the **Health Act 2006**. Law regulates the social life of the community much more than in the past. This is a feature of the 'nature of law' which should not be overlooked.

Checklist ✔

Ensure that you are acquainted with the following topics:

- the role of law in the postmodern social environment;
- law's deep penetration into the social life of the nation in the modern Western state;
- the meaning of the phrase 'normativity of law';
- the views of Kelsen, Bentham, Hart and Raz on the 'normativity of law';
- the relationship between the 'normativity of law' and human rationality.

QUESTION 28

Discuss the role of law in the postmodern social environment.

Answer Plan

Law is traditionally analysed in legal theory as having great instrumental worth in achieving mighty social goals, such as civil peace or the co-ordination of society, but law's particular role in postmodern Western societies needs consideration. The collapse of faith in modern Western democracies in religion and political ideology has left a vacuum which is partly filled by the secular law. The law thus becomes an expression of social union in increasingly fragmented societies divided on ethnic, class and financial lines. Dworkin has argued that given the fragmentation of modern societies there is a great need for the law to speak with the voice of 'integrity': so that each citizen's position in the eyes of the law is defined by the same coherent principles. Law, thus conceived by Dworkin and others, almost becomes a substitute religion, a 'belief system' for a sceptical fragmented society.

A skeleton plan is suggested:

- ❖ Introduction;
- ❖ the decline of 'faith' in Western liberal democracies and the rise of law as a secular substitute;
- ❖ the role of law in maintaining social unity in the face of substantial fragmentation in the social world of the society;
- ❖ critics of Western societies who object to the treatment of democracy and its product – secular Western law, as a 'quasi-religion' in Western democratic societies;

- ❖ law's role in defining the social space through legal notions such as property, ownership, contract, rights, duty, fault and guilt;
- ❖ conclusion, the overwhelming social power of law in the postmodern social environment.

ANSWER

The law's claim to legitimate authority is not only a necessary feature of law wherever it is found but that claim by the law to an overarching authority is arguably necessary for the survival of modern Western societies in what is termed 'the post modern social environment'.

The condition of modern Western societies is such that widespread faith in political ideology, religious belief and even liberal progress itself have largely disappeared and into that 'faith' gap comes the law to provide a kind of secular certainty for people. As Bernard Lewis puts the point about religious faith in *The Crisis of Islam* (2003):

> most Muslim countries are still profoundly Muslim, in a way and in a sense that most Christian countries are no longer Christian.

Roger Cotterrell comments in *Law, Culture and Society* (2006):

> post modern ideas about the collapse of grand narratives might suggest that the authority or validity of all large-scale structures of knowledge has been put in question. . . . It could be argued that legitimacy through legality remains the only possibility of stable authority in the postmodern social environment' and Cotterrell comments of law's 'social power in a world that has lost faith in other discourses.

The 'collapse of grand narratives' is a theme of postmodern writing on law, stressing how in the Western world public faith has been lost in the explanatory and justificatory power of political ideology, religious faith, even science itself. Jean- Francois Lyotard has put the matter thus: 'grand narratives have lost their credibility'. Thus in the Western world persons no longer believe in the narrative version of history provided by the Bible, Marx's 'Das Kapital' or even in the eventual solution of all mankind's problems by science. The law then provides a form of a substitute belief system for a society without shared beliefs. As the French writer Emmanuel Levy (1871–1944) comments, law is **'un substitut pratique de la religion' – a practical substitute for religion**.

However, although the law provides something to believe in a postmodern world, where faith has collapsed, it may not ultimately provide a real substitute for proper belief systems. As Cotterrell comments in *Living Law* (2008):

> in the most pessimistic post modern views, law may be all there is to believe in. But that is not much...the endlessly pragmatic adjustment of regulation to increasing social complexity.

Indeed, modern statute law may be an appropriate object of belief for a morally empty consumer goods-obsessed modern world. As Cotterrell comments modern law's 'moral emptiness makes it a form of knowledge entirely appropriate to a morally empty world'. Modern statute law's transience, disposability and infinite adaptability mirrors the transience, disposability and infinite adaptability of the market-driven consumer society.

Law's social power in the post modern social environment is that in an era of substantial social fragmentation and diversity the law of the state represents the 'last universal' – the symbol of a formal unity. Indeed Professor Dworkin draws on this idea of 'unity through the legal order' in modern Western democracies when he argues that law should have integrity as he defines the idea. Dworkin in *Justice in Robes* (2006) comments:

> Every contemporary democracy is a divided nation, and our democracy (USA) is particularly divided. We are divided culturally, ethnically, politically and morally. We nevertheless aspire to live together as equals, and it seems absolutely crucial to that ambition that we also aspire that the principles under which we are governed treat us as equals.

Therefore Dworkin is not merely maintaining that his vision of law as integrity is necessary to justify the coercive authority of the state as expressed through law, but that the very sustainability of a vastly diverse society depends on government through the rule of law.

In a 'world of strangers', which is the modern state, citizens of vastly different political, ethnic and belief systems can at least owe their primary allegiance to an impersonal, secular and impartial legal order of publicly administered rules. Leslie Green comments in 'Legality and Community' (*Oxford Journal of Legal Studies*):

> As other and narrower loyalties weaken citizens of modern states who have nothing else in common might look to the civic order itself as an expression of social union.

The elevation of the law to an almost 'religious' status in modern society has been a very long process. Ian Ward comments in 'God, Terror and Law' (*Oxford Journal of Legal Studies*) of the Eighteenth Century Enlightenment:

> in the place of God, or at least alongside, was the law.

For critics of Western society this deification of the law in Western societies is a symbol of deep moral crisis. The radical Islamic writer Abu Muhammed al-Maqdisi comments in his book *Democracy is a Religion*:

> Democracy is a religion that is not Allah's religion. . .they and their followers rule according to the religion of democracy and the constitution's laws upon which the government is based. . . Their master is their God, their big idols who approve or reject legislation.

Indeed one aspect of law, namely human rights legislation, almost has the status of a 'world religion'. Indeed human rights law has been called 'the ideology at the end of history' (see Cotterrell, *Law, Culture and Society* (2006)). As John Tasioulas comments in *The Moral Reality of Human Rights* (2007): 'discourse of human rights has acquired in recent times . . . the status of an ethical lingua franca'. As Professor Raz comments in *Human Rights in the Emerging World Order* (2010):

> human rights . . . have become a distinctive ingredient in the emerging world order where they generate new channels for political action in the international arena.

Law's power in the postmodern state derives from three factors:

(1) the widespread collapse in faith in political ideology, religion or even science to solve mankind's problems;
(2) law's backing by the coercive authority of the modern state, a coercive authority that is inescapable and ever present;
(3) the law's claim to be based on rationality, or at least the result of rational debate.

A final theme of postmodern writing on law has been on how the authority of law actually constitutes the social order. The law has the power to **'create the social'** in the consciousness of the population by shaping such ideas as property ownership, responsibility, contract, rights, fault and guilt. The authority of the law is, on this view, the very foundation of social life. This is not a particularly novel claim. Professor Raz wrote, back in 1979, in *The Authority of Law*:

> **the law claims to provide the general framework for the conduct of all aspects of social life and sets itself up as the supreme guardian of society.**

Given that modern statute law is complex, technical and ever-changing it is not surprising that some doubt has been expressed whether natural law theory, with its emphasis on universal principles of natural law discoverable by reason, has much relevance to the image of modern statute law we are exploring here. Cotterrell in *The Politics of Jurisprudence* (2003) asks 'is natural law dead?' and penetratingly observes of the eclipse of natural law theory:

> **The problem is that even if there are universal principles of natural law they may not offer a convincing guide or grounding for complex, highly technical, ever-changing modern law.**

Law's role in the postmodern social environment as a complex, highly technical and ever-changing set of norms has the potency to test the continuing validity of one of the great schools of jurisprudential thought – namely natural law. Arguably natural law has little to say by way of guidance through so-called universal moral principles to a system of modern law that is complex, highly technical and ever-changing.

NOTES

Roger Cotterrell in *The Politics of Jurisprudence* (2003, 2nd edition) discusses the role of law in the postmodern social environment at pp 250–257. Cotterrell returns to the same theme in *Law, Culture and Society: Legal Ideas in the Mirror of Social Theory* (2006) pp 19–26. Cotterrell returns again to the role of law in the postmodern society in *Living Law* (2008) pp 108–109 and see his essay on Emmanuel Levy at pp 73–84 of *Living Law*.

QUESTION 29

Explain the 'normativity' of law.

Answer Plan

This question involves discussion of the important jurisprudential question of how the law is normative – the 'normativity' of law: its 'oughtness', its bindingness. The sanction-based explanation of the law's normativity offered by Bentham and Austin has been widely discredited. Kelsen's career-long efforts to explain the law's normativity through the basic norm (or 'grundnorm') occupies the greater part of his legal theory. The most satisfactory account of the law's normativity resides with Professor Hart and Professor Raz. Hart's idea, drawn from the seventeenth century's Thomas Hobbes, explains law as a 'peremptory, content-independent norm'. In other words the fact that a law is issued from an authoritative source is meant in itself to be a binding reason to obey that law on the part of citizens. As Hobbes said in Chapter 25 of his *Leviathan* (1651):

> Command is when a man saith do this or do not do this yet without expecting any other reason than the will of him that saith it.

As Hart comments:

> For to have such authority is to have one's expression of intention as to the actions of others accepted as peremptory content independent reasons for action.

The word 'peremptory' means just cutting off deliberation, debate or argument and the word with this meaning came into the English language from Roman law. Therefore the law-maker's expression of will is not intended to function within the hearer's deliberations as another ordinary reason for doing the act but the law promulgated by authority is intended to function as the overriding reason for doing or not doing the required or prohibited act. Professor Hart means by 'content independent' that the bindingness, the 'normativity' of the law, does not depend upon the content of the law – what the law actually commands – but rather that the 'normativity' of the law is due to its promulgation by an authority with the authority to issue laws to the populace: the 'bindingness' of the law does not depend on whether the law commands the morally good or the morally bad, but rather it is the fact of authoritative promulgation in itself that is meant to bind citizens.

Hart's account of the normativity of law (such an account of the 'normativity' of law is not found in the *The Concept of Law* (1961): where Hart merely describes the linguistic difference between being 'obliged' to do something by a gangster and being under an 'obligation' of law) found in *Essays on Bentham* (1982) resembles closely Professor Raz's idea of the law as offering the citizens 'exclusionary reasons for action'. An 'exclusionary reason' is meant to exclude other valid reasons for not complying with the exclusionary reason emanating from authority. Raz argues that law by its nature claims legitimate moral authority in that it purports to give the law's subjects exclusionary reasons for compliance with the law's edicts. Whether the law has in fact such legitimate moral authority is a different question.

The answer to the puzzle of the law's normativity lies in the law's self-image, what the law itself claims: the law claims to be a structure of legitimate moral authority and it is this claim which is intended to bind citizens and explains the 'oughtness' of law: law's 'normativity'.

A skeleton plan is suggested.

❖ Introduction;
❖ the concept of the 'normativity' of law;
❖ the failed 'sanction based' explanations of law's normativity;
❖ Kelsen's extensive attempts to solve the problem of the law's 'normativity' through the 'basic norm' '(grundnorm');
❖ Raz's persuasive account of the law's normativity through what the law itself claims (the law claims through the acts and speech of legal officials such as judges, who act as if they have legitimate authority and talk as if they had such legitimate authority): a claim to be the legitimate moral authority in a community;
❖ how the law's normativity relates to the rational powers of persons.

ANSWER

June 2009 marked the publication of the second edition of Professor Raz's *The Authority of Law*. The central argument of Raz's work into the nature of law has been the law's claim to authority over the society it purports to govern. The law's claim to authority is presented as a conceptual truth about the essence or nature of law wherever it is found in human societies.

For Raz the law's claim to authority helps to explain a central puzzle of legal theory, namely the normativity of law. The question about the normativity of law is the question of what sense to give to the bindingness of law, its duty imposing nature. In other words, what sense can be given to the mystery 'oughtness' of law. The law is a realm of obligation and duty, the law acts not as our advisor but as an authority that must be obeyed. By framing the answer to the law's normativity in terms of what the law itself claims over its subjects, law's self-image, then Raz, by stating that the law by its nature claims legitimate authority, provides a coherent account of the law's normativity.

According to Raz the law claims to bind its subjects by offering them 'exclusionary reasons' for action. In other words it is the fact that a law has been issued from a recognised authority in that society that is meant to be taken by citizens as a standard for the conduct of the individual to the exclusion of any reasons, moral or personal that the citizen may have for non-compliance with that particular law.

Two points need to be made at this stage, concerning the alleged claim to legitimate authority of the law wherever it is found, suggested by Raz:

(1) the fact that the law claims authority over persons in a particular society does not entail that the law actually has legitimate authority in any given society. Raz argues that the law often claims more than can be morally justified. Raz has argued that the actual legitimate reach of any legal system calls for careful reflection. Raz argues that law by its nature claims legitimate authority not that it in fact has such legitimate authority. A person can claim something without actually having the legitimacy to make that claim for example;

(2) the argument by Raz that the law claims authority seems to involve a strange personification of a non-living entity. How can 'the law' claim anything in the sense that a person may make a claim? Indeed in an article entitled 'Why Law Makes No Claims' (in *Law, Rights and Discourse*, edited by Pavlakos 2007) Neil MacCormick claims that the law is a state of affairs which cannot make claims: 'law claims nothing'. MacCormick is right in maintaining that law as such is incapable of raising, in a literal sense, any claim. In a literal sense claims can be raised only by subjects having the capacity to speak or act. However Raz means that legal officials (particularly judges) talk as if, and act as if, they have the legitimate authority which the law grants them. Law can and does raise a claim to legitimate authority for the claim is made by the law's representatives. As Raz comments in *The Authority of Law*, second edition:

> the law claims to have legitimate authority, in the sense that legal institutions both act as if they have such authority, and articulate the view that they have it.

Those writers, such as Austin and Bentham, who viewed law as a species of command from a sovereign to an inferior, held that law's normativity, its 'bindingness', resided in the threat of the application of coercion from the sovereign in the light of the subject's non-compliance. However, as Raz persuasively argues in *Practical Reason and Norms* (1990) the 'sanction based' account of law's normativity is not adequate to explain how the law binds its subjects. As Raz comments:

> the fact that so far as sanctions go the law is merely an auxiliary reason is not intended to belittle the importance of legal sanctions. They are a most important means of securing social co-ordination and of providing people with reasons for conforming to the law. . . But the fact that a law is backed by a sanction is never

an exclusionary reason. It is a simple first-order reason. The inevitable conclusion is that, despite the undoubted importance of sanctions and the use of force to enforce them in all human legal systems, the sanction-directed attempt to explain the normativity of law leads to a dead-end.

Raz's argument boils down to this: although sanctions imposed by authorities for non-compliance to laws are important, the law in fact intends its subjects to comply to its edicts because they are precisely the law's edicts irrespective of any sanction for non-compliance.

Another major attempt to explain law's normativity is to be found in Kelsen's idea of the basic norm, or in German 'the grundnorm'. Kelsen argued that it was necessary for anyone who accepted the 'normativity' of a particular legal system to presuppose that the legal system was valid, in other words for an individual to accept the normativity of a legal system he had to assume that there was a basic norm which gave normative charge to the whole legal system. Neil MacCormick in *Institutions of Law* (2007) comments approvingly of Kelsen:

> the most basic understanding of norms ought to be in terms of the norm-user . . . Hans Kelsen after tackling heroically the great mystery of the ought, increasingly fell away from his initial insight.

Kelsen explained the foundational significance of the basic norm to his own pure theory of law in *Introduction to the Problems of Legal Theory* (1934):

> the pure theory of law works with this basic norm as a hypothetical foundation. Given the presupposition that the basic norm is valid, the legal system resting on it is also valid. The basic norm confers on the act of the first legislator – and thus on all other acts of the legal system resting on this first act – the sense of 'ought'. . .rooted in the basic norm, ultimately is the normative import of all the material facts consisting the legal system.

For Kelsen the 'basic norm' gave sense to normative statements such as 'the law says X ought to be done'. Kelsen was fond of drawing parallels between his basic norm and religious faith. Although many persons do not believe in God, those persons who **do believe** in God presuppose in their religious faith the basic norm that 'God's commandments ought to be obeyed'. Similarly those who have 'faith' or 'belief' in the justified normativity of their own legal system presuppose a basic norm that the constitution of that legal system ought to be obeyed. In other words normativity like beauty is in 'the eye (or rather mind) of the beholder'. Two points need to be made concerning 'the basic norm':

(1) the basic norm is never created by any law creating body, it is not created by anyone, it is merely a presupposition of someone who believes in the legal system of a state (and for Kelsen the legal system and state were synonymous). As Kelsen explains:

> the Pure Theory aims simply to raise to the level of consciousness what all jurists are doing (for the most part unwittingly) when . . . they understand the positive law as a valid system.

Unlike all other norms in a legal system the basic norm is not created but found in the consciousness of a person who believes the coercive order of his state is a valid legal order.

Therefore, the demands of the gangster and the taxman can be distinguished: those subject to the demands of the gangster do not presuppose such demands are valid, whereas those who are subject to the demands of the taxman can see them as valid if they see them as part of a valid legal order justified by the basic norm in the person's consciousness.

(2) Kelsen was keen to stress that it is not necessary to accept the basic norm of any legal system. Kelsen's aim was to try and explain what a person meant when they said they accepted a coercive order as a valid legal order – Kelsen's answer was deceptively simple: that person accepted the basic norm of his legal system. However Kelsen allowed for the fact that the anarchist, for example, rejected the validity of all legal systems and saw in law only coercive order. However not all persons are anarchists and Kelsen's basic norm offered an account of how a person could interpret the coercive order of his state as a valid legal order.

Kelsen seeks to explain the normativity of law by viewing the answer through the lens of how the law's subjects, the citizens, view the legal system. This is perhaps getting the issue the wrong way round and it is more fruitful to ask, with Professor Raz, what the law claims itself, the law's self-image holding the key to explaining law's normativity: the law is normative because it claims legitimate authority. Whether that normativity is justified is a separate question.

The key to the normativity of law is in the law claiming to provide valid reasons for action. Following the approach of Raz all normative phenomena, such as morality or the law, are normative because they provide persons with reasons for action. This explanation of law's normativity coheres well with the status of persons as rational agents. As John Gardner comments in 'Nearly Natural Law' (*American Journal of Jurisprudence* (2007)):

we human beings are rational beings. We have a highly developed capacity to respond to reasons. This is an important aspect of our nature... Our highly developed capacity to respond to reasons includes the capacity to use norms to guide our actions.

Neil MacCormick in *Institutions of Law* (2007) comments in a similar vein that response to norms is inherent within humans:

human beings are through-and-through norm-users, capable of achieving a kind of voluntary order among themselves by common observance of common orders.

Indeed, MacCormick gives a definition of law in terms of normativity; law is for MacCormick 'an institutional normative order' and 'a normative order is possible, because humans are norm-users'.

The explanation of the normativity of law provided by Raz in that the law claims to provide 'exclusionary' reasons for action, i.e. legitimate authority fits the way in which law acts in the practical reasoning of rational persons to a much greater degree than the sanction backed model of law provided by Austin or Bentham or the concept of the 'basic norm' offered by Kelsen.

Indeed, following Raz's analysis, the idea of acting on reasons provided by the law not only is consistent with the actual role played by law in a rational individual's practical reasoning but indeed responding to reasons is also constitutive of being a person, for we engage with the world through our reason-driven intentions. Our rational powers, which the law employs when it directs its orders at us, are constitutive of personhood itself. Therefore the question concerning the 'normativity of law' strikes at the very essence of what it means to be a person.

Aim Higher ★

Students can gain extra marks by noting that the 'normativity of law' is one of the most important topics in legal theory. Students will note that Kelsen's explanation of normativity in terms of the 'basic norm' (grundnorm) has attracted the most attention in terms of Kelsen's legal philosophy. Students can avoid the pitfall of thinking that the command theory of law espoused by Austin and Bentham explains the 'normativity of law' satisfactorily, when in fact that theory empties the law of normativity by making the bindingness of law turn on the existence of sanctions.

NOTES

Professor Raz's demolition of the 'sanction based' account of normativity offered by Bentham and Austin is found in *Practical Reason and Norms* (1990, 2nd edition) pp 161–162. Professor Hart's account of law's normativity (not to be found in *The Concept of Law* (1961): which may be regarded as one of the crucial omissions of that flawed masterwork) is to be found in *Essays on Bentham* (1982) pp 244–258: Hart's account of a law as a 'peremptory content-independent norm' is very similar to Raz's idea of law as an 'exclusionary reason for action'. A very readable account of Kelsen's lifelong attempt to explain the normativity of law is to be found in the online and free *Stanford Encyclopedia of Philosophy*, an essay by Andrei Marmor entitled 'The Pure Theory of Law': http://plato.stanford.edu/entries/lawphil-theory/

11 Contemporary American Jurisprudence and Political Philosophy

INTRODUCTION

The questions in this chapter concern jurists who typify certain strands of thought in contemporary American jurisprudence. Those selected are Rawls (b 1921) and his pupil, Nozick (b 1938). These jurists share no common platform: Rawls and Nozick have diametrically opposite views on matters such as the distribution of wealth.

Checklist ✔

Ensure that you are acquainted with the following topics:

- Rawls's 'original position' concept;
- Rawls's two principles of justice;
- primary social goods;
- American Critical Legal Studies;
- Nozick's 'minimal state'.

QUESTION 30

'Rawls's theory of justice is a credible, radical alternative to the conception of justice based on classical utilitarianism.'

▶ Is it?

Answer Plan

Rawls is a contemporary philosopher who is interested particularly in questions of social justice. His theory is based on the necessity of perceiving questions of justice to be more important than questions of happiness (which are central to utilitarianism); what is *right* is a matter of priority, whereas what is *good* is a secondary matter. The theory of justice associated with Rawls is, therefore, in contrast to the utilitarian concept. Essentials of the theory are based on a set of limitations which must be explained in an answer to the question. The following skeleton plan is used:

- ❖ Introduction;
- ❖ essence of Rawls's approach;
- ❖ the well ordered society;
- ❖ justice viewed in rational terms;
- ❖ social contract;
- ❖ 'original position' and the 'veil of ignorance';
- ❖ primary social goods;
- ❖ principles of justice;
- ❖ priority of justice and liberty;
- ❖ credibility of the theory;
- ❖ conclusion, Rawls's theory as an alternative to utilitarianism.

ANSWER

The problem of what ought to be the principles of social justice – basic to ethics and jurisprudence – is subjected to a detailed analysis by Rawls in *A Theory of Justice* (1971). An elaborate, systematic argument emerges in which Rawls provided an alternative to earlier doctrines of justice as conceived by utilitarians such as Bentham, for whom a 'just system' required legal institutions directed at the creation of 'the greatest happiness for the greatest number'. Rawls's approach is epitomised in the statement: 'Justice is fairness.' His theory is, without doubt, a radical alternative to utilitarian justice; whether it is credible is less certain.

The society which Rawls uses for purposes of analysis is a more or less self-sufficient association of individuals who stand in a relationship one to the other and which is characterised by recognition of the binding nature of certain rules of conduct which are generally acted upon. Rawls assumes that this society wishes to decide a set of principles upon which to construct 'social justice'. The principles are to be used in assigning rights and duties and in defining the distribution of burdens and benefits considered appropriate for social co-operation. A well ordered society is seen as one which is designed to advance the good of its members and is regulated by 'a public conception of justice'. Each individual accepts the principles of justice and is aware of their general acceptance. Society's basic institutions seek to satisfy these principles. Essentially, a public conception of justice constitutes the 'fundamental charter' of society. Here, at once, is a concept at variance with the doctrine of classical utilitarianism.

Rawls is concerned to show that the 'principles of justice' required for such a society would be precisely those that would be chosen by 'rational persons'. The circumstances in which the choice is made give Rawls's theory a highly unusual basis. He utilises the theory of 'the social contract' to suggest that principles of justice rest on *a compact* made by society's members. The realisation of these principles constitutes the very *object*, the very *reason*, of the compact. We are to imagine, says Rawls, a hypothetical situation in which those who have entered the compact are deciding a fundamental charter for their society. The people involved are rational and free, and desirous of furthering their own interests. Their initial position is one based on equality – '*the original position*'.

If the principles of justice to be decided upon are to be objective and fair, then, says Rawls, those in the 'original position' must accept *limitations* and must step behind a 'veil of ignorance'. None of the participants knows (and, therefore, acts as though he does not know) any of his special circumstances. The veil eliminates any prejudices. One's place in society, class, position and intelligence are 'unknowns' for the purpose of this exercise. Since all participants in the inquiry accept this limitation, none of them will fashion principles deliberately to suit his own particular condition. The principles of justice which emerge will be the result of a 'fair' agreement. Rawls assumes, however, that those in the 'original position' will be capable of maintaining a 'sense of justice'. They will, apparently, without question, see justice as 'fairness'. Rawls assumes, further, that those in the 'original position' will have no information as to the particular circumstances of their society, that is, they are presumed not to be aware of its level of culture and civilisation. Nor do they know the generation to which they belong, so that they must derive principles with which *they* are prepared to live. It is assumed, however, that they know the general facts about society and that they understand the basic principles of economics, politics and psychology. 'The veil' will ensure that they are not prejudiced by 'arbitrary contingencies'.

Because the participants intend to evolve their charter of justice on the basis of rationality, Rawls suggests that the communal structure which will be evolved as a result of the reflective equilibrium of the group will be concerned with *the rational distribution of 'primary social goods'*. These are things which every rational person is presumed to want more of; they have a use whatever a person's rational life plan may be; their distribution is always a matter of concern. The 'primary social goods' are rights and liberties, opportunities and powers, income and wealth. For every person, 'the good' is the satisfaction of rational desire; whatever one's ends, the primary goods are, in rational terms, the necessary means. (At a later stage, Rawls added 'the most important of the primary goods – self-respect'; this would include 'a person's sense of his own value, his secure conviction that his good, his plan or life is worth carrying out'.)

From Rawls's perception of the overall 'good' and his view of 'primary goods' comes his belief that there will emerge from the deliberations of those in the 'original position' two vital principles of justice. *The first principle will be a resounding affirmation of equality and fairness as basic to justice.* Each individual must have an equal right to the most extensive total system of equal, basic liberties compatible with a similar system of liberty for all (a principle similar to that which is basic to Mill's *On Liberty*). This involves a maximisation of liberty deliberately intended to furnish maximum freedom of speech and conscience. 'Liberty for all' may have to be restricted, but *only for the sake of liberty itself*, as where, for example, freedom of speech requires a system of public order regulations (see the **Public Order Act 1986**, for example). The maintenance of public order must be accepted as a necessary condition for each person to achieve his ends. Further, less-than-equal liberty may be justified but only where it is acceptable to those who have the lesser liberty; resulting inequalities in one liberty must be shown to have the effect of a greater overall protection of other liberties as a direct result of a restriction (the **Road Traffic Act 1988** provides an example). (Rawls argues that persons in the original position who, according to his hypothesis, will not know their true position in society will fear that when they return to the real world, they might be slaves deprived of all freedoms. Hence, they will seek to pronounce that slavery is incompatible with justice.)

The *second principle of justice* (as amended by Rawls after publication of his book in 1971) is as follows: *social and economic inequalities are to be arranged so that they will be to the greatest benefit of the least advantaged persons, consistent with a 'just savings principle', and are attached to offices and positions open to all under conditions of fairness and equality of opportunity.* Rawls recognises that those in the 'original position' will be aware of the facts of inequality and differences among individuals and will wish to ensure that these differences do not result in injustice. There is no suggestion that wealth and income ought to be divided equally; but any unequal division will be justifiable only if *all* persons are better off as a result, that is, the unequal division is to result to everyone's advantage. The 'just savings principle' involves justice operating not only among the members of society represented in the 'original position', but among those of succeeding generations also; savings involve a recognition of the responsibilities of one generation to the next.

Rawls is aware that there may be conflicts of principle. A resolution of such conflict may be effected, he suggests, by the application of 'principles of priority'. This concept is referred to as 'lexical' – that is, the first principle must be satisfied *totally* before any consideration can be given to the second. (The term 'lexical' refers to a dictionary: the first letter is 'lexically first', so that no compensation at the level of subsequent letters can erase the negative effect ensuing from the substitution of another letter for the first.) The first priority rule is *the absolute priority of liberty*: one may restrict liberty *only* for the sake of liberty. The second priority rule is that *justice shall prevail over efficiency and welfare*. In a conflict of principles of liberty and social need, liberty has an unalterable priority, and must not be exchanged for other benefits. Concerns derived from 'maximisation of utility' must give way to the overriding necessity for liberty. To depart from the principle of equal liberty cannot be justified, therefore, by the promise of greater economic and social advantage except, perhaps, where it is necessary to enhance the quality of civilisation 'so that in due course equal freedoms can be enjoyed by all'.

The credibility of Rawls's theory of justice has been questioned persistently. The 'original position' seems so hypothetical, so artificial, and so very difficult to visualise that it is perceived by some jurists as weakening the basis of the theory. Is it possible to imagine persons from whom individual histories, environmental links and values have been removed? Is what remains sufficient to constitute a 'rational person' from whom reasoning can be expected? Those in the 'original position' are not in possession of data appropriate to the task of working out principles of justice, say the critics. And if, as Rawls suggests, those 'behind the veil' must be presumed to know the principles of psychology, they will be aware of the results of speculating *in vacuo*.

It is not at all certain, continue the critics, that those in the 'original position' would come to the 'liberal-democratic' conclusions suggested by Rawls. Why would they necessarily prefer liberty to equality? Why would they not invoke a 'winner-takes-all' philosophy? Suppose that some of those in the 'original position' concluded, on the strength of their 'allowed knowledge', that there can be no true liberty save on the basis of economic sufficiency, or that material goods are of relatively small worth?

There is doubt, too, as to whether pure ratiocination 'behind the veil' would produce anything like Rawls's principles of justice. Has Rawls confused 'liberty' and 'liberties'? Is it that the logic of 'liberty as indivisible' has been overlooked? And would rational thought produce, inevitably, Rawls's catalogue of 'primary social goods'?

Dworkin, in *Sovereign Virtue: the Theory and Practice of Equality* (2000), finds the device of the original position implausible as the starting point for a philosophical interpretation of justice. It requires a more profound theory behind it which will attempt to explain *why* the original position possesses its particular features and *why* the principles chosen by people in that position should be categorised as 'principles of justice'.

It is certain that Rawls has produced a radical alternative to the rigidities of utilitarianism. The exponents of that philosophy were prepared to accept inequalities if the result would be the maximisation of the happiness of the greatest number. Rawls's principles constitute a rejection of this view. He sees liberty as a means to the promotion of society's good but, unlike the utilitarians, he is not prepared to put it aside so as to 'increase' that good. Liberty, for Rawls, is a good *in itself* and may not be limited save in the few circumstances he mentions. This is indeed a radical alternative to the simplistic views of utilitarianism; whether it is 'credible', given the hypothetical circumstances postulated by Rawls as necessary for the emergence of principles of justice, must remain arguable.

NOTES

A useful introduction to the fundamentals of Rawls's views is given in *Reading Rawls*, edited by Daniels. *John Rawls' Theory of Justice*, by Blocker and Smith, is a complete exposition of the theory. Wolff analyses the theory in *Understanding Rawls: a Reconstruction and Critique of a Theory of Justice*. Davies and Holdcroft, Chapter 9, explore Rawls's theory in detail. See, also, *Rawls and Rights*, by Martin, and *Modern Theories of Justice*, by Kohn (which considers criticisms of Rawls's theories). Ricoeur's *The Just* is a series of essays by a French jurist (translated by Pellaner) which includes an analysis of Rawls's theory.

QUESTION 31

'Nozick's theory of justice is really a political manifesto in the guise of jurisprudential fables.'

▶ Outline the theory and comment on the criticism.

Answer Plan

Nozick was a pupil of Rawls and rejected his teacher's insistence on the need for governmental intervention so as to achieve a redistribution of wealth. The concepts of individual libertarianism formed the basis of Nozick's view of society. Man's rights are of great importance, but their protection requires no more than the exercise by a 'minimal state' of 'night watchman functions'. Liberty and equality are not to be confused, and the right to property is inseparable from liberty. Nozick's appeal to politicians on the right of the political spectrum cannot be denied. An answer to the question involves an explanation of the 'minimal state' and a discussion of the 'fable' of its development. Nozick's attitudes to property and its distribution require comment. The following skeleton plan is suggested:

- ❖ Introduction;
- ❖ Nozick's principal theses;
- ❖ right to acquisition and possession of property;
- ❖ creation of the 'minimal state';
- ❖ distributive justice;
- ❖ Nozick's appeal to the political right wing;
- ❖ criticism of Nozick's 'poetic fantasies';
- ❖ his 'taxation and forced labour equivalence';
- ❖ conclusion, criticism of Nozick's 'parable of individuality'.

ANSWER

A 'just society', according to Nozick, is one based on *individualism*. The natural rights of the individual are to be considered inviolable, and each person may enjoy those rights subject only to certain moral 'side restraints' concerning the rights of others. The only type of state which is acceptable to those who believe in the virtues of liberalism is that which functions in a *minimal mode*; attempts by the state to redistribute wealth are generally unjustifiable and it is very doubtful whether liberty and equality are always compatible. These are the theses elaborated by Nozick in *Anarchy, State and Utopia* (1974). Ideas of this type have been used to underpin some political ideologies that have emerged in Western societies in recent years, but it is doubtful whether Nozick intended to produce a political manifesto as such. It is the *basis* and the *implications* of his ideas which have produced criticism from jurists and others.

Nozick assumes, for the purposes of his theory, that persons exist as 'distinct entities'. Adopting and adapting Locke's fable of the 'state of freedom' which accompanied the 'state of nature' in which man originally existed, he draws attention to the 'law of nature' which allows no individual to act in ways which bring harm to another's life, liberty or possessions. We have our 'natural rights' – freedom from violence against the person, freedom to hold property and freedom to enforce our rights against those who violate these basic freedoms. The freedom to hold property is based on 'legitimate acquisition': *just initial acquisition*, by which an individual acquires the ownership of that which was previously unowned; *legitimate transfer*, for example, by gift or exchange; and *rectification of former unjust distribution*, as where a person has obtained property unjustly and it has been returned to its proper owner. *'Justice in holdings*' (in acquisition, transfer and rectification) constitutes the individual's natural right to possessions.

None of these rights may be interfered with in the absence of the individual's consent. A person's 'distinctiveness' ensures that he ought not to be treated as a means to an end; hence, the concept of one person's natural abilities being available for exploitation merely for the benefit of, say, those within society who lack some advantage, is unacceptable. There can be no justice where social 'goals' or 'end state' demand that one person may claim rights in another. No individual has a right to something the realisation of which requires the use of things and activities involving other individuals' rights and entitlements. 'There is no justified sacrifice of some of us for others.' We may have a right to life (that is, the right not to be deprived of it by others), but not to the means needed to sustain life.

If goal-based societies are to be rejected, what principle ought to be favoured in the search for justice? Nozick suggests the principle of 'historical entitlement'. In order to test the presence of justice within a society, it is necessary to ask whether that society emerged in 'just fashion', whether its workings infringe rights and whether property is acquired and held there on the basis of 'justice in holdings'. The touchstones are, according to Nozick, total respect for individual rights and the existence of moral 'side constraints', forbidding any actions which negate individual rights. The right to liberty and the right to property are interdependent: take away one, and the other is rendered meaningless. (It is interesting to note that in 1830 Bentham had argued that property and law 'are born and must die together'.) An important expression of the individual's right to liberty is to be found in his right to acquire and keep property; indeed, says Nozick, an extension of private property may be interpreted as a growth of freedom.

What of the state in Nozick's theory? He approves only of the 'minimal state' which, he suggests, best realises the aspirations of many libertarian visionaries. 'The minimal state is inspiring as well as right.' He sees the 'minimal state' as expressing an 'invisible hand process' (the phraseology is that of Adam Smith, who used it to personify 'beneficent Providence'), which allows development of society without the violation of individual rights. Nozick uses his 'state of nature' fable to show how the 'minimal state' emerges. Initially, groups formed for themselves 'mutual protection associations' in which each member acted so as to defend all other members of the association. Eventually, there emerged 'protection agencies', their services paid for, acting as 'protection associations' and dealing with complaints by association members against one another. Conflicts among protection associations began, and one association emerged as the strongest and, therefore, dominant. Outside the protection associations were, of course, 'independents' who chose initially not to join. Finally, the dominant protection association agency took over control of all persons within its area of operations; the 'independents' received compensation for their loss of independence by being allowed to join the dominant association. The state was born. It has since developed in spontaneous fashion, its growth mirroring the self-interest of individuals.

The 'minimal state' is, in effect, no more than a 'night-watchman state': it operates only on a range of minimal activities. It will protect from force, fraud and theft; it will enforce contracts; it enjoys a monopoly of force; but it will not become involved in any form of economic redistribution. It has come into existence by morally permissible means and without violation of anyone's rights; it must operate so as to keep those rights inviolate. Nozick rejects any growth of the state beyond these narrow confines. That there ought to be a state is unquestioned, and to argue otherwise is to plunge into the errors of anarchy; but that there ought to be a 'supra-minimal state' is unacceptable, if liberty is to prevail.

Nozick's rejection of any form of state other than that of the 'night-watchman' type emerges in his attitude to 'distributive justice' – that is, where poorer, weaker citizens are assisted through the fruits of taxation and redistribution of resources. This is unacceptable to Nozick. The 'difference principle' advocated by Rawls, which allows an arrangement of economic and other advantages so as to assist those who are less well off, is perceived as an unwarranted interference with the norms of distribution and a violation of individual liberties. Indeed, a state which acted in this way so as to effect a 'patterned distribution of wealth' is to be regarded as intrinsically immoral. The task is not to redistribute resources, but rather to protect persons' rights to what they already possess. If an individual has obtained his property by 'just initial acquisition', he is entitled to keep it and it may not be utilised by others through a process of redistribution, save by his agreement. Where each person's holdings are just, then the total set of holdings is just. The 'fair redistribution of resources' is, in Nozick's eyes, a mask for the violation of liberty.

In a celebrated aphorism, Nozick states that taxation of earnings of labour is on a par with forced labour. To take the earnings of, say, x hours of labour is like taking x hours from the person; it is like forcing that person to work x hours for the purposes of another, to ends not his own. The fact that others may intentionally intervene to threaten force to ensure that taxes are paid makes the tax system equivalent to forced labour. Those who create wealth have inviolable rights over its possession and utilisation. Redistribution on grounds of 'social justice', 'difference principles' or 'welfare claims' is essentially unjust. Justice does not exist where processes involving redistribution of property or its fruits without consent are common.

Nozick's thesis, appearing at a period in American history during which legal, political and ethical argument seemed to be moving ineluctably in favour of an increased degree of state intervention, was unpopular among many jurists. On the agenda of public discussion were topics such as socialised medicine, free legal aid, improved welfare benefits and positive 'reverse discrimination' in favour of disadvantaged ethnic communities, all of which pointed to the need for intensified government intervention and a redistribution of social resources. Nozick's parable of the 'minimal state' and its social and legal consequences were highly unpopular. It was suggested by one lawyer that a subtitle for Nozick's book might be 'Forward to the 1770s', referring, presumably, to the period which saw the publication of Adam Smith's *Wealth of Nations*, with its emphasis on economic libertarianism. But it is not easy to accept the view that Nozick's writings constitute a political manifesto for the right wing. The fact that they may have given ideological comfort to those who espouse the politics of non-interventionism is no more proof of the 'political manifesto' charge than the purloining by the Nazis of extracts from the writing of Savigny is proof that he would have approved their political creed.

Objection has been taken to Nozick's theses on the ground of lack of supporting data; his views on the emergence of the state have been dismissed as 'little more than poetic fantasy'. There is no direct proof of the state's *evolution* as envisaged by Nozick. It may sound convincing, and it has a ring of authenticity, particularly in its insistence on 'survival' as being the aim of earlier societies. But there is little direct evidence in favour of the 'protective association' thesis. Indeed, no society has ever been created in the fashion envisaged by Nozick. Further, Nozick does not explain in convincing fashion the *derivation* of fundamental rights. Where and how did they originate? And why does his enumeration of fundamental rights exclude, say, the right to work, education and shelter? Why does he provide no catalogue of fundamental duties? Given the reciprocity and relationships without which our type of society would be doomed, would it not have been useful to postulate the duties arising 'naturally' from the right to have one's liberties respected?

Additionally, is it possible to keep a state in its 'minimal' form? Is it not mere wishful thinking to suggest that a 'night-watchman state' will not seek to grow as its tasks increase in scope and complexity? How will the 'minimal state' cope with problems of internal and external security save by a significant extension of its activities? Just as the state emerged, in Nozick's terms, by imposing restraints on the 'independents' outside the original 'protective associations', how will it be possible for a state to carry out its basic functions of 'night-watchman' without infringing the rights of some individuals? Above all, how can the 'minimal state' be *controlled* by those on whose behalf it operates?

Nozick's 'discovery' of an equivalence of taxation and forced labour has been dismissed as a delusion. Thus, taxation can be avoided by a person freely choosing not to undertake taxed employment; 'forced labour' arises from no free choice. Taxation may be viewed legitimately as a contribution to the welfare of others; forced labour is in no sense a contribution of this nature. Taxation is not an undignified violation of human rights; forced labour robs the individual of dignity and rights. Similarly, Nozick's claim that an extension of ownership of private property increases liberty may exemplify the error, pointed out by many contemporary jurists, of assuming that the conditions of freedom for *single* individuals can be defined *before* considering conditions of freedom for *all* individuals within a community. What is the nature of the 'freedom' enjoyed by a minority of individuals within a community which deprives the majority of its citizens of dignity?

It may be that Nozick's 'parable of individuality' rests on his refusal to accept that 'no man is an island entire of itself'. His concept of 'inviolable, individual rights' seems to ignore the social setting which is required to give substance to those rights. The relationship of rights and duties is indeed fundamental to our type of society. A perception of redistribution of social resources as invariably 'unjust' acts, it has been said, as a justification of a society without charity, philanthropy and compassion. The rejection of redistribution in the form of welfare activities by the state will, it is argued, rob sections of the community of the 'meaningful life' (which can be moulded in accordance with individual choice) to be found at the very heart of Nozick's philosophy. Nozick's elevation of individualism guided by the 'minimal state' is probably of limited value for an understanding of the complex web of rights, duties, relationships and reciprocity which we term 'society'.

Common Pitfalls

Students can avoid the pitfall of thinking that Nozick is an anarchist because he argues against the modern redistributive welfare state and because his book is entitled *Anarchy, State and Utopia*. Nozick was not an anarchist but believed in the 'minimal' or 'nightwatchman' state where the state exists to protect citizens against crime internally and the threat of foreign attack from without, but where the state in Nozick's scheme cannot redistribute wealth without violating citizen's 'rights'. For Nozick the two fundamental questions in political philosophy are (1) is the state justified at all? (2) if so justified, what is the reach of the state: can the state redistribute wealth through taxation of the wealthy? Students can gain extra marks by pointing out that Nozick was in the tradition of conservative thought going back to Hobbes that sees government restricted to its traditional tasks: the maintenance of legal order within the community and the defence of the community's integrity against attack from the outside.

NOTES

The concept of the 'minimal state' is discussed in Davies and Holdcroft, Chapter 11. Paul has edited a collection of essays entitled *Reading Nozick*. Criticisms of Nozick's theory of justice are contained in *Courts and Administrators: A Study in Jurisprudence*, by Detmold. Lessnoff's essay, 'Robert Nozick', in *The Political Classics*, edited by Forsyth and Keens-Soper, and Wolff's *Robert Nozick* explore implications of Nozick's philosophy.

Rights

12

INTRODUCTION

In this chapter, the questions concern problems arising from the concept of 'rights'. Some jurists have referred to jurisprudence as 'the science of rights', seeking to stress, presumably, the significance of human rights in any legal system and in any analysis of the purposes and functions of the law. The questions relate to Dworkin (b 1931) and his rights thesis, to the circumstances in which the overriding of individual rights might be justified, and to arguments concerning 'the right to euthanasia'.

Checklist ✔

Ensure that you are acquainted with the following topics:

- basic, inalienable rights;
- the overriding of rights;
- Dworkin's 'principle of integrity';
- the controversy concerning euthanasia.

QUESTION 32

How has Dworkin utilised his 'rights thesis' in his exploration of the concept of equality?

Answer Plan

Dworkin (b 1931), an American jurist, holds chairs in Law and Philosophy at New York University, and Jurisprudence at University College, London. His writings in jurisprudence are concerned with the fundamental nature of rights and their significance in law and society. He is concerned, in particular, with the interface of jurisprudence and political ideas and has written extensively on current problems relating to abortion, euthanasia, civil rights and equality. His most recent major publication deals specifically with equality – 'the endangered species of political ideals'. The required answer should be based on a short account of his views relating to rights and his belief that equality and liberty are vital, substantial ideals, and are aspects of a single concept of the quality of social life. The following skeleton plan is suggested:

- ❖ Introduction;
- ❖ Dworkin's rejection of theories of positivism and natural rights;
- ❖ standards, principles, and significance of dignity of citizens of a community;
- ❖ entitlement to rights;
- ❖ problem of equality;
- ❖ possible conflict of liberty and equality;
- ❖ conclusion, affirmation of principle of integrity as basis of entitlement to rights.

ANSWER

Dworkin's jurisprudential writings seek to explore the essence of rights and to place them within a wider setting of social and political ideology. His work ranges beyond that generally associated with current American legal theory in that he rejects the view of jurisprudence as a 'pure academic discipline' which should have little to say of immediate significance for political realities. For Dworkin, law and political ideology have close links: both co-exist as aspects of social aspirations and activities, and neither can be understood fully without reference to the other. Law in practice is for him 'an unfolding narrative' which can be interpreted only by comprehending its social setting. An analysis of rights, in particular, demands examination of their place within the wide culture, and very purpose, of social and political awareness.

In an examination of rights, Dworkin declares, little is to be gained from theories which suppose that rights have some special metaphysical character: the old theories of natural law that rely on this supposition are of no value. The doctrines of natural law, suggesting that lawyers tend to follow criteria that are not entirely factual when they ask whether propositions are 'true', or that law and justice are identical, in the sense that makes it impossible to consider an unjust proposition of law to be 'true', tell us nothing about the fundamentals of rights. The *a priori* reasoning associated with the natural law is unacceptable; if we wish to make an effective investigation of a legal structure and its validity, then empirical study is required.

If we examine rights in the setting of positivist theory, we are met with the assertion that law consists of rules, and that this is reflected in concepts of rights. Legal rules are applied automatically once appropriate conditions are met. 'Event A will bring in its train penalty B.' Thus, **s 16** of the **Terrorism Act 2000** states clearly that a person commits an offence if he uses money or other property for the purposes of terrorism; the appropriate penalties are set out in **s 22**. The 'rules' of the statute dictate particular results and, other things being equal, the statutory penalty under **s 16** will be inflicted on persons found guilty. In a more specific sense of the term 'rules', the **Civil Procedure Rules 1998** state that a person who makes a false statement of truth, or who causes such a statement to be made, without an honest belief in its truth is guilty of contempt of court (**r 32.14(1)**). Given the requisite conditions, application of the rules then follows. But Dworkin rejects totally the claim that law consists in its entirety of rules of this nature. In making his generalised criticism of positivism, which fails to explain rights, he declares that, in making a basic attack on that doctrine, he will seek to show that the notion of a single fundamental test for law ('law as rules') misses the important role of those *standards* that are not rules.

The legal system, and the place of rights within it, requires an explanation involving not only the discrete rules and statutes enacted by its officials, but also consideration of the general principles of justice and fairness that these rules and statutes, taken together, presuppose by way of implicit justification. Thus, 'policy' is of great importance as an element of law: a policy is 'a kind of standard that sets out a goal to be reached, generally an improvement in some economic, political or social feature of the community'. Thus, the **Pollution Prevention and Control Act 1999** has a clear social goal of 'preserving the coherence of our industrial pollution control systems'. To ignore communal aspirations and policies within the terms of a statute is to ignore the real meaning of law.

'Principle' is of great significance for Dworkin: from an understanding of its role stems a comprehension of the essence of law and the relationship of rights and justice. A principle is a standard that is to be observed, not because it will advance or secure an economic or political situation deemed desirable, but because it is 'a requirement of justice or fairness or some other dimension of morality'. Principles are fundamental to law; they have a dimension of weights so that it is for the courts to assess their weights in relation to a particular dispute, and to balance them. Thus, it may be necessary to balance the principle that a person may use his land as he wishes against the principle that no one may use his property in a way which inflicts injury on another. Rights may emerge from considerations of the weight of principles.

Existence of a firm dividing line between law and morality, which features in many statements of positivism, is rejected by Dworkin. A judge engaged in the task of adjudication may have to make moral judgments. The very process of balancing principles and policies may involve him in a consideration of the community's general attitudes to questions of right and wrong, which express commonly held views on morality. Judgments ought not to vitiate social standards and this involves, according to Dworkin, the important matter of 'law as integrity' and rights as expressing a 'community of principles'. The concept of 'law as integrity' asks the judge to assume, so far as this is possible, 'that the law is structured by a coherent set of principles about justice and fairness and procedural due process', and it asks him to enforce these in the fresh cases that come before him. For each statute that the judge is asked to enforce, he should construct some justification that 'fits and flows through that statute', and is consistent with other legislation in force.

The positivist contention that judges make law and, therefore, have a duty to fashion rights is not accepted by Dworkin. The judge has no occasion, he maintains, to utilise legal reasoning to produce new law (which is a task for the community's elected legislature). His task is to balance policies and principles so as to discover the correct solution to the problems emerging in a hearing. His task is to apply *principles* which may not be altered at his whim.

The law is to be interpreted as the embodiment of rights and responsibilities. Rights do not emanate from sources outside mankind. An individual's entitlement to rights in civil society depends on the practice and the justice of its institutions, political and legal. Existing political rights are enforced (but not created) by judicial decisions. Jurisprudence guides the community in its attempt to discover which rights a particular political theory assumes that citizens possess. It is within this context that questions of rights in relation to, say, freedom of speech or racial equality have to be examined. The right of freedom of speech has emerged over the centuries as respect for human dignity has intensified. The framework of rights bolstering racial equality represents, in similar fashion, respect for fairness.

Abstract rights stem from abstract principles; concrete rights are an expression of the weight of facts in relation to general principles. The courts do not fashion new rights; they tend to discover them within the existing law through an examination of an individual's entitlements under particular circumstances.

Dworkin's view of rights is predicated on his belief in the need for society to protect, through political and legal action, *the dignity of its members*. Some rights, which affect a person's individuality, should rarely be violated, even when it may appear that the welfare of society is in question. If rights make sense at all, then an invasion of a relatively important right is very serious indeed: an invasion of this nature necessitates treating a man as less than a man or as less worthy of concern than other men. 'The institution of "men's rights" rests on the conviction that this is a grave injustice ... and that it is worth paying the incremental cost in social policy or efficiency that is necessary so as to prevent it.' It is this aspect of Dworkin's rights thesis that underpins his treatment of the problem of equality in society.

In his examination of equality (*Sovereign Virtue: the Theory and Practice of Equality* (2000)), Dworkin argues that we must not turn our backs on equality, *no matter what the cost*. Our jurisprudence must propagate the argument that no government is legitimate 'that does not show equal concern for the fate of all those citizens over whom it claims dominion and from whom it claims allegiance'. Without equal concern for citizens, a government is little short of a tyranny. Equal concern for all is essential if we are to act so as to redeem our political virtue. This has little to do with ensuring that all persons have the same wealth, for Dworkin does not see equality in those terms. It has everything to do with 'equality of resources', of making available to all the resources of society, including the framework of rights which will ensure the triumph of 'ethical individualism'. Human lives must be successful, rather than wasted, and 'one person has a special and final responsibility for that success – the person whose life it is'. The principle of equality does not attach to a person's property and his property rights, but to the hope that his life shall come to something rather than being rendered ineffectual.

A government has the duty, according to Dworkin, to adopt laws and policies that will ensure that the fates of its citizens are, so far as this is capable of achievement, insensitive to who they otherwise are – in terms of gender, race, economic backgrounds. Further, governments must act through the courts and legislative institutions to ensure that the fates of citizens are sensitive to the choices they have made.

Dworkin emphasises that he is interested in liberty in its 'negative sense', that is, in its relation to freedom of constraint; his general belief is that people's liberty over matters of fundamental personal concern ought not to be infringed. Nevertheless, he argues *against* the view that liberty is a fundamental value that must *never* be sacrificed to equality. In general, there should be no conflict between liberty and equality: equality is unlikely to exist in a society from which liberty is absent. But in a genuine contest between liberty and equality, liberty may have to lose out.

What are the circumstances in which rights to liberty might conflict with rights to equality? Dworkin suggests that this might arise where two conditions co-exist: first, that 'on balance' the position of some group within the community could be improved by eliminating some existing liberty, and, secondly, that the principle of equal concern for the rights of that group requires that this step ought to be taken.

Essentially, this will be a matter of balancing political and legal rights. As an illustration, Dworkin gives the example of a society in which private and state medical provision exist together. If the poorer citizens within that society would enjoy better medical care were private medicine to be abolished, then the principle of equal concern demands that this step be taken. To refuse to carry out this step implies, according to Dworkin, acceptance of the view that the lives of the poor are less important than the lives of others. The principle of liberty has little value except for the contribution it makes to the life of society; in a conflict of this nature, the principle of egalitarianism, which reflects concern for the rights of all, must prevail.

It is jurisprudential argument of this nature which has led Dworkin to emerge as a prominent supporter of policies of 'affirmative action' in the USA. Policies of this type (known also as 'reverse discrimination' or 'positive discrimination') have been defined by Katzner as 'a call to offset the effect of past acts of bias by skewing opportunities in the opposite directions'; they involve giving preferential treatment to disadvantaged groups so as to compensate for past discrimination. Dworkin sees legal-political action of this type as giving expression to his belief that there are circumstances in which the right to equality in resources (for example, the right to higher education) requires a fundamental reappraisal of the purposes of the liberty to which the community is committed.

The essence of Dworkin's teaching in this area of jurisprudence suggests that *rights arise from the community's respect for the principle of integrity*. In his words: 'Integrity insists that each citizen must accept demands on him, and may make demands on others, that share and extend the moral dimensions of any explicit political decisions.' When the good citizen is faced with the question of deciding how he ought to treat his fellow citizen when interests collide, he must act so as to fulfil the common scheme of justice 'to which they are committed just in virtue of citizenship'.

Aim Higher ★

Students can gain extra marks by pointing out the difference between 'treating people as equals' and giving them 'equal treatment'. The need for 'equality of opportunity' in life chances, such as careers so as to treat people as equals, might require the practice of 'reverse discrimination' so as to give persons from disadvantaged ethnic or social backgrounds extra help in achieving university or work placement places. Students can gain extra marks by pointing out that whereas the state must always 'treat citizens as equals' this does not necessarily entail 'equal treatment' of citizens.

NOTES

Dworkin's views on rights are set out in *Taking Rights Seriously* and *Law's Empire*. His examination of equality is contained in *Sovereign Virtue: the Theory and Practice of Equality*. Davies and Holdcroft, Chapter 10, sets out Dworkin's basic rights thesis; Harris, Chapter 4, summarises the reasoning behind the thesis. See, also, *Ronald Dworkin*, by Guest, and 'Professor Dworkin's theory of rights', by Raz in (1978) 26 Political Studies 123.

QUESTION 33

Comment on some of the jurisprudential issues raised in recent years by debates on the so-called 'right to euthanasia'.

Answer Plan

Debates on 'rights at life's edges', relating to abortion and euthanasia, have intensified in recent years as extensive improvements in medical technology have come to public notice in the USA and Britain. A difficulty in answering a question of this nature is to avoid concentrating on purely religious or moral points of view to the exclusion of jurisprudential issues concerning 'rights'. The writings of Dworkin and Grisez include valuable summaries of the arguments surrounding euthanasia – the deliberate termination of a life of intense pain and incurable suffering in circumstances which would currently attract sanctions under the criminal law. The following skeleton plan is used:

- ❖ Introduction;
- ❖ definitions;
- ❖ situation in English law;
- ❖ Dworkin's thesis of rights and human dignity;
- ❖ the case against euthanasia as presented by the Catholic jurist, Grisez;
- ❖ the problems of death with dignity;
- ❖ conclusion, the chance of agreement by both sides in the dispute.

ANSWER

Current debates on euthanasia tend to turn upon the recognition or rejection of *a right* to the termination of one's life where suffering has become intolerable. Supporters of euthanasia generally argue from the principle of human autonomy and its implications, while opponents emphasise the moral and legal dangers of interfering with 'life at its edges'. The central debate has been summarised in the writings of the American jurists, Dworkin, who lends general support to the legalisation of euthanasia (set out in his *Life's Dominion* (1993)) and Grisez, who rejects a right to euthanasia (as set out in the text, *Life and Death with Liberty and Justice* (1985, 1st edition)).

Active euthanasia involves the deliberate killing of one person by another – for example, where X, who carries out the killing, genuinely believes that Y, who is suffering from a grave, pitiable disease or defect, would be 'better off dead'. *Voluntary active euthanasia* involves Y, who is legally competent, giving his informed consent to being killed by X, or being assisted by X to take his own life, in conditions characterised by Y's very grave illness. *Involuntary euthanasia* involves the killing by X of Y, who is seriously ill, in circumstances where X does not consult Y, or overrides his (Y's) judgment.

The situation in English law in relation to so-called 'mercy killing' seems clear. In *Airedale NHS Trust v Bland* (1993), Lord Goff stated:

> It is not lawful for a doctor to administer a drug to his patient to bring about his death, even though that course is prompted by a humanitarian desire to end his suffering, however great that suffering may be . . . So to act is to cross the Rubicon which runs between, on the one hand, the care of the living patient and, on the other hand, euthanasia – actively causing his death to avoid or end his suffering. *Euthanasia is not lawful at common law.*

Dworkin's thesis, outlined in *Life's Dominion*, may be viewed as resting upon the closing peroration in his *Law's Empire* (1986), in which he speaks of the significance of the fraternal attitude which should unite the community even though it be divided on matters of interest and conviction. Aware of the very wide gulf which currently divides the pro- and anti-euthanasia jurists and other members of the community, he urges consideration of a measure of conciliation and unity, believing that the fundamental respect for human dignity which appears to characterise both sides of the argument may assist in bridging the gap. Dworkin's major concern is for *an extension of rights* that will recognise human autonomy and dignity.

Three main types of situation in which people may have to decide about their own, or some other person's, death are noted by Dworkin. The first type of situation involves a decision by a *conscious or competent* individual. The laws of almost all Western countries generally prohibit the direct killing of a person (by a physician or other person) at that (conscious and competent) person's request. A physician who acts in this way is perceived by the law as having betrayed his unequivocal duty. The second type of situation involves a decision taken by a physician in relation to a person who is *unconscious and dying*. The person may be in a persistent vegetative state, that is, incapable of sensation or thought (see, for example, the *Airedale NHS* case, in which the House of Lords emphasised that continuing treatment was not in the patient's best interests). The third situation involves a patient who is *conscious but incompetent*, as in the case of a patient suffering from the dementia associated with Alzheimer's disease.

Dworkin suggests that decisions concerning death in these types of situation involve a consideration of three issues, the first of which is *autonomy*. A person's undoubted *right* to make important decisions for himself should be taken, it is argued, as including freedom to end his life when he wishes ('at least if his decision is not plainly irrational'). Where a person is unconscious, Dworkin suggests that we can respect his autonomy only by posing a question as to what he himself would have decided in relation to this situation before his competence disappeared (for example, by reference to a 'living will' which sets out his wishes as to what ought to be done in circumstances of this nature).

A second issue involves the argument concerning a person's '*best interests*'. Dworkin is aware that some persons may wish to remain alive for as long as possible, no matter in what condition they may live: a paternalistic view that they may be 'better off dead' suggests that they do not know their own interests. In some cases, however, as where a person is permanently unconscious, those responsible for him (including his immediate family) may feel genuinely that a termination of life would, in the specific circumstances, be preferable *in his interests* to a continued existence in conditions of severe distress.

The third issue is that of *the sanctity of life*. The argument that euthanasia and suicide are contrary to God's will, in that the termination of a life before its natural end runs contrary to the duties imposed by God's gift of life, is powerful. Its expression in jurisprudential terms suggests that there should be no right based upon the recognition and protection by the law of an act which seems contrary to God's commands. Dworkin's considered reply is based on a belief that the idea of the sanctity of human life 'has a secular as well as a religious interpretation'. Respect for the sanctity of human life can involve acceptance of the view that human beings must be allowed to end their lives *appropriately* and, where possible, not in circumstances which are a denial of the values they have considered as characterising their lives. Attention ought to be given to the argument that persons ought to be allowed 'to die proudly when it is no longer possible to live proudly'. In considering juristic rights which might be involved in the deliberate ending of a life, Dworkin reminds us that the principal question posed by calls for the legislation of active euthanasia is how life's sanctity should be understood *and* respected. To make an individual sufferer die in a manner of which others approve, but which he believes to be an appalling contradiction of his own existence, 'is a devastating, odious form of tyranny'.

Dworkin gives particular attention to euthanasia in the context of the lives of those who have lost the very capacities which ought to be protected by the right to autonomy: he has in mind those who are living 'a life past reason'. Ought we to continue to recognise the right of a person to take a decision which is contrary to his interests so as to afford a measure of protection for capacities which he clearly lacks? How can we know the 'best interests' of a person who is in a permanent state of dementia? Have persons a right *not* to exist for long periods in degrading conditions which create or perpetuate indignity or which make them unconscious of that indignity? Our understanding of the significance of the kind of life a person has lived should bring us to an insistence that he must not be treated in a manner which 'in our community's vocabulary of respect, denies him dignity'.

Hence, Dworkin concludes, there must be engendered a right – in the name of that freedom which is a cardinal requirement of self-respect – for a person to be allowed to die in a way which we think shows self-respect. Both sides in the euthanasia debate accept the profound significance of concern for the sanctity of human life; disagreement emerges from a consideration of how to *interpret* that concern. The laws which the community makes must express an understanding of *why* life is sacred and *why* rights and freedom are of significance in 'life's dominion'.

Grisez, writing from the standpoint of neo-Thomist jurisprudence, is an opponent of euthanasia. Fundamental to his view is the teaching of the Catholic Church, restated in 1995 by the Pope in his Encyclical, *The Gospel of Life*: 'I confirm that euthanasia is a grave violation of the law of God, since it is the deliberate and morally unacceptable killing of a human being.' In jurisprudential terms, Grisez denies the existence of rights which allow or might allow the deliberate killing of persons at their own request or for merciful motives.

Grisez notes the difficulty of defining 'death' in terms which are acceptable to jurists and others who are concerned with the question of euthanasia. Medical technology allows, for example, the maintenance of 'vital functions' in persons who might otherwise have been pronounced dead. A typical definition of death, from the 1960s, is that given in *Black's Law Dictionary*:

> The cessation of life; defined by physicians as a total stoppage of the circulation of the blood, and a cessation of the animal and vital functions consequent thereon, such as respiration, pulsation, etc.

This would not now be acceptable to physicians. In English law, death has not been defined in precise terms by statute. Some English jurists have drawn attention to the value of the definition given in the Kansas Statutes 1971: 'A person will be considered medically and legally dead if, in the opinion of a physician, based on ordinary standards of medical practice, there is the absence of spontaneous brain function.'

The American Bar Association has used the following definition in recent comments on the question of legalised euthanasia: 'For all legal purposes, a human body with irreversible cessation of *total* brain function, according to usual and customary standards of medical practice, shall be considered dead.' Grisez emphasises the difficulties involved in defining precisely what is meant by euthanasia in the absence of a definition of death which is widely acceptable in legal institutions. Is death a 'process' or a 'single event'? Is the philosopher Wittgenstein 'correct' in assuming that death is not a part of life, but merely its limit? It is not easy to speak of a 'right to terminate life' when its very boundaries have not yet been marked with acceptable precision.

Grisez places emphasis on the significance of the jurisprudential principle of *justice* in relation to the arguments against euthanasia. If voluntary active euthanasia is to be legalised, then there would be a strong chance that 'persons who do not wish to be killed are likely to become unwilling victims', so that they might be denied the protection of the law of homicide which they now enjoy: that denial would constitute a grave injustice. Further, because physicians are not infallible, a wrong diagnosis could be made which constituted the sole significant factor in rendering a case 'hopeless', thus bringing it within the class of cases in which euthanasia is held desirable. And may not individual sufferers be easily pressured into consent, thus leading to a killing which is essentially unjust? Is it sufficient to rely on 'the good judgment and humanistic motives' of all concerned in order to ensure that justice will be done in the process of ending a life?

In his *Sanctity of Life* (1957), the jurist Glanville Williams suggested legislation to be based on the following clause: 'It shall be lawful for a physician after consultation with another physician, to accelerate by any merciful means the death of a patient who is seriously ill, unless it is proved that the act was not done in good faith with the consent of the patient and for the purpose of saving him from severe pain in an illness believed to be of an incurable and fatal character.' Such a formulation, argues Grisez, may not sound dangerous until it is recalled that what Williams is proposing is an amendment to the law which prohibits murder. 'Once this fact is taken into account, the danger is obvious.' How could the prosecution prove beyond reasonable doubt that the physicians did not act in good faith, or that they did not believe the illness to be incurable or fatal?

Grisez suggests a careful consideration of the 'thin end of the wedge' argument – namely, that there can be no guarantee that the legislation of voluntary euthanasia will not move incrementally into a policy which legalises non-voluntary euthanasia. He notes the road travelled by the enthusiastic advocates (physicians and jurists) of eugenics in Germany who moved with ease from support for proposals in the 1920s for 'death with dignity' to the acceptance of arguments in favour of sterilisation and euthanasia for incurable mentally ill persons who were regarded as 'mere caricatures of real persons'. The road to eventual genocide was prepared at an early date. Grisez stresses the differences between euthanasia and genocide, but notes the way in which leading members of the German medical profession easily moved their stance, often with the support of prominent jurists.

The arguments of proponents of euthanasia, expressed in the aphorism 'death with dignity', are analysed by Grisez in the light of the neo-Thomist view of man as entitled to dignity and, therefore, to those rights which embody this entitlement, *because* he is made in the image of God. Dignity implies inherent worth: all persons have dignity and all are entitled to respect. But respect for dignity must involve a refusal to impose on non-competent sufferers a judgment of others that it would be better for them if they were dead. Further, dignity may be made manifest in one who is suffering by 'maintaining his uniqueness against the power of suffering and death' with a display of courage and patience. Grisez suggests that the work of hospices demonstrates in impressive fashion that 'there certainly can be dignity in dying without voluntary active euthanasia'. There is, he claims, no necessity for any person to die in misery, deprived of human dignity. To see euthanasia as a solution to the problem of 'death with dignity' is to adopt a technically easy solution in a manner 'which least comports with the dignity of persons'. To provide 'appropriate and excellent care' for the dying is to respect their dignity in full measure.

In juristic terms, the plea from both sides in the debate involves a recognition of the equal dignity to be attached *through the medium of legal rights* to all persons. The predicament of suffering is to be approached in a spirit of justice and understanding. Without a basis of justice, any attempt to deal with the problem of mortal suffering will, in the words of Grisez, expose people to the natural forces of the struggle of all to survive, 'a struggle in which the fittest to survive are those who survive, but the fittest to live with human dignity are more than others likely to die'. There is little difference between this view and that of Dworkin: there is probably a good chance of agreement on ends, but whether the gulf between their points of view concerning legal means can be bridged easily remains problematic.

Legal argument continues, fuelled by cases such as *Re A (Children)* (2000), in which the Court of Appeal considered, primarily, the lawfulness of a proposed surgical operation on conjoined twins which would result inevitably in the death of one of them. The court decided that the operation would be lawful. The comments of

Ward LJ sought to reaffirm the sanctity of life principle in circumstances in which the law, presented with an acute dilemma, 'had to allow an escape through choosing the lesser of two evils'. Some jurists, commenting on the decision, expressed concerns at what they perceived as a movement along the road to legalised euthanasia.

Elements of an important strand of judicial thought emerged in the discussions leading to the publication, in January 2000, of the **Medical Treatment (Prevention of Euthanasia) Bill**. Clause 1 stated: 'It shall be unlawful for any person responsible for the care of a patient to withdraw or withhold from the patient medical treatment or sustenance if his purpose or one of his purposes in doing so is to hasten or otherwise cause the death of the patient.' 'Medical treatment' was defined as 'any medical or surgical treatment, including the administration of drugs or the use of any mechanical or other apparatus for the provision or support of ventilation or of any other bodily function'. The Bill did not complete the necessary stages of passage through the Commons, but, again, concern was voiced in many quarters on judicial decisions which seemed, effectively, to support a right to end life, while opponents of the Bill felt that existing legal barriers against euthanasia were adequate.

NOTES

The following short selection from the vast range of the literature on euthanasia is suggested as background reading: *To Die or Not to Die*, edited by Berger (1990); *The Human Body and the Law*, by Myers (1990); 'Against the right to die', by Velleman, in (1992) 7 Journal of Medicine and Philosophy; 'Involuntary euthanasia', by Robertson, in (1975) 27 Stanford L Rev; *The Morality of Killing: Sanctity of Life, Abortion and Euthanasia*, by Kohl; *Voluntary Euthanasia and the Common Law*, by Otlowski; 'Sex, death and the courts', in Dworkin's recently published *Sovereign Virtue: the Theory and Practice of Equality*, in which he poses and seeks to answer the question: 'May a "moral majority" limit the liberty of individual citizens on no better ground than that it disapproves of the personal choices they make?' The Journal of Medical Ethics carries regular articles on the medico-legal issues raised by discussions on euthanasia.

13

Law and Morality

INTRODUCTION

In this chapter attention is drawn to the age-old question of the links between law and morality. Ought the law to reflect morality? Ought it to change as social morality changes? Ought the institutions of the law to be viewed as guardians of morality? The Wolfenden Report of 1957 precipitated an intensive debate on the law and sexual morality in which Hart and Devlin (a former judge of the Court of Appeal and the House of Lords) appeared as advocates of different attitudes to this problem. A question in this chapter considers the arguments for the basis of toleration in liberal democratic states and the 'natural lawyers' reply to those liberal arguments.

Checklist ✔

Ensure that you are acquainted with the following topics:

- the Wolfenden Report;
- the 'seamless web of morality';
- the 'right-thinking' man;
- JS Mill's 'harm principle';
- Dworkin's argument for liberal toleration based on 'equal concern and respect';
- Raz's argument for toleration based on 'respect for autonomy';
- the 'natural law' tradition on this issue.

QUESTION 34

In the discussion which followed the publication of the Wolfenden Report (1957), Devlin posed as a fundamental question: 'What is the connection between crime and sin and to what extent, if at all, should the criminal law of England concern itself with the enforcement of morals and punish sin or morality as such?'

▶ How did Devlin answer this question, and what reactions did his answer elicit from Hart?

Answer Plan

In the controversy which followed publication of the Wolfenden Report (1957), Devlin (1905–1992) spoke for those who rejected its findings. His personal ground of opposition was the failure of the Report to justify the philosophy upon which it appeared to be based. In support of his opposition, he raised the fundamental problem of the relationship of crime, morality and the law. Hart (1907–1992) sought to support the recommendations of the Report and, in so doing, attempted to expose some of Devlin's arguments as fallacious. The answer ought to concentrate on the essential features of Devlin's three questions and his answers, together with an outline of Hart's stand on the law–morality link as he perceives it. The following skeleton plan is used:

- ❖ Introduction;
- ❖ background to the controversy;
- ❖ Devlin's interrogatories and answers;
- ❖ Hart's counter-arguments;
- ❖ summary of the debate;
- ❖ conclusion, the unresolved questions concerning the social significance of morality.

ANSWER

The *Wolfenden Report on Homosexual Offences and Prostitution* (1957) suggested the decriminalisation of specific homosexual acts between consenting adults in private, and stressed the significance of two particular principles. The first of these was that the function of the criminal law, in the area with which the Report had been concerned, was to preserve public order and decency, to protect the public from that which was injurious or offensive and to safeguard the vulnerable against corruption and exploitation. The second principle was that there must remain a realm of private morality which is not the law's business (but to say this was not to condone in any way private immorality). Devlin criticised the thinking behind the Report; Hart supported the general proposals of the Report and sought to attack the principles from which Devlin argued.

There are, said Devlin, certain moral principles which our society does require to be observed; their breach can be considered as an offence against society *as a whole*. The law does not punish *all* immorality; it does not condone *any* immorality. It is always necessary to investigate the links between sin and the purpose and tasks of the criminal law. Devlin put three questions. The *first* asked whether a society had the right to pass judgment at all on matters of morals, and whether there ought to be a public morality, or whether morals should always be a matter for private judgment. The *second* question asked whether, if society has a right to pass a judgment, it may use the law to enforce it. The *third* question asked whether the weapon of the law should be used in all cases or only in some and, if only in some, what principles should be kept in mind.

Devlin answered the first question with a resounding 'Yes'. The Report took for granted the existence of a public morality. If the bonds of that morality are relaxed too far, then members of society will drift apart. These bonds are a part of the 'price of society' and, because mankind has a need of society, the price must be paid.

The second question produced an uncompromising answer. A society *is* entitled to use the law in order to preserve its morality in precisely the same way that it uses the law to safeguard anything else considered essential to its existence. It is not possible, says Devlin, to set any theoretical limits to the government's power to legislate against immorality. A society has an undeniable right to legislate against internal and external dangers – the law of treason provides an example. The loosening of communal bonds may be a preliminary to total social disintegration and, therefore, a society should take steps to preserve its moral code.

The third question involves the circumstances in which a government ought to act in the event of a threatened disintegration of its moral basis. How may the moral judgments of society be ascertained? Devlin suggests that reference be made to the judgment of 'the right-minded man' (not to be confused with 'the reasonable man'). He may be thought of as 'the man in the jury box'. Let *his* judgment prevail and, for the purposes of the law, let immorality be thought of as what 'every right-minded man' considers to be immoral.

At this stage of his argument, Devlin refers to certain 'elastic principles' to be kept in mind by a legislature. First, there ought to be toleration of the maximum individual freedom consistent with society's integrity. Secondly, only that which lies 'beyond the limits of tolerance' ought to be punished; these limits will be reached when an activity creates disgust among 'right-minded persons'. Not everything can be tolerated, and general, widespread disgust marks the point at which tolerance must be questioned. It should be remembered, too, that the limits of tolerance may shift from generation to generation. Thirdly, privacy must be respected and this needs to be balanced against the need to enforce the law. Finally, the law is concerned with minima, not maxima; society should set its standards above those of the law.

Hart reacted by questioning the basis of Devlin's axioms. He was concerned, in particular, with Devlin's implicit 'legal moralism' – the attempt to prevent and prohibit conduct because it is perceived as immoral, even though it harms no person. Hart objected to Devlin's stress on 'intolerance, indignation and disgust' as marking the boundaries for tolerance. Hart reminds legislators that the popular limits of tolerance shift; they are not static over long periods of time. Devlin's concept of morality as a 'seamless web', which will collapse unless the community's vetoes are enforced by law, is not accepted by Hart. He denies that breaches of morality will necessarily affect the integrity of society as a whole. Devlin's analogy, which was drawn between the suppression of treason and the suppression of sexual immorality, was 'quite absurd'. It was 'grotesque' to suggest that homosexual activity could lead to the destruction of society. To offend against one aspect of society's moral code is not necessarily to jeopardise its entire structure. Devlin ignores, according to Hart, the fact that there cannot be, logically, a sphere of 'private treason', but there is, undoubtedly, a sphere of 'private morality and immorality'.

Hart is moved to argue, further, that legal punishment which may follow on sexual misdemeanour may provide disproportionate personal misery. This must not be disregarded. Indeed, he claims, blackmail and other evil consequences of criminal punishment may outweigh the harm caused by the practices classified as sexual offences.

Hart's argument continues with a caution to legislators. Devlin's criterion for the 'immorality' of a sexual practice is, apparently, the disgust it produces in the mind of 'the right-thinking man'. Given this criterion, the legislator must ask himself certain questions. What is the *nature* of the general morality embraced by 'the right-thinking man'? Is it based in any way on ignorance, superstition or misunderstanding? Does that morality engender the misconception that deviants from its codes are in some other ways dangerous to society? Is the weight of the misery attendant on punishment for homosexual offences well understood? (It should be remembered that Hart was writing before the **Sexual Offences Act 1967**.) Hart concludes with a warning against 'populism' as an arbiter of how we should live. There is, he suggests, a danger of 'populism' in Devlin's reliance on the feelings of 'the right-minded man'; it should be resisted.

To summarise: Devlin sees the preservation of morality as vital to society's well-being; morality is very much more than mere integument, it expresses essential aspects of the bonds which serve to unify society; the law has an important, inescapable role to fulfil in safeguarding society from attempts to shatter its shared morality. Hart does not accept Devlin's fundamental assumption that morality in its entirety forms a unique 'seamless web'; deviants from a conventional sexual morality are not necessarily antagonistic in other ways to society as a whole and its demands; there is always the danger of entrenching irrational and harmful prejudices in the guise of a legal stance designed to safeguard 'basic patterns' of morality. Devlin turns his attention on society as a whole; Hart, on the individual. Devlin accentuates, therefore, the significance of a shared public morality and its maintenance; Hart underlines (as did the Wolfenden Report) the important distinction between public and private behaviour, public and private areas of morality, and reminds legislators that there is a private area which ought not to be the concern of the law.

The debate has not ended. Its preoccupations are revived particularly on those occasions upon which legislators make proposals relating to basic changes in the law in areas concerned with sexual behaviour. The debate which preceded the passing of the **Sexual Offences Act 1967** (the provisions of which reflected the recommendations of the Wolfenden Report) was a reminder of the intensity of feeling which surrounds this area of the criminal law. Devlin's supporters continue to insist that 'the suppression of vice is as much the law's business as the suppression of subversive activities'. They are reminded by their opponents of Spinoza's warning, some three centuries ago, that: 'He alone knows what the law can do who sees clearly what it cannot do . . . He who tries to fix and determine everything by law will inflame rather than correct the vices of the world.' Hart's supporters repeat his view that: 'To use coercion to maintain the moral status quo at any given point in history would be artificially to arrest the process which gives social institutions their value.' They are warned by opponents of Holmes's reminder that a sound body of law must correspond with the community's actual feelings and demands. They are urged to remember that legal and moral rules 'are in a symbiotic relationship – people learn what is moral by observing what other people tend to enforce'.

Essentially, the debate turned on the *social significance of sexual morality* and, in particular, on the importance for society of private reactions to a generally accepted code of moral behaviour. But some jurists saw the debate as drawing attention to a deeper question for general jurisprudence – namely, how far legality ought to be considered simply in terms of *restraint*. Is it to be 'the whip of the animal trainer or the voice of conscience'? The path from the authoritarian 'must' to the autonomous 'ought' is tortuous. It is suggested that, for some jurists, the principal value of the debate might reside in its insistent reminder that the concept of law as a means to an end demands continuous examination of that end; for others, there is the reminder of the continuing separation of law and morality – in Korkunov's words: 'The distinction between morals and law can be formulated very simply. Morality furnishes the criterion for the proper evaluation of our interests; law marks out the limits within which they ought to be confined. To analyse out a criterion for the evolution of our interests is the function of morality; to settle the principles of the reciprocal delimitation of one's own and other people's interests is the function of the law.'

NOTES

The key texts in this area are Devlin's *The Enforcement of Morals*, Hart's *Immorality and Treason* and *Law, Liberty and Morality*. The Wolfenden Report (Cmnd 1957) contains the precise recommendations which were discussed in the subsequent debate on law and morality. Riddall, Chapter 14, summarises the debate on enforcement of morality. Mitchell's *Law, Morality and Religion in a Secular Society* treats in detail some of the questions posed by Hart and Devlin. Lee's *Law and Morals* is a useful summary of the fundamental questions; it contains a bibliography relating to the problems. Shiner's essay, 'Law and morality', in *A Companion to Philosophy of Law*, edited by Patterson, asks whether 'morality' is a jurisprudentially neutral term. Grey's *The Legal Enforcement of Morality* examines the legislature's 'right' to enforce morality by law.

QUESTION 35

What is the modern philosophical basis of toleration in liberal democratic states?

Answer Plan

The issue of whether, and to what extent, the state should tolerate so-called victimless immoralities has been of concern to philosophers at least since the publication of John Stuart Mill's *On Liberty* (1859). The roots of toleration, at least in the religious context, can be traced back to Locke's analysis in *A Letter Concerning Toleration* (1667). Modern debate was re-ignited with the Hart–Devlin debate in the 1950s and 1960s over proposals to decriminalise homosexuality in England. Modern theorists, such as Dworkin and Raz, have sought to give strong foundations to liberal toleration but their approach is opposed by a continuing strand of 'natural law' thought which seeks to emphasise the continuing relevance of man's sinfulness in the eyes of God and the need to suppress immoral conduct. The debate between liberals and conservatives on this matter could not be of more relevance today. A skeleton plan is suggested.

❖   Introduction;
❖   discussion of Locke's arguments for religious toleration;
❖   discussion of Mill's 'harm principle' and its drawbacks;
❖   discussion of Raz's argument for liberal toleration based on a concern for autonomy;

❖ discussion of Dworkin's 'equal concern and respect' argument for liberal toleration;

❖ discussion of the views of 'natural lawyers' such as Finnis;

❖ discussion of 'original sin';

❖ conclusion, viewpoint taken will depend on view of human nature taken, whether optimistic or pessimistic.

ANSWER

The question of how far and on what basis the state should tolerate so-called 'victimless' immoralities, such as drug abuse, homosexuality and suicide, has been a source of great philosophical inquiry for many jurists and philosophers.

The starting point for the historical origin of toleration is often taken to be John Locke's (1632–1704) *Letter Concerning Toleration* (1667) which was later joined by a *Second Letter* and a *Third Letter*. Between 1642 and 1649 there was a civil war in England partly arising from conflicting religious beliefs. When the dust of conflict had settled, and Charles II was restored to the throne in 1660, philosophers such as Locke naturally asked the questions: 'How is civil society even possible between those of different faiths?' and 'What can conceivably be the basis of religious toleration?'

The alternative to religious toleration was unpalatable: unending civil war. Therefore, the historical origin of political liberalism is the seventeenth century in England, something like the modern understanding of liberty of conscience and freedom of thought, began then. It is possible to speak of 'the liberalism of fear' born out of the fear associated with religious persecution and cruelties. John Locke, in 1667, wrote *A Letter Concerning Toleration* in which he argued:

> God has given no man authority over another, no man can abandon the care of his own salvation to the care of another, a church is a voluntary society, and no man is bound to any particular church and he may leave it as freely as he entered, only faith and inward sincerity gain our salvation with God.

In England in the 1660s there was a widespread belief that civil order and tranquillity required religious uniformity. Locke argued for the opposite: freedom of religious worship. Locke had two main arguments, which were original to Locke, for religious toleration: (1) the true faith cannot be forced, and (2) the government has no more reason to think that it is right in religious matters than anyone else.

Locke thought that any attempt to force a particular religion onto persons was inconsistent with the true ends of religion for, as Locke commented, 'the way to salvation not being any forced exterior performance, but the voluntary and secret choice of the mind'. This is an explicitly religious argument to justify religious toleration and Locke argues that neither the example of Jesus nor the teaching of the New Testament suggests that the use of force is a proper way to bring persons to salvation. Locke gives another more philosophical argument for religious toleration: that the identity of the true religion was itself a matter of dispute and that the government has, in the words of Locke, 'no more certain or more infallible knowledge of the way to attain it than I myself'. This observation that governments may be wrong about which is the true religion is bolstered by the observation that governments are motivated by the quest for power, not truth, and are therefore unlikely to be sound in the pursuit of religious truth. History is full of examples of the use of religion by government for political ends.

As a result of these observations, Locke believed that 'in religious worship every man hath a perfect liberty which he may freely use without or contrary to the magistrate's command'.

It is possible to see, in the context of religious freedom advocated in Locke's writings, the origin of freedom of opinion which is the hallmark of modern democratic liberal states.

The next landmark in philosophical writings concerning toleration was published in 1859 by John Stuart Mill, *On Liberty*. Mill stated the view that the only justification for the intervention of the state through the criminal law restraining an individual's actions was 'to prevent harm to others'. The individual's own physical or moral welfare was not a sufficient reason for state intervention. Of course, an individual's family and friends could use moral persuasion and psychological pressure to dissuade any individual from pursuing a course of conduct harmful to himself, but the state could only intervene if there was 'harm to others'. Mill bases his doctrine, 'the harm principle', on the value of freedom in itself to human beings: 'The only freedom which deserves the name is that of pursuing our own good in our own way so long as we do not attempt to deprive others of theirs, or impede their efforts to obtain it.'

There are serious problems, though, with the 'harm principle' as a rational basis for toleration in modern Western society:

(1) As Professor Hart pointed out in *Law, Liberty and Morality* (1962), the psychology of a human being employed by Mill is defective, in that Mill's conception of a human being was endowed with the settled temperament and character of a

middle-aged middle-class man not unlike Mill himself. However, many individuals need protection from their own foolish choices, such as addiction to opiates, and therefore some 'paternalism' in the state is needed. The fundamental point that Mill overlooked is that not every individual is the model of rationality and maturity envisaged by Mill in *On Liberty*.

(2)   Mill's theory also has to answer the fundamental objection 'what is to count as "harm to others"?' Does 'harm' include only physical harm or does it include harm to the ethical environment of the community?

As Professor Dworkin has commented in a 1989 article ('Liberal community' in California Law Review) some liberals have thought that liberal tolerance can be fully justified by John Stuart Mill's 'harm principle', which holds that the state may properly restrain someone's liberty only to prevent his harming others, not himself. This, it is argued, rules out legislation making homosexual acts criminal. However, as Dworkin points out, this argument is sound only if we limit harm to physical harm to person or property. Every community has an ethical environment, and that environment makes a difference to the lives its members can lead. A community which tolerates homosexuality, and in which homosexuality has a strong presence, provides a different ethical environment from one in which homosexuality is forbidden, and some people believe themselves harmed by the difference.

The failure of Mill's 'harm principle' to provide a satisfactory foundation for liberal toleration has led to the development of other theories. Professor Raz, a believer in liberal toleration, writes in 'Liberalism, scepticism and democracy' (1989, Iowa Law Review) that toleration springs from a concern with the well-being of citizens based on a respect for personal autonomy. The state should be careful in the means it adopts to promote virtue. Those means should not infringe a person's autonomy, which is the foundation of his or her well-being. Government should neither criminalise nor employ coercion to discourage victimless immoralities. Raz argues that, by attaching the stigma of criminal conviction, by disrupting a person's life through the process of trial and conviction, criminal coercion affects the general control people have over the course of their lives. Such an infringement of personal autonomy may be justified by the need to protect the autonomy of others. However, when the matter concerns victimless offences, then respect for the autonomy of the individual dictates a policy of toleration by government.

Therefore, for Raz, liberal toleration stems from a concern with the well-being of citizens in that the criminal conviction and punishment for victimless immoralities can interfere substantially with the control (the autonomy) that a person has over his own life.

Professor Dworkin has deployed a number of arguments over the years to argue for 'liberalism', but the most celebrated justification was the argument based on 'equal concern and respect' which is found, for example, in the article 'Liberalism' (reprinted in *A Matter of Principle* (1985)). The argument is that the state has a fundamental duty to treat its citizens with equal concern and respect and this includes respecting the lifestyle choice of citizens, including homosexuality. As Dworkin writes in 'Liberalism': 'The constitutive morality of liberalism is a theory of equality that requires official neutrality amongst theories of what is valuable in life.' This is in distinction to the 'conservative' or 'perfectionist' view that society must help its members to achieve what is in fact good. A proponent of 'perfectionism' is the natural lawyer, Professor Finnis (whose leading work is *Natural Law and Natural Rights* (1980)), and he severely criticises Dworkin's 'equal concern and respect' argument for liberal toleration. Finnis denies that laws prohibiting drug abuse (for example, opiates such as heroin), suicide or homosexuality violate a person's self-respect or denies that citizen 'equal concern and respect'. Finnis comments in his 'Maccabean Lecture' for the British Academy in 1985:

> the phenomenon of conversion (repentance) or, less dramatically, of regret and reform, shows that one must not identify the person (and his worth as a human being) with his current lifestyle. A person prevented from using illegal drugs, committing suicide or engaging in homosexual acts on this view cannot think that the law does not treat him as an equal for the justifying concern of the law is an effort to uphold morality for the good, the worth and the dignity of everyone without exception. To condemn and prohibit the sin is not to manifest contempt for the sinner in classic Catholic theology.

Therefore, Finnis argues that legislation prohibiting homosexuality may be based on a sense of equal concern and respect – the equal worth and human dignity of those persons whose conduct is outlawed precisely on the ground that such immoral conduct as homosexuality actually degrades human worth and dignity. The tradition in Western Christian thought from Aquinas (1225–1273), and supported by Finnis, is that persons who are prone to vice and resistant to verbal persuasion not only can be restrained from depraved actions by coercive threats but also can be led by an acculturation (called 'habituation' by natural lawyers) to make willingly, through their own authentic free choice, the good choices which earlier they made only under coercion and threats. Therefore, Finnis argues that the concept of the state showing 'equal concern and respect' to citizens can lead to the prohibition of homosexuality rather than the same concept leading to the legalisation of homosexuality, as Dworkin argues.

The natural lawyers' view of a 'paternalistic state' prohibiting possession of drugs, suicide and homosexuality is based on a concept found in the Bible itself. The key concept for natural lawyers of 'original sin' can be traced back to the Old Testament (see Psalm 51, verse 5) and was endorsed by St Augustine (354–430) in the fifth century (see Augustine's monumental work, *The City of God*, for his views on 'original sin'). The view of 'original sin' is that man in his natural non-religious state is inherently sinful and prone to evil conduct and that this is an 'inherited' characteristic of every human being who is not saved by Divine grace. Pelagius, a monk of the fifth century, famously disagreed with Augustine's notion of original sin and argued that man is born with a natural tendency towards goodness and charity. However St Augustine's view of the universality of 'original sin' has been very influential and supports the natural lawyers' view that the state needs to use coercion to enforce morality. Ultra-conservative 'Augustinians' believe that the individual is incapable of behaving well without the repressive intervention of the state and its laws, and that 'sins' such as abortion, homosexuality and suicide need to be rigorously suppressed. The authoritarian state is an Augustinian construct. The Augustinian view of 'original sin' was ratified by the Council of Carthage in 418 AD. The criminal law of England was broadly Augustinian before the 1960s, but has become increasingly Pelagian from the mid-1960s with the decriminalisation of homosexuality, attempted suicide, abortion and more tolerant legal attitudes towards the possession of illegal drugs. Lord Devlin, the Law Lord (1905–1992), in his book *The Enforcement of Morals* (1965), can be viewed as taking a traditional 'natural law' approach to the issue of the toleration or suppression of activities such as homosexuality when he wrote that 'the suppression of vice is as much the law's business as the suppression of subversive activities'. This echoes the comment of Oliver Cromwell (1599–1658) as Lord Protector in 1656 that 'the suppressing of vice and encouragement of virtue' was on a par with the security of the peace of the nation as the ends of his government (Cromwell quoted in *Cromwell and the Interregnum*, edited by David L Smith (2003)).

The view of the prevalence of 'original sin' in human beings is supported by the great natural law thinker St Thomas Aquinas, who is quoted by Finnis (in *Aquinas* (1998)) as holding:

> there is in us a natural inclination towards what is appealing (*conveniens*) to bodily feelings (*carnali sensui*) against the good of practical reasonableness (*contra bonum rationis*).

As Finnis comments, like all great exponents of natural law and moral objectivity, Aquinas expects immoral customs and practices to predominate. This belief in the pervasiveness of 'original sin' was challenged by the men of the Enlightenment in the eighteenth century. Indeed, as Professor Henry Chadwick comments in his book, *St Augustine* (1986), the men of the Enlightenment thought the actual perfecting of man was hindered by belief in original sin and disliked Augustine very much. The men of the Enlightenment were displeased when the Enlightenment philosopher, Immanuel Kant (1724–1804), decisively assented to the belief that human nature is distorted by a pervasive radical evil. Kant had asserted that from the crooked timber of humanity nothing completely straight can be made. The doctrine of 'original sin' was well expressed by the great Bible translator, William Tyndale (1494–1536) in his work *A Pathway to the Holy Scripture* (1530) when he wrote: 'By nature through the fall of Adam are we the children of wrath, heirs of the vengeance of God by birth, yea and from our conception . . . so are we hated of God for that natural poison which is conceived and born with us before we do any outward evil.' As the great Puritan thinker of the mid-seventeenth century, John Owen (1616–1683), commented in his book *The Holy Spirit* (1674): 'Original sin is the habitual inconformity of our natures to the holiness of God.'

The recognition of 'original sin' as a pervasive human characteristic will generally lead to the adoption of conservative or even authoritarian views on the state and the enforcement of morals. This is the view of the classical 'natural lawyers', such as Aquinas and Finnis. The rejection of the 'original sin' doctrine (Pelagianism) will lead to an optimistic view of human beings and a rejection of the concept of 'sin' at all, leading to 'liberalism' in the enforcement of morals and toleration of homosexuality, abortion and suicide. This is the view of Raz and Dworkin. Ultimately, the question as to whether, and to what extent, the state should enforce morality will depend on which view of human nature is taken by the theorist, whether pessimistic or optimistic.

Common Pitfalls

Students can avoid the pitfall of thinking that JS Mill's 'harm principle' is in itself a workable theory for defining the limits of state power over the individual and his lifestyle choices, since everything depends on what counts as 'harm'. In other words 'the harm principle' has to be embedded in a normative theory of what counts as relevant 'harm' to others – for example is it just physical harm or harm to the social environment? Students can gain extra marks by pointing out that legal theorists such as Raz and Dworkin, who take a permissive attitude towards abortion, homosexuality and illegal drug use, are in fact in the tradition of eighteenth century Enlightenment thinkers such as Rousseau and William Godwin who argued against institutions which repress the innate moral goodness of persons.

NOTES

The views of Locke concerning religious toleration can be found in *The Stanford Encyclopedia of Philosophy* website entries on Locke (http://plato.stanford.edu/), especially Alex Tuckness's essay 'Locke's political philosophy'. For a general discussion of Locke's arguments concerning religious toleration, see *John Locke: an Essay Concerning Toleration*, edited with an introduction and notes by J R Milton and Philip Milton (Oxford University Press (2006)). The 'Everyman' edition of JS Mill's *On Liberty* contains a useful interpretive essay by the philosopher, Isaiah Berlin.

Dworkin's views are reflected in the essay 'Liberalism' (1978), collected in *A Matter of Principle* (1985). The view of Raz on liberal toleration can be found in *The Morality of Freedom* (1986). The conservative views of Professor Finnis can be found in the 1985 Maccabean lecture on Jurisprudence to the British Academy and in the approving reference Finnis gives to the concept of 'public morality' in Chapter VIII of *Natural Law and Natural Rights* (1980). The views of St Thomas Aquinas on human immorality can be found in Finnis's work *Aquinas: Moral, Political and Legal Theory* (Oxford University Press (1998)).

Index

a priori reasoning 212
abortion 59, 217
absolutism 28, 29, 31–4, 35
abstract rights 214
abuse of powers 35
accepted social practice 132
acculturation 234
acid metaphor, duty 173, 174, 175, 176
active euthanasia 218, 219, 222
Adam, fall of 236
adequacy, in legal philosophy 179
adjudication, Dworkin's theory of 65, 116, 142,
    144, 145; and natural law 59–60, 61, 62
aesthetics 53, 55
affirmative action, US 216
age of statutes 67, 80–1
alienation 166
American Declaration of Independence 36
American jurisprudence: functional 176; Nozick's
    theory of justice 204–10; Rawls' theory of
    justice 199–204
American Realism 173–83; Cardozo, on nature of
    judicial process 178–83; Holmes, on path of
    the law 74, 173–8
analytical jurisprudence 45
anarchy 31, 158
anthropology 175
apparent goods 54
Aquinas, St Thomas 6, 15, 45, 49–51, 55, 59, 234,
    235, 236; *Summa Theologica* 40, 41, 46, 47;
    theory of law 40–4
archetypal (standard) legal system 131
aristocracy 23
Aristotle 39, 40, 41, 46, 48
associative obligations 171
Atkin, Lord James 60, 77

Augustine of Hippo, St 6, 47, 235
Austin, John 4, 31, 190; and common law/statute
    66, 70, 71, 72; institutional perspective of 10,
    14; and legal positivism 111, 112, 113, 114,
    118–21, 123, 131, 140, 149; and normativity of
    law 193, 196
authority 50, 81, 123, 155–72; justification for
    156–64, 185, 187; man-made law 39, 118, 119;
    moral obligation to obey law, philosophical
    treatment 164–72; service conception of 149,
    162, 163
autonomy 123, 150, 233; and authority 160, 161;
    and rights 218, 219; *see also* individualism

'bad' law 25, 30, 50–1
balancing interests 84, 213; and American
    Realism 179–80, 181, 183
basic norms 11, 194–5, 196
Beccaria, Cesare 106
belonging, feeling of 170
Bentham, Jeremy 31, 68–71, 190, 193, 200;
    codification of law, vision for 69, 71; common
    law, attack on 65–73, 113; and legal positivism
    111, 112, 114, 118–20, 130, 131, 140, 149; and
    punishment 101, 102, 103, 106–10; and
    utilitarianism 83, 89, 90; and viewpoint of
    legal theorist 10, 14
best interests, and euthanasia 218, 220–1
Bible 103, 187, 232, 235; and authority 156, 157, 158,
    159, 163
bindingness of law 192
Bingham, Lord Thomas Henry (Tom) 79, 80, 82
Bix, Brian 45, 52
Blackstone, Sir William 68, 69, 76
bodies in motion 27–8
body politic 34

brain function, and death 221
breaches of law 170

Calvin, John/Calvinism 158
capital punishment 108–9
Cardozo, Benjamin 143, 173; on nature of judicial
    process 178–83
Catholic Church 40, 41, 43, 54, 220
central case legal system 48, 49, 50, 134
Chadwick, Henry 235
chain novel 60
Charles I, King 157, 159
Charles II, King 27–8, 231
Christiano, Tom 164
Cicero, Marcus Tullius 21, 39; *De Legibus* 25, 26;
    De Republica 23, 26, 43; on state and nature
    of law 21–6
civil law 29–30, 31, 75
civil society 27, 28, 29, 231
codification of English law, Bentham's plan for
    69, 71, 113
coercion 12–13, 102, 119, 120, 122, 123, 146
Cohen, M. R. 176
Coke, Sir Edward 67
Coleman, Jules 6–7, 132
command theory 4, 66, 70, 71, 111, 113, 114, 117–23,
    125, 146; criticism of 121–4; whether virtue as
    a theory of law 117–21
common good concept 15, 90, 102, 137; and
    natural law 47, 48, 50, 54–5, 56
common law and statute 60, 131, 218; and
    Bentham 65–73, 113; and Dworkin 45, 57, 61,
    62; eclipse of common law 67, 79; experience
    74–5; incrementalism of common law 67, 76,
    77; legislation, dominance of as primary
    source of law 66, 78–82; strengths of
    common law 73–8; transition to statute
    dominated system 114
communitarianism 171
competence, and euthanasia 219
Concept of Law, The (Hart), 4, 18, 48, 112, 116, 143;
    attempts to improve upon analysis in
    128–39; and command theory 118, 120, 122,
    123, 125; descriptive theory of law in 17, 19,
    124–8; and social benefits of law 14–15;
    see also Hart, H. L. A.
concrete rights 214
confessions 75
conflicts of principle 203

consent 158, 166, 167, 168, 206
consequences, and punishment 106, 108
consistency 76
content of law, identification 7
contract law, and common law 74
co-operation, fair system of 97
Cotterrell, Roger 17, 62–3; and common law
    and statute 72, 74, 78, 82; and role of law 187,
    188, 190
court functions 176
Covenant theory *see* Social Contract (Covenant)
    theory
criminal law 75, 76, 107–8, 109; and morality
    225–30, 232, 235
Criminal Law Revision Committee, Eleventh
    Report 75
Cromwell, Oliver 27, 158, 235

Davies, Sir John 67
death: defined 220–1; with dignity 218, 222; *see
    also* euthanasia; murder
death penalty 108–9
definition, in law 176
democracy 23, 33, 34, 188, 189
Denning, Lord Alfred 78, 79, 80
deontological moral theories 93
desert philosophy of punishment 103, 104
detached institutional perspectives 9, 10, 15
deterrence and punishment 101, 103–4, 108
Devlin, Lord Patrick 225, 226–9, 235
Dewey, John 173
difference principle 207
dignity 214; death with 218, 222
Disraeli, Benjamin 50
distributive justice 207
divine law (*lex divina*), 42
Divine Right of Kings 157
division of powers 34–5
drug abuse 231, 234
duress, common law defence of 76
duty 173–8
Dworkin, Ronald 102, 155, 171, 185, 203–4, 236;
    adjudication theory 59–60, 61, 62, 65, 116, 142,
    144, 145; and common law 45, 57, 61, 62;
    equality concept, and rights 211–17; and
    euthanasia 217, 218, 222; *Law's Empire* 3, 45,
    61, 115, 132, 140, 141, 145–6, 170, 218; lawyer's
    perspective of 9, 10, 11, 12–14, 62; and legal
    positivism 57–8, 112, 115–16, 117, 124, 125, 127,

131–2, 137, 138, 140–8; whether a 'natural lawyer,' 6, 56–63; on toleration 230, 233, 234
Dyzenhaus, D. 61

Edmund-Davies, Lord Herbert 75
engaged institutional perspectives 9, 10, 15
Enlightenment 68–9, 118, 189, 235–6, 236
equal treatment 216
equality 96, 204; Cicero on 24, 25; Locke on 33, 34–5; and rights 211–17
eternal law (*lex aeterna*), 42
European Union (EU), legitimacy of legislation 79
euthanasia 211, 217–23; active, voluntary or involuntary 218, 220–1, 222; and best interests 219, 220–1; legalisation of 218, 221, 222–3; and sanctity of life 219–20, 222
evil 27; primary or secondary 107
evolution, method of 179
exclusionary reasons for action 124, 191, 192–3, 196
Exodus 103
experience, and common law 74–5
expression, freedom of 84–8, 91, 202, 214
external point of view, analysis of law from 124, 128

fables, jurisprudential, and Nozick's theory of justice 204–10
fairness 14, 49, 91, 166, 169; justice as 95, 97, 200, 201, 202
felicific calculus 107
fiduciary relationship of government 36
Finnis, John 6, 39, 45–6, 56, 234, 236; and authority 155, 166–7; on human goods, self-evident 47–8, 49, 52–4, 55; institutional perspective of 9, 10, 15; and legal positivism 112, 115, 116, 121, 129, 130, 134, 135, 137, 138, 139, 142, 144, 145; *Natural Law and Natural Rights see Natural Law and Natural Rights* (Finnis)
fit, judicial criterion of 144–5
flourishing, human 51, 53
fragmentation 186, 188
Frank, Jerome 183
free will 160
freedom of constraint 215
freedom of speech 84–8, 91, 202, 214
French Revolution 90
Freud, Sigmund 31

Friedmann, Wolfgang 31, 34
friendship 48

Galligan, Denis 3, 70–1, 120, 129, 134–5; institutional perspective of 9, 10, 15, 16
Gama, Raymundo 2
gapless theory of law 143
Gardner, John 17–18, 65, 117, 195–6
George, Robert P. 59
Glorious Revolution 1688, 32
goal-based societies 206
God, and the law 34, 43; and Aquinas 41, 46; and Cicero 25, 26; and Hobbes 29, 30, 31; *see also* religion/religious faith
Godwin, William 161
Goff, Lord 218
'good' law 26, 29
Goodhart, A. L. 176
government and the state 21, 85, 87, 93, 102, 215; authority *see* authority; Cicero on state and nature of law 21, 21–6; coercion by 12–13, 102, 119, 120, 122, 123, 146; Hobbes on Social Contract theory 27–32, 125–6, 156, 158, 162; justification for authority of state 156–64; justification for intervention by 84, 85, 87–8; Locke's theory of the state and nature of law 32–7; minimal state 98, 99, 159, 204, 206–9; paternalism 86, 234; philosophical basis of toleration in liberal states 230–7; Social Contract *see* Social Contract (Covenant) theory; torture, use of 91–2
grand narratives, collapse of 187
Gray, John Chipman 34, 173
Green, Leslie 12, 50, 51, 137, 149, 156, 165, 172, 188–9
Greenawalt, Kent 58–9, 63, 155, 165, 172
grievous bodily harm 76
Grisez, Germain 217, 218, 221, 222
Grotius, Hugo 119

habituation 234
Hailsham, Lord (Quintin McGarel Hogg) 76
Hale, Sir Matthew 67, 76
Hamilton, Walton 36
Hand, Billings Learned 68
happiness, and utilitarianism 83, 90, 91, 107–8, 109, 199–200
hard cases 58; in legal positivism 115–17, 127, 140–6, 150
Hare, R. M. 91

harm, prevention of 85, 86, 87, 108, 232–3, 236
Hart, H. L. A. 3, 70, 99, 169, 191; *Concept of Law
see Concept of Law, The* (Hart); institutional
perspective of 9, 10, 12, 14–15, 17, 18; and legal
positivism 111, 113, 116, 132, 133, 137–8, 141–3,
146, 154; and morality and law 225, 226, 228,
229; and natural law 49, 50, 51; and
punishment 100, 101, 103–4, 105; recognition
rule of 114, 126–7, 132, 143; on rules, primary
and secondary 123, 133–4, 149
'hidden' law 146
highest good concept 25
Hill, Christopher 157, 159
historical entitlement principle (Nozick), 206
history 72, 176, 181
Hobbes, Thomas 18, 21, 58, 70, 155; and legal
positivism 111, 112, 113, 118, 119, 120, 125–6,
139, 151; *Leviathan* 14, 27, 32, 36, 81, 125, 151,
153, 157, 159, 163, 191; Locke contrasted 31,
32, 36, 158; on Social Contract 27–31, 32,
125–6, 156, 158, 162; and viewpoint of legal
theorist 12, 14
Holmes, Oliver Wendell 143, 173, 229; on common
law and statute 73, 74–5, 78; on path of the
law 74, 173–8
homosexuality 59, 226, 230, 231, 233, 234
Honderich, Ted 103, 104
Honore, Tony 130–1
hospices 222
human goods, self-evident 47–8, 49, 52–4, 55
human law (*lex humana*), 43
human nature, Hobbes on 28–9, 32, 158; *see also*
state of nature
human rights 189; and utilitarianism
88–100, 90, 91
Hume, David 31, 89, 139, 167

ideal form of law 15, 16, 49, 129, 134
idolatry 43
illegality 167, 170
immorality 225–30, 228, 231
impartiality of the law 183
implied consent 167
incapacitation, and punishment 105
individualism 31, 205, 209, 214–15
inflammatory material 86
institutional (external) legal perspectives 9, 10,
12, 14–18, 62
integrative jurisprudence school 178, 179

integrity 14, 93, 170; and legal positivism 137,
140, 146; and natural law 60, 61, 62; rights
thesis (Dworkin), 214, 215–16; and role of
law 186, 188
internal point of view, analysis of law from 123,
124, 128, 132–3, 134, 137, 141
interpretation of law 117, 132, 144, 176
involuntary euthanasia 218
irrefragable undertakings 175

James, Mr Justice 75
James, William 173, 177
James I, King 157
John XXII, Pope 46
judge-made law 72, 80, 113, 119
judicial process, Cardozo on 178–83
judicial thinking 179–80
jurisprudence: American *see* American
jurisprudence; precursors *see* precursors of
modern jurisprudence; purpose 2–3; as
science of law 25
just savings principle 202
justice 26; as fairness 95, 97, 200, 201, 202;
principles 95–6, 97, 201, 204, 214, 220 –1;
social 200, 207; and utilitarianism 84,
88–100, 91
justification, judicial criterion of 144, 145

Kant, Immanuel 93, 101, 102–3, 104, 159–60, 236
Kelsen, Hans 3, 131, 151; *Introduction to the
Problems of Legal Theory* 11, 12, 152, 154;
lawyer's perspective of 9, 10, 11–12, 13; and
normativity of law 190–1, 194–5
Klosko, George 165, 171–2
knowledge 40, 53, 54, 55
Korkunov, Nikolai 229–30

Lacey, Nicola 129
Laski, Harold 12
law: central and peripheral cases 48, 49, 50, 134;
higher functions of 115; Holmes, on path of
74, 173–8; ideal form 15, 16, 49, 129, 134;
instrumental approach to 152; whether
intrinsic value in 151–4; moral justification to
obey, philosophical treatment 164–72; and
morality 225–37; nature of 21–6, 185–97;
normativity of 11, 190–7; role in postmodern
social environment 186–90; sources *see*
sources of law; and state, Cicero on 21, 21–6;

supremacy of 41; value of 126–7; viewpoint of legal theorist concerning, identifying 9–18; *see also* natural law

law-states, constitutional 16

Lawton, (Lord Justice) Frederick 75

lawyer perspectives *see* participant (lawyer) perspectives

legal duty 175

legal orders, modern 16

legal positivism 5, 45, 48, 111–54; command theory *see* command theory; definitions 112–17; and Dworkin 140–8; inclusive 132; and Raz 148–51; sources thesis *see* sources thesis; *see also Concept of Law, The* (Hart)

legal theory: perspectives on *see* perspectives on legal theory; purpose 185

legislation (statute law), 86, 107, 188; and common law *see* common law and statute; dominance of 66, 78–82; European Union derived 79; and legal positivism 113–14

Leiter, Brian 144

Levy, Emmanuel 187–8

Lewis, Bernard 187

lex injusta non est lex (unjust law is not a law), 6, 44, 47, 50, 51, 55, 56

lex naturalis see natural laws

lexical concepts 203

liberalism 94–5, 97, 205, 234

liberty 203, 204, 215, 227; Locke on 32, 35; Mill on 84–8; *see also under* Mill, John Stuart

lifestyle choices 234

Locke, John 21, 27, 70, 155, 205; and authority 156, 158–9, 162, 167, 168; Hobbes contrasted 30, 31, 32, 36, 158; and state and nature of law 32–7; and toleration 230, 231–2; *Treatise of Civil Government* 32, 37, 121

logic, and common law 74, 75, 76

lower courts 116

Lyotard, Jean-Francois 187

MacCormick, Neil 4, 19, 133; institutional perspective of 9, 10, 16, 18; and natural law 52–6; and normativity of law 193, 196

MacMillan, Lord 143

Magnus, Albertus 40

Maitland, Frederic William 22–3

mala in se/mala prohibita 108

man-made law 39, 118, 119

Mansfield, Lord William 61, 67, 78

manslaughter 76

al-Maqdisi, Abu Muhammed 189

Mark Antony 22

Marx, Karl 159, 187

McHugh J 80

medical treatment 223

mercy killing 218

Mill, John Stuart 83, 84–8, 90, 108–9; *On Liberty* 84, 202, 230, 232, 233

mind maps 10

minimal state 98, 99, 159, 206, 209; as night-watchman state 204, 207, 208

mischief, of a criminal act 107

monarchy 23–4, 34

Montesquieu, Baron de 35, 118

moral philosophy 23

moral phraseology 175

morality and law 7, 76, 93, 225–37; and legal positivism 112, 115, 117, 118, 120; moral obligation to obey law, philosophical treatment 164–72; and natural law 41, 43, 48; seamless web, morality as 228; sin and crime 225–30; toleration, modern philosophical basis 230–7

motion, law of (Hobbes), 28

murder 76, 94, 103, 108, 182, 222; imprisonment of innocent for 75

Murphy, Mark 46, 51

Nagel, Thomas 94, 96

natural law 5, 26–8, 39–63, 190, 211–13; Aquinas, theory of 40–4; caricature version 52–3, 56; current relevance of theory 44–52; Finnis, critique of views 52–6; Holmes on 174–5; and legal positivism 115, 118

Natural Law and Natural Rights (Finnis), 5, 15, 19, 44, 45, 47–9, 51, 58; and authority 161, 166; and legal positivism 115, 116, 121, 139; MacCormick on 52–6; *see also* Finnis, John

natural rights 35, 205

nature, law of 33, 34, 35

Nazi regime 48, 208

negligence 77

neo-Scholastic school of jurisprudence 40

neo-Thomist view of man 222

New Testament 232

Newton, Sir Isaac 36

Nielsen, Kai 47

Nobles, Richard 70, 73

normativity of law 11, 12, 13, 67, 185, 190–7; exclusionary reasons for action 124, 191, 192–3, 196

Nozick, Robert 83, 90, 94, 199; *Anarchy, State and Utopia* 89, 92, 97, 98, 100, 160, 169, 205, 209; theory of justice, as political manifesto 204–10

Old Testament 103, 159, 235

Oliver, Lord 77

opinion, expression of 85–6

original position (Rawls), 95, 96, 201, 202, 203–4

original sin 31, 46, 139, 158, 235, 236

oughtness *see* normativity of law

'overlapping consensus' (Rawls), 94, 95, 96, 97

Owen, John 236

pactum unionis/pactum subjectionis 34

pannomion (all the laws), 113

Panopticon 109

participant (lawyer) perspectives 9, 10–14, 15, 62

paternalism 86, 234

path of law (Holmes) 74, 173–8

Pelagius (monk) 235, 236

penology, contemporary school 110

persistent vegetative state 218–19

perspectives on legal theory: institutional (external), 9, 10, 12, 14–18, 62; participant (lawyer), 9, 10–14, 15, 62

philosophical anarchism 155, 156, 160, 161, 165, 166

philosophy 23, 25, 42, 179

Pilgrim Fathers 29

Plamenatz, John 109

Plato 21; *Crito* 155, 157, 164, 168

play 53, 55

pleasure and pain 98, 107, 109

police, use of torture by 91–2

policy 213

political liberalism 94–5, 97

Pollock, Sir Frederick 71

populism 228

pornography rights 59

posited law *see* man-made law

positive (man-made) law 118, 119; natural law contrasted 39

Postema, Gerald 69, 72, 113, 144

postmodern social environment, role of law in 186–90

powers, separation/division 35–6

practical rationality 46, 53, 54

Pragmatism 177

precedent 180–1

precursors of modern jurisprudence 21, 21–36; Cicero on state and nature of law 21, 21–6; Hobbes, on Social Contract *see* Social Contract (Covenant) theory; Locke's theory of the state and nature of law 32–7

prediction, as object of a study of law 174

pre-legal society (Hart) 125, 126, 127, 153

press, freedom of 91

primary social goods 201–2, 203

priority, principles of 203

privacy/private morality 226, 227

property rights 34–5, 36, 119, 204, 205

protection agencies/associations 206–7, 208

Providence, divine 23, 25, 26

public morality 227

punishment: and deterrence 101, 103–4, 108; and incapacitation 105; justification for imposition on individuals 101–6; 'mixed theory,' 104, 105; and rehabilitation 105; and retribution 101, 102–3, 104, 108; and utilitarianism 106–10

Pure Theory of Law (Kelsen) 11

Quinton, Anthony 73, 81, 137, 138, 139

racism 86

Radcliffe, Lord 143

rationality 203; practical 46, 53, 54; rational coherence, principles 181; *see also* reason

Rawls, John 83, 90; original position 95, 96, 201, 202, 203–4; overlapping consensus of 94, 95, 96, 97; *A Theory of Justice* 89, 92, 97, 169, 200; utilitarianism and theory of justice of 199–204; veil of ignorance 95, 96, 201

Raz, Joseph 2–3, 4, 7, 19, 48, 58, 62, 236; and authority 155, 156, 157, 160–2, 163, 164, 169–70; and common law/statute 65, 81–2; and legal positivism 111, 112, 113, 114, 115, 116, 121, 122–3, 124, 128, 132, 133, 141, 143, 148–51, 153–4; and normativity of law 191, 193–4; and role of law 189–90; and toleration 230, 233; and viewpoint of legal theorist 10–11, 12, 13–14

Realism, American *see* American Realism

reason 25, 118, 160, 182; Aquinas on 40, 41–2, 43

recognition, rule of 114, 126–7, 132, 137, 143

rehabilitation 105
Reid, Lord 143
religion/religious faith 53, 55, 76, 194; Catholic Church 40, 41, 43, 54, 220; and euthanasia 219–20; God, and the law 25, 26, 30, 31, 35, 41, 42, 43, 46; law replacing faith 187–8, 189; original sin 32, 46, 139, 158, 235, 236; religious toleration 230–7; see also Bible
resources, redistribution 207
respect for law 166
restraint, legality as 229
retribution and punishment 101, 102–3, 104, 108
reverse discrimination 208, 216
rights: Dworkin's rights thesis and equality concept 211–17; euthanasia 211, 217–23; natural 35, 36, 205; violation of 36; see also human rights
Roman law 191
Rousseau, Jean-Jacques 27
rule of law 15, 34, 35
rule utilitarianism 91–2
rules: laws as 41; primary and secondary 123, 126, 133–4, 149
Russell, Conrad 67

sanctions 123, 193–4; see also punishment
sanctity of life, and euthanasia 219–20, 222–3
Savigny, Friedrich Karl von 208
Scarman, Lord James Leslie 60–1, 78–9
Schauer, Frederick 71, 72
Schiff, David 70, 73
science of theology 41
scientific rationalism 41
security 31, 33
Sedley, Stephen 78–9
self-evident goods see human goods
self-respect 202
separability thesis, legal positivism 117
separateness of persons 89, 98, 99
separation of powers 34–5
service conception of authority 149, 162, 163
sexual morality/immorality 228–9
Simonds, Lord Gavin Turnbull 68
Simpson, Brian 131
sin: and crime 225–30; original 32, 46, 139, 158, 235, 236
slavery 202
Smith, Adam 206, 208
Smith, David L. 235

smoking in public places, ban on 185
social benefits of law systems 14–15
Social Contract (Covenant) theory 21, 159; Hobbes on 27–32, 33, 125–6, 156, 158, 162; Locke on 34, 35–6, 162, 167; Rawls on 95, 201
social justice 200, 207
Socrates 155, 157, 164, 168
sources of law: common law 73–8; legislation, dominance of 78–82
sources thesis 5, 6, 48, 57–9, 185; and legal positivism 111, 112, 114, 115, 116, 117, 118, 120, 123, 149, 150
sovereign, commands of see command theory
sovereign power, indivisibility of 29–31
speech, freedom of 84–8, 91, 202, 214
Spinoza, Baruch 229
stability in law 180, 183
Stammler, Rudolf 26
stare decisis 180
state see government and the state
state of nature 27, 28, 32, 34, 36, 156, 157–8, 159, 206; and legal positivism 125–6, 153
statute law see common law and statute; legislation (statute law)
sterilisation 222
Stoics 23
Strachey, Lytton 71
suicide 231, 234
Sumner, Lord John 75
supremacy of law, principle of 41

tacit consent 167, 168
Taggart, M. 61
Tasioulas, John 189
taxation 49, 98–9, 208–9
terrorism 86, 92
Thomist view of law 43
toleration, modern philosophical basis, in liberal democratic states 230–7
tort, action for 75, 77
torture, use of 91–2, 94
totalitarianism 31, 36
tradition, method of 179
treason 227, 228
truth 85–6
Twining, William 2, 16
Tyndale, William 236
tyranny 26, 36, 43

uniformity of the law 183
unilateral acquisition, theory of 34
United States: affirmative action in 216;
    American Realism *see* American Realism;
    Declaration of Independence 36;
    jurisprudence *see* American jurisprudence;
    Supreme Court 63, 174
unity, principle of 40–1
unjust laws *see lex injusta non est lex* (unjust law
    is not a law)
unlawful acts 167, 170
utilitarianism 83–100; appeal of 89, 90, 91;
    critique 88–100; 'Jim in the jungle,'
    imaginary account of 92–3; justice and
    human rights 88–100; Mill, on freedom of
    individual 84–8; and punishment 106–10;
    and Rawls' theory of justice 199–204
utility principle 84, 91, 107

value of law 126–7
veil of ignorance (Rawls) 95, 96, 201
'victimless' immoralities 231
virtue 23, 26
voluntary active euthanasia 218, 221, 222
voting, and consent 168

Waldron, Jeremy 71–2
Ward, Ian 189
Weber, Max 159
Weinreb, Ernest 55–6
Wheeler, J 180
Wilkinson, Michael 136
Williams, Bernard 89, 92, 93, 100
Williams, Glanville 221
Wittgenstein, Ludwig 221
Wolfenden Report (1957) 225, 226, 229, 230
Woolf, Robert Paul 160, 165